THE NATURE OF CANADA

THE
NATURE OF
CANADA

EDITED BY

COLIN M. COATES

GRAEME WYNN

a UBC Press imprint
Vancouver . Toronto

28 27 26 25 24 23 22 21 20 19   5 4 3 2

Printed in Canada on FSC-certified ancient-forest-free paper (100% post-consumer recycled) that is processed chlorine- and acid-free, with vegetable-based inks.

Library and Archives Canada Cataloguing in Publication

Title: The nature of Canada / edited by Colin M. Coates, Graeme Wynn.
Names: Coates, Colin MacMillan, editor. | Wynn, Graeme, editor.
Description: Includes bibliographical references and index.
Identifiers: Canadiana (print) 20189069392 | Canadiana (ebook) 20189069406 |
ISBN 9780774890366 (softcover) | ISBN 9780774890373 (PDF) |
ISBN 9780774890380 (EPUB) | ISBN 9780774890397 (Kindle)
Subjects: LCSH: Human geography – Canada. | LCSH: Human ecology –
Canada. | LCSH: Traditional ecological knowledge – Canada. |
LCSH: Nature – Effect of human beings on – Canada. | LCSH: Human
beings – Effect of environment on – Canada.
Classification: LCC GF511 .N38 2019 | DDC 304.20971—dc23

Canadä

UBC Press gratefully acknowledges the financial support for our publishing program of the Government of Canada (through the Canada Book Fund), the Canada Council for the Arts, and the British Columbia Arts Council.

Printed and bound in Canada by Friesens
Set in Monotype Sabon and Futura by Artegraphica Design Co. Ltd.
Copy editor: Lesley Erickson
Proofreader: Helen Godolphin
Indexer: Celia Braves
Cover designer: Jessica Sullivan

On Point Press, an imprint of UBC Press
The University of British Columbia
2029 West Mall
Vancouver, BC V6T 1Z2
www.ubcpress.ca

For our immediate families,
who helped us understand the nature of Canada:
Megan, Mab, and Bryn
Barbara, Louise, and Jonathan

And for those (including Olivia Mills) who follow,
in the hope that they, too,
may come to know something of the country
through these pages

CONTENTS

——

THE NATURE OF CANADA

INTRODUCTION

THIS BOOK GRAPPLES WITH two deceptively simple but ultimately complicated questions. How have people engaged with Canadian nature, and what do these engagements reveal about the nature of Canada (and Canadians)? We are not the first to explore these questions. Generations of scholars, creative writers, cultural commentators, and others have pondered them, but most took the idea of nature for granted. Rather than limiting and fixing its meaning, in the way that nineteenth-century naturalists pinned butterflies to cardboard in their efforts to put life in order, they lived and worked with a degree of imprecision. Forsaking rigid definition in favour of the Humpty Dumpty–like assumption that "when I use a word, it means just what I choose it to mean," they bolstered the common claim that nature is "perhaps the most complex word in the language."

Nature is many things. It is the air we breathe, the water we drink, and the earth upon which we walk. In another register, it marks the essential qualities or innate disposition of a person or thing. The gifted athlete is "a natural"; a calm friend has a "placid nature." Traditionally, the term marked a distinction between the natural and artificial elements of Earth. To enter the wilderness was to "return to nature" – a place unaltered by humans.

In this sense, nature is the antithesis of culture, everything not made by humankind. But people shaded new and different meanings onto this

3

black-and-white distinction over time. At the turn of the twentieth century, Canadians thought of nature in many different ways, including as a benevolent provider (Mother Nature), as a storehouse of resources, and as a place of worship. More recently, the pervasiveness of human influence upon the earth – seen in the pollution of remote oceans, the dissemination of species across continents, and global climate change – has blurred the boundaries between the natural and "made" worlds. To make this point, the American environmentalist Bill McKibben's 1989 book bore the title *The End of Nature*. At pretty much the same time, rising interest in the use of language to categorize the world and establish its taken-for-granted realities spawned the claim that nature is a social construction – nothing more than a widely accepted idea constituted by language rather than a pre-existent reality described by the word. Today – as the essays in this book reveal – the concept of nature retains its chameleon-like qualities. In addition to earlier connotations such as "unspoiled nature," "Mother Nature," or "the essence of things," the term signals the environment (the habitat of persons, animals, or plants), the landscape (the surface upon which cultures inscribe their marks), and a mix of biological processes. Furthermore, nature is now widely understood as a hybrid object – produced by the complex interactions between biological, chemical, physical, and organic processes on the one hand and by people pursuing their diverse interests on the other. Together, these forces constitute the web of life.

Among those Canadians who thought to ponder the questions at the heart of this book, many, like us, found inspiration in what they saw around them, even as they learned from earlier efforts to consider "nature in some one of its many relations with humanity." Take Charles G.D. Roberts as a solitary but shining example. A leading light among the Confederation poets of the late nineteenth century, Roberts won fame on two fronts. He was celebrated for his poetic sensibility to the relations between humans and the natural world. And he was equally well known for his animal stories, intended to lead "us back to the old kinship of earth." He understood the long European traditions of writing in both of these genres. Like those who shaped these traditions, Roberts wanted to illuminate the "many vital relationships between external nature and 'the deep heart of man.'" But he gave voice to a very Canadian sensibility as he wrestled with the tensions between permanence and transience and sought ways "to catch within the transitory, something of the permanent in nature."

As students of and commentators on Canada's environmental history, we follow in Roberts's footsteps. But our point of departure is quite different. We make no claim to share his poetic and creative genius. We are also conscious that circumstances have changed, that new flakes of knowledge and understanding have accumulated where Roberts once trod, changing the landscape that he dinted.

By far the most consequential of these new flakes began to form in the 1940s. Gradually, they accumulated until they began to fall in an intense flurry. The storm was seeded by Northrop Frye, the outstanding literary critic of his generation. Frye was famous for his efforts to identify the typical forms and myth-making designs of literature. Reviewing a 1943 anthology of poetry as he wrestled with this larger challenge, he identified a consistent, ominous theme in Canadian verse – nature was an ever-present threat to human existence. More than this, it seemed that Canadians paired "the unconscious horror of nature" with "subconscious horrors of the mind" as they attempted to give imaginative shape to a cruel and meaningless world. As Frye expressed it: "Whatever sinister lurks in nature lurks also in us." For Frye, the "outstanding achievement" of Canadian poets lay in their "evocation of stark terror."

Seventeen years later, in 1960, Warren Tallman, an American-born poet and professor of English at the University of British Columbia, added an existential twist to Frye's austere perception of Canadians as fallen people in a fallen world. While reading a handful of important novels, he was struck by the vast, implacable nature of Canada. The engulfing silence, he concluded, bore in upon people oppressed and isolated by the grim, primeval, and tragic qualities of their surroundings. In his view, transplanted Europeans who tried to set roots in the northern reaches of the continent were met with profound indifference. The country's harsh climes blunted the universal human desire that drove people on "their strange journeys toward fulfilment." Influenced by American modernism, Tallman insisted that "the continent itself – the gray wolf whose shadow is underneath the snow – has resisted the culture, the cultivation, the civilization which is indigenous to Europe but alien to North America." Tallman and Frye found few signs in Canadian letters of humans refusing "to be bullied by space and time." There was all too little "affirmation of the supremacy of intelligence and humanity over stupid power."

Claims such as these soon became convention. In a contribution to a sweeping history of English Canadian literature published in 1965, Hugo McPherson found the essence of postwar fiction in the "struggle against the violence, or the snowy indifference of nature." Later in the same volume, Frye concluded that literature reflected the way that Canada had developed as a conglomeration of small and isolated communities, as a collection of "closely knit and beleaguered societies" surrounded by and confronted with "a huge unthinking, menacing and formidable physical setting." The consequences were momentous. Huddled together for defence against a sinister, menacing nature, Canadians had developed a narrow, cowering garrison mentality that hardened moral conviction and stifled originality.

As Canadians celebrated the centenary of Confederation, many of the country's intellectuals grew anxious about the mushrooming influence of American culture on Canadian society. Seeking to assert a distinctive Canadian identity, a new generation of writers argued that the country and its people had been forged in the struggle with merciless nature. Foremost among them was Margaret Atwood. Her powerful influence was exercised in two short but important works. In 1970 she published *The Journals of Susanna Moodie,* which the publisher described as "perhaps the most memorable evocation in modern Canadian literature of the myth of the wilderness, the immigrant experience, and the alienating and schizophrenic effects of the colonial mentality." In this cycle of poems, "the rocks ignore," and the land is "a large darkness" that presents "vistas of desolation." Those who attempt to cultivate and humanize the wilderness will be "surrounded, stormed, broken / in upon" if they cease toiling for even a moment to contemplate the overwhelming, formidable nature that encircles them.

Two years later, in a popular guide to Canadian literature, Atwood responded to contemporary angst about what it meant to be Canadian by noting that we "are forever taking the national pulse like doctors at a sickbed." She identified survival as the central symbol of Canadianness. Taking this multifaceted and adaptable idea as the title of her book, she found the leitmotif of Canadian experience in the simple act of "hanging on, staying alive" in the "face of 'hostile' elements." The archetypal Canadian story was not about "those who made it" but about "those who made it back," back, that is to say, "from the awful experience – the North, the snowstorm, the sinking ship – that killed everyone else." In this telling, "death by nature" was a Canadian obsession. Fatalities attributable to nature in the guise of a monster, dangerous woman, or ice goddess haunted the Canadian imagination. Survival was a welcome relief – although it failed to generate much sense of excitement, adventure, or security. Canadians, Atwood told her readers, were victims (actual or potential) of forbidding forces beyond their control. They lived in a state of "almost intolerable anxiety." Revealingly, if not perhaps surprisingly, Canadian heroes almost invariably died or failed. For all that, Atwood's sweeping assertions struck a responsive chord. Canadians seemed ready to understand tales of survival in the bush as metaphors for the necessity of hanging on in the face of growing economic and social domination by the United States.

In the light of a later day, many of these claims seem exaggerated. Vivid though the "survival in a garrison" motif may be, it diminishes the variety of Canadian experience and reduces strong and resourceful pioneers to pawns of their environmental circumstances. The motif is reductive and geographically deterministic. The Frye-Atwood story about Canadians frightened and browbeaten by nature is also ahistorical in its projection of twentieth-century political, social, cultural, and psychological concerns onto nineteenth-century lives. Those who have attempted to shore up the thesis by softening its claims acknowledge that nature has been a haven and an opportunity as well as a threat in the development of Canada. But such concessions bypass larger concerns. For Frye, Canada had no Atlantic seaboard. Europeans coming into the country edged into it "like a tiny Jonah entering an inconceivably large whale"; they were "silently swallowed by an alien continent." But not every newcomer had the "intimidating experience" of entering the country this way, and developing communities soon helped to temper the forbidding qualities of the reluctant land.

By much the same token, many settlers along the St. Lawrence and elsewhere embraced the "book of nature." Rather than being cowed by their settings, they sought to "gather wisdom from the expanded leaves of creation." Some believed that "every flower ... hath its instruction." Not until late in the nineteenth century were these impulses nudged aside by evolutionary ideas about the survival of the fittest and "nature red in tooth and claw." As these new views permeated colonial imaginations, they provided grist for dramatic claims about nasty, amoral nature. But earlier impulses were never banished.

In short, Canadians have understood their settings in radically different ways, and many of them have known a great deal about nature in the places where they lived and worked. Indigenous groups envisaged the fish of the rivers and the trees of the forests as kin. Farmers watched the weather and recognized the rhythms of the seasons. Natural history buffs collected, catalogued, and studied many elements of the environment, from flowers to molluscs to butterflies. Urban dwellers knew the sounds and smells of lives lived in close proximity. Fishermen found wonder and mystery in the sea as they studied its tides and sensed its moods. Prospectors turned the

stones of time into valuable commodities by transmuting rocks into resources. Engineers calculated the strength of strata and the flow of waters
as they planned dams that would (to some extent) tame nature. But they
rarely committed their innermost thoughts about their relationship with
nature to paper or other records. Perhaps the most we can say, then, in echo
of Prairie novelist Rudy Wiebe, is that whether farmer or writer, "the way
a man feels with and lives with that living earth with which he is always
labouring to live" is always deeply personal. The sum of these understandings is both as wide as the horizon and as deep as time.

Those who wrote in the nineteenth century of the development of
British North America and what would become Canada generally shunned
such complexities. Their works emphasized the achievements of settlers
who subdued the wilderness. In these accounts, Indigenous peoples were
mostly an irrelevance, and nature was a barrier to progress, advancement,
and improvement. By contrast, many of the books written after the First
World War by the first generation of professionally trained Canadian historians gave the environment a strong role in shaping society. Many of their
contemporaries believed that environments moulded humans and societies
in particular ways. Working in a country that Prime Minister William Lyon
Mackenzie King described as having "too much geography," Canadian
scholars emphasized the importance of geographical considerations (such
as distance, space, and the harshness of the climate) to the story of their
country. Among them, Arthur R.M. Lower, the most nationalistic English
Canadian historian of his day, saw the history of Canada (and that of the
"New World" more generally) as a product of the environment. The "war
with the wilderness," he wrote in 1938, had been "the ever-present factor,
the constant influence shaping the mentality and conduct of every inhabitant." Lower's contemporary, Harold Innis, perhaps the most celebrated
Canadian student of economic development, characterized the Canadian
Pacific Railway as an enormous commitment of human energy to "the
conquest of geographical barriers." In Innis's histories, geography provided

"the grooves which determine the cause and to a large extent the character of economic life." In the 1960s, a new generation of historians turned their interests to urban and social concerns and to issues in labour, class, ethnic, and women's history. Mostly city-born and -bred, they exhibited what a senior Prairie historian dubbed a "pavement mentality." They were oblivious to "the revolution of the seasons ... and the relevance of time and place." Dismissive and overstated though it was, this claim more or less reflected shifting emphases in Canadian scholarship. Less intentionally, it also identified some of the foundations from which important changes in individual and societal attitudes towards nature sprang in the closing decades of the twentieth century.

John Crosbie, prominent Newfoundlander and sometime federal cabinet minister, captured the essence of these changes with characteristic wit and exaggeration when he said, in the 1980s, "Ten years ago we didn't know about the environment – but now it is all around us." Crosbie's witticism pointed to a sea change in public attitudes towards life on Earth. Late in the twentieth century, Canadians and others began to regard nature in new ways. In broad terms, they expanded the scale of their concern from the relatively local to the continental and the global. Scientists developed new ways of thinking that stressed the interdependence of component parts in a system. Ecologists emphasized that everything was connected to everything else. Many worried at the destructive power of human ingenuity, epitomized by the Promethean fire of nuclear warheads. Demographers chimed in with concerns about the "population bomb," which threatened disaster as human reproduction outpaced the earth's capacity to feed its people. New images from space drove home the finite, fragile, and ultimately beautiful qualities of "our only planet," silhouetted against the black void of the universe. All of this spawned unease about the unprecedented toll that humans were (and are) exacting from the earth. Arguments for rethinking the relationship between humankind and our habitat gained strength. The environment became an important focus of political and societal concern. The level of disquiet and engagement has waxed and waned, but environmentalism, as this emergent consciousness came to be known, has reshaped how Canadians (and others) interact with nature.

The environmental movement also stimulated new ways of thinking about the world. Because scholars are influenced by contemporary concerns, many turned their attention to the ways in which peoples and environments have interacted through time. Historians first traced changes in the ways that people thought about their physical surroundings – as wilderness, as garden, or as pastoral middle ground, for example. Before long, they came to recognize nature's capacity to affect human lives. In this they neither echoed Arthur Lower's muted environmental determinism nor mirrored Harold Innis's sense of the landscape (or geography) as an obstacle to be overcome. Rather than being a setting that determined the script or a stage upon which human dramas were enacted, nature became a participant in the play. Dynamic rather than static, it changed according to its own rules (the so-called laws of nature), which signalled resistance or adaptation to human actions. Simple examples include the recolonization, by shrubs and trees, of pastures cleared by arduous human toil; the sudden upsurge of certain animal populations after ecological disturbances such as the clearing of forest or the removal of predators; or the clogging of irrigation ditches with weeds. Whether nature had agency remained a matter of debate. Those who felt the word *agency* implied volition doubted that it did. But the hybrid, interactive quality of human-nature systems was widely recognized. So, too, was the notion that any understanding of the world reflects the context in which it is formulated and can, therefore, be challenged or revised.

Ecologists and other scientists also began to recognize contingency and chaos in the natural world and to write historical accounts of Earth and humans. So-called Big Histories encompassed millions, even billions, of years. All of this opened exciting new conversations across the fences that had long separated different fields of knowledge. The result was an expansion in both the range of inquiries and the ways in which people thought about past and present, humans and nature. Although historians were relatively cautious about expanding the temporal and spatial range of their inquiries, they forged a recognizable new field commonly known as environmental history, which embraced new methods of understanding human experience. Information from ice cores and tree rings is being used alongside textual records to trace the influence of nonhuman factors in stories of the human past – and vice versa. Recent years have seen a remarkable upsurge of historical writing along these lines in Canada, much of it by contributors to this book. Inspired by a changing intellectual climate and driven by contemporary societal concerns about the depletion of important resources, the runaway growth tendencies of modern industrial economies, and the plundering and defacement of the earth, their work reflects a deeper, abiding interest in the relationship between humans and the material world they have inhabited, imagined, and changed.

The essays featured here explore how our interactions with nature have changed over time. They chart the dependence and influence of Canadians on land, air, and water; their connections to plant, animal, avian, and microbial species; and their attitudes towards the places that sustain them. Challenged to offer new insights in short, pithy essays, the authors, including ourselves, jettison common scholarly blinkers in favour of more provocative argument. We grapple with changes unfolding at various scales, from the local to the global, and at various rates, from the near instantaneous to the almost infinitesimally slow. Together, we explore a range of issues, ranging from the creation of the continents to the economic bases of Canadian development to climate change. We also ponder important ideas that have shaped how Canadians view the wilderness, the city, the environment, and appropriate forms of knowledge about these things. Each essay invites you to think anew about what we know of the development of Canada, and each will help you grapple with the increasingly urgent challenge of reframing relations between humans and nature.

We open with what might be described as a little Big History of Canada. By considering deep time – the eons, eras, periods, epochs, and ages of the geological time scale that encompasses billions of years – "Nature and Nation" raises two essential points. First, that profound and not-so-long-ago-unimaginable natural processes have been essential to the development of the nation as we know it. And second, that our human tenure on the globe and the place now known as Canada has been but a fleeting moment. This juxtaposition – of our species' short-lived existence and our dependence on the rock of ages – drives home the resilience of nature. This long (but ever foreshortening) view also emphasizes the precariousness of humankind's existence on Earth. We cannot escape this truth.

Many scientists argue that we are living in a new geological epoch, the Anthropocene, distinguished by the transformative, quickening impact of human activity on Earth ecosystems. Precisely when the Anthropocene began remains a matter of debate. But few now doubt that shrinking Arctic sea ice, retreating glaciers, rising sea levels, and increasing global mean temperatures are signs of significant change. Canadians have not been solely responsible for these changes. We do, though, share culpability with others. Time and again in the pages that follow we see newcomers to northern North America (non-Indigenous peoples) pursuing economic and social development with scant regard for the environmental costs. In some sense, this trend began with the earliest encounters, when fish and furs, whales and birds seemed inexhaustible. There were efforts to regulate and control exploitation, but many of them were flawed in conception, implementation, or both. Particular casts of mind favoured transforming the earth. Settler-farmers were praised for converting "waste lands" into productive acres, even though cutting forests increased run-off and erosion and resulted in silted streams and altered ecologies.

After the Second World War, these trends continued and picked up speed with the embrace of ever-more powerful technologies that spawned demand for improvements in transportation and new markets for minerals and fossil fuels. Science, technology, and the development imperative have greatly improved the material circumstances of most (though certainly not all) Canadians. Compare the conditions in which we live with those of the eighteenth and nineteenth centuries. We have larger, warmer houses; move more easily across the vastness of the country; consume at unprecedented levels; and know countless luxuries unimaginable to our predecessors. Clearly, the toil and persistence of those who came before us helped to make the country what it is today. But the day of reckoning approaches. As "Time Chased Me Down, and I Stopped Looking Away," the luminous final essay in this volume, reminds us, we can no longer afford to turn blind eyes to the cumulative and continuing impact of humans on the natural world.

Between these discussions of deep time and time slipping away, we reflect on the ways that people have interacted with Canadian nature through the decades and consider what various groups and generations of individuals thought about those interactions. Together, we reveal some of the choices and chances, ideas and forces that lie behind many of the most vexing challenges now facing Canadians. "Painting the Map Red" and "Listening for Different Stories" jointly establish the broad parameters of human engagement with Canadian nature. The first focuses on three maps that illuminate, in turn, early European encounters with northern North America, the progress of newcomer settlement and economic development into the twentieth century, and the ways that maps (and histories) reflect the views of the victors rather than the vanquished in any struggle for power and territory. That is why it is important, as Julie Cruikshank argues with remarkable eloquence in the essay that follows, to listen for different stories in and of the past. The message is simple: environmental despoliation (and a great deal of individual and social anguish) might have been tempered had greater heed been paid to Indigenous views of nature.

For all the attention lavished on explorers in traditional histories of the continent, acquisitiveness trumped inquisitiveness as the driver of newcomer interest. Fish, whales, and furs drew sailors and traders – "merchant adventurers" all – across the Atlantic, into the icy edges of the Arctic islands, and across the interior. The prospect of farms, independence, and at least modest prosperity (the very realization of what philosophers of liberalism call possessive individualism) lured hundreds of thousands more to settle the land. In the process, as the cartographic installation discussed in "Painting the Map Red" makes clear, Indigenous peoples were marginalized and dispossessed. Forests were felled to erect and heat buildings but also, with increasing fervour in the nineteenth century, to meet market demands for wood in Britain and the United States. Later, precious and base minerals and a succession of fuels (coal, oil, gas, uranium, and bitumen) served to foster development and economic growth.

Some of the first Spaniards to reach South America heard of a mythical king, El Hombre Dorado, who dusted himself in gold. Successive iterations of this story transmuted the golden man into a golden city and, eventually, an empire, Eldorado. There was gold far to the north, but until the Fraser and Yukon gold rushes of the late nineteenth century, Canada's Eldorado was much more prosaic than its Andean namesake. In *The Nature of Canada*, we deal in different ways with some of the resources that constituted Canada's wealth and underpinned its development: fish from the sea and furs from the forest (in "Eldorado North?"); metals, minerals, and fossil fuels from the earth (in "Never Just a Hole in the Ground" and "The Power of Canada"); and the various products, animal and vegetable, that came from toil in hard-won fields (in "Back to the Land"). Together, these discussions help us calibrate the technological forces and guiding assumptions that have shaped the trajectory of Canadian economic growth, even as they allow us to measure the environmental consequences of the path we have taken.

Of course, in the moment, consequences may be unintended, unforeseen, or unrecognized. The essays "Nature We Cannot See" and "Every Creeping Thing ..." turn on this specific point, although it is one that has larger relevance to most environmental studies. Debilitating and deadly pathogens have made their way into northern North America unwanted and unheralded for centuries. After hitching rides across the oceans on human transporters, many of them wrought havoc on the unsuspecting and unprepared inhabitants of the new world in which they were unleashed. From first to last, from the sixteenth to the twentieth centuries, these invisible invaders spawned terror and panic among the populations they infected, and people struggled to understand the nature of their afflictions. The unintended consequences of the various communication corridors – railways, pipelines, airlines, and telecommunications networks – that opened up and tied together the spaces of the nation have been less dramatic but hardly less significant for the animal inhabitants of the continent. Humans impact nature in many ways, on countless scales, and often in a surprising fashion.

Ideas and assumptions are crucial guides and mediators of human action, and they rightly figure large in our discussions of the interactions between humans and nature. But ideas can be tricky things, shape-shifting will-o'-the-wisps or chameleon-like notions that present different hues in different circumstances. Wild nature is something that (most people believe) Canada possesses in abundance. But the accumulation of PCBs and other chemical substances in the bodies of polar bears, the clutter of ocean-borne detritus on beaches, and the poisoning of lakes by acid rain suggest that few parts of nature are truly wild or untouched by human influence any more. Indeed, Canadians' attitudes towards the vast, "empty" spaces of their country are nothing if not ambiguous. Many regard these spaces as frontiers for exploitation. Others consider them pristine places of bare rock, sparkling lakes, and clear air that allow the spirit of the wild to endure among predominantly urban Canadians. How can we set aside and treasure wilderness parks but encourage more and more people to visit them? These conundrums lie at the heart of "The Wealth of Wilderness."

If nature is "that 'given' world we have marred but not made," as novelist and poet Janice Kulyk Keefer so beautifully characterized it, cities are the most marred of places, especially in contrast to wilderness parks. But it is a matter of degree. In cities, nature is everywhere – in street trees, in cracks and crevices, in the air and water that courses through them, in the birds that fly above us and feed on discarded crumbs, and in the pets and parks and gardens that we meet at every turn. Cities are classic hybrid spaces. Like parks, they are designed according to certain precepts, to achieve certain ends. In "Imagining the City," you'll see that even our largest urban places were envisaged before they were built and that their realization changed ideas about the appeal, or otherwise, of different forms of urban design, and about urbanism more generally.

Ideas have the power to shape actions and worlds. The high modernist impulse, which combined the celebrated power of science and the transformative capacity of brute force technologies, was felt worldwide. Its consequences in Canada were as monumental as the St. Lawrence Seaway and Power Project and as personal as the loss of a family orchard. High modernism is generally criticized for denying the complexity and diversity of nature and riding roughshod over local concerns. In "Questions of Scale," it is presented as both a powerful abstraction and a practice grounded in detailed (albeit scientific) knowledge of particular places that did much to remake the country. "A Gendered Sense of Nature" turns our attention to Voice of Women and Greenpeace, two parallel but surprisingly intertwined protest movements generated by the testing of nuclear armaments in the 1960s, a pivotal moment in the development of environmentalism, both in Canada and globally. The essay deepens our understanding of the ideas at play and the issues at stake during these years. In arguing that gender shaped how the protest actions were conceived and executed, it also raises an important, often bypassed question: Do men and women have different environmental histories?

In 2012, a well-known leader of the Canadian environmental movement lamented the failure of that cause, but the authors of "Advocates and Activists" take a more moderate view. Yes, logging, pollution, and the despoliation of nature (the target of countless protest marches, barricades, and oppositional struggles over half a century and more) continue. And human blockades and various efforts to alert the public to the damage being inflicted on the natural world have failed to halt economic expansion. Ecological understanding may not be top of mind for most twenty-first-century Canadians, but many of them appreciate our collective need to tread more lightly on the earth. Nature is no longer assaulted as relentlessly as it once was. Debates that were framed in simple confrontational terms – prosperity versus protection, development versus wilderness, economy versus environment – are now a lot more complicated. This complexity stems, in large part, from increased recognition of Indigenous voices in discussions of resource development, territorial claims, and social and environmental justice.

The world is real, but we can't escape the fact that people make sense of it in diverse ways. Individuals interpret their surroundings differently, depending on their context, beliefs, and experiences. Consider, for example, the concept of wilderness. Travel to England, and you'll find sign-posted "wilderness walks" within the walled courtyard gardens of country houses. On the west coast of Canada, a document produced by the University of British Columbia describes a campus bordered by wilderness, presumably a reference to the second- and third-growth forests of Pacific Spirit Park, immediately to the east. Tended by rangers, cut through by heavily used roads, and threaded with trails thick with joggers, cyclists, dog walkers, and bird watchers, the park is hardly more wild than Vancouver, the busy, booming metropolis on its eastern edge. But as the discussion in "Climates of Our Times" reminds us, even seemingly secure and scientific ideas such as "the climate" are intellectual constructions with particular histories. Armed with this insight, we can better comprehend how we frame and understand larger issues such as climate change. We can also recognize that all knowledge is made, not given. Our understanding of the world reflects the circumstances in which it was produced and speaks to particular times and places.

The Nature of Canada offers several insights to help meet the challenges of living more sustainable lives in Canada. First, beware of simplifying fictions such as "Economics is more important than ecology," "The complexities of nature can be ignored," or "We can have it all" (whether it be sustainable mines or wild places that are at once pristine and exploited). Likewise, remember that wilderness, climate, and nation are not real and incontrovertible things but rather complex, contingent, and constructed concepts. Second, the cultural and material dimensions of our existence are deeply intertwined. For all the power of our intellects and imaginations, we depend on nature. This dependence was more obvious in times past, when, for example, family hearths were warmed by wood hewed, chopped, and hauled by members of the household. But we are no less dependent on nature's bounty today, even though we generally have few links to the processes that produce electricity and gasoline. Third, human-nature interactions are embodied experiences. Males and females, young and old, rich and poor, Indigenous peoples and newcomers have (and have had) different experiences of, relations with, and beliefs about the environment. Fourth, environmental transformations help to constitute society and the power relations threaded through it. Fifth, personal and societal aspirations must be reconciled with environmental realities to sustain human life on Earth. The human drive to domination must take nature's limits into consideration. Sixth, it is hard to find transcendent truths to light our way forward. Finally, the significant shifts in human attitudes to and interactions with nature traced in these pages offer hope that changes for the better remain possible.

Inconsistencies – paradoxes – confront us at every turn, but the manner in which we face, respond to, and attempt to resolve the environmental challenges ahead will be shaped by history and who we understand our-selves to be. Collaboration and coexistence rather than confrontation will be essential as we rethink the human-nature relationship. We hope that these pages will encourage you to think again and anew about the causes and consequences of our interactions with the earth. The futures of Canada, of Canadians, of humankind, and of the only world we have are at stake.

REFERENCES AND FURTHER READING

The "most complex word in the language" claim is from Raymond Williams, *Keywords: A Vocabulary of Culture and Society* (Oxford: Oxford University Press, 2015 [1976]), 164. The labyrinth of environmental thought, generally, is discussed in Raymond Williams, "Ideas of Nature," in *Problems of Materialism and Culture*, edited by Raymond Williams, 67–85 (London: Verso, 1980), and Roderick F. Nash, *Wilderness and the American Mind* (New Haven: Yale University Press, 1967). Keith Thomas traces its lineaments in England in *Man and the Natural World: Changing Attitudes in England, 1500–1800* (Harmondsworth, UK: Penguin Books, 1984). See also Richard White, "From Wilderness to Hybrid Landscapes: The Cultural Turn in Environmental History," *The Historian* 66, 3 (2004): 557–64.

The nature's "many relations with humanity" quote is from Sir Charles George Douglas Roberts, "Introductory Essay: The Poetry of Nature," in *The World's Best Poetry*, vol. 5, *Nature*, edited by Bliss Carman, John Vance Cheney, Sir Charles George Douglas Roberts, Charles Francis Richardson, Francis Hovey Stoddard, and John Raymond Howard, ix–xv (Philadelphia: John D. Morris, 1904). "The old kinship of earth" is from C.G.D. Roberts, *The Kindred of the Wild* (Boston: Page, 1902), 29; see also Thomas R. Dunlap, "'The Old Kinship of Earth': Science, Man and Nature in the Animal Stories of Charles G.D. Roberts," *Journal of Canadian Studies* 22, 1 (1987): 104–20, and Misao Dean, "Political Science: Realism in Roberts's Animal Stories," *Studies in Canadian Literature* 21, 1 (1996): 1–16. "Something of the permanent in nature" is from Lorraine McMullen, "'The Poetry of Earth': A Note on Roberts' Sonnets," *Studies in Canadian Literature/*

Études en littérature canadienne 1, 2 (1976): https://journals.lib.unb.ca/index.php/ scl/article/view/7846/8903.

Frye's "evocation of stark terror" appeared in "Canada and Its Poetry," *Canadian Forum,* December 1943, 210, and was reprinted in Northrop Frye, *The Bush Garden: Essays on the Canadian Imagination* (Toronto: Anansi, 1971). Warren Tallman's arguments were articulated in a two-part article, "Wolf in the Snow," *Canadian Literature* 5 (Summer 1960): 7–20, and 6 (Autumn 1960): 41–48. The "stupid power" quote is from Frye, *The Bush Garden,* 142. The garrison mentality is articulated in Frye, "Conclusion to a *Literary History of Canada*," in *The Literary History of Canada: Canadian Literature in English,* edited by Alfred G. Bailey, Claude Bissell, Roy Daniells, Northrop Frye, and Desmond Pacey (Toronto: University of Toronto Press, 1965), 318–32 [reprinted in Frye, *Bush Garden,* 213–48], which also envisages tiny Jonah entering an inconceivably large whale and characterizes this as an intimidating experience.

Margaret Atwood's *The Journals of Susanna Moodie* (Toronto: Oxford University Press, 1970) is a remarkable work. Her *Survival: A Thematic Guide to Canadian Literature* (Toronto: Anansi, 1972) popularized Frye's vision. Similar arguments appear in Marsha B. Klein, *Beyond the Land Itself: Views of Nature in Canada and the United States* (Cambridge: Harvard University Press, 1970), and D.G. Jones, *Butterfly on Rock: A Study of Themes and Images in Canadian Literature* (Toronto: University of Toronto Press, 1970). Atwood's "death by nature" appears in *Survival* and is transformed into "Death by Landscape" in her *Wilderness Tips* (Toronto: McClelland and Stewart, 1991); see also Faye Hamill, "'Death by Nature': Margaret Atwood and Wilderness Gothic," *Gothic Studies* 5, 2 (2003): 47–63. The "snowy indifference of nature" is remarked upon in Hugo McPherson, "Fiction 1940–1960," in Bailey et al., *Literary History,* 233. The "reluctant land" phrase echoes Cole Harris, *The Reluctant Land: Society, Space, and Environment in Canada before Confederation* (Vancouver: UBC Press, 2008).

Carl Berger's *Science, God, and Nature in Victorian Canada* (Toronto: University of Toronto Press, 1983) is an illuminating survey of natural history in nineteenth-century Canada and includes a useful discussion of those in awe of "the book of nature." "Wisdom from the leaves of creation" is from Joseph Howe, *Western and Eastern Rambles: Travel Sketches of Nova Scotia, 1828–31,* edited by M.G. Parks (Toronto: University of Toronto Press, 1973), 54. Janice K. Keefer's *Under Eastern Eyes: A Critical Reading of Maritime Fiction* (Toronto: University of Toronto Press, 1987), 62–90, has a useful discussion of the importance of the book of nature and the limits of the survivalist vision. Rudy Wiebe's "the way a man feels" is in "Passage by Land," *Canadian Literature* 48 (Spring 1971): 27.

The claim that "If some countries have too much history, Canada has too much geography" was made by Prime Minister Mackenzie King in a speech to the House of Commons, Ottawa, June 18, 1936. Carl Berger's *The Writing of Canadian History: Aspects of English-Canadian Historical Writing since 1900,* 2nd ed. (Toronto: University of Toronto Press, 1986) provides a thoughtful introduction to historical writing in and about Canada and includes chapters on Lower (112–37) and Innis (85–111). See A.R.M. Lower, *The North American Assault on the Canadian Forest: A History of the Lumber Industry between Canada and the United States* (New Haven: Yale University Press, 1938), 1, for "war on the wilderness," and H.A. Innis, *A History of the Canadian Pacific Railway* (London: P.S. King and Son, 1923), 287, for "conquest of geographical barriers." Innis grooves geography in his "On the Economic Significance of Culture," *Journal of Economic History* 4, supplement (December 1944): 84. The "pavement mentality" view belongs to W.L. Morton. See "Seeing an Unliterary Landscape," *Mosaic: A Journal for the Comparative Study of Literature and Ideas,* Manitoba Centennial Issue, 3, 3 (1970): 1–10. John Crosbie's witticism is reported in J. Stan Rowe, "Wilderness as Home Place," in *Home Place: Essays in Ecology,* edited by J. Stan Rowe (Edmonton: NeWest Publishers, 1990), 29.

For brief assessments of the rise of environmental history, see J. Donald Hughes, *What Is Environmental History?,* 2nd ed. (Cambridge: Polity Press, 2015) and, for Canada, Matthew Evenden and Graeme Wynn, "'54:40 or Fight': Writing within and across Borders in North American Environmental History," in *Nature's End: History and the Environment,* edited by Paul Warde and Sverker Sörlin,

215–46 (London: Palgrave, 2009). The idea of Big History (sometimes character-ized as "from nothing to everything") is widely associated with David Christian – see his *Maps of Time: An Introduction to Big History* (Berkeley: University of California Press, 2004) – and has gained visibility through the Bill Gates–sponsored Big History Project. See https://www.bighistoryproject.com/home.

There is a rapidly expanding literature on the Anthropocene. For a beginning, see John R. McNeill and Peter Engelke, *The Great Acceleration: An Environmental History of the Anthropocene since 1945* (Cambridge: Belknap Press of Harvard University Press, 2014); Gaia Vince, *Adventures in the Anthropocene: A Journey to the Heart of the Planet We Made* (London: Chatto and Windus, 2014); and Elizabeth Kolbert, *The Sixth Extinction: An Unnatural History* (New York: Henry Holt, 2014).

The characterization of nature as "that 'given' world we have marred but not made" is in Keefer, *Under Eastern Eyes*, 65.

Deep Time.
This striking graphic presents four and a half million years of Earth history
as recorded in rocks. The story rests on two main sources: knowledge of the
rate of decay of radioactive isotopes and the fossil remains of plants and
animals that evolved from cells and organic structures that existed about
three billion years ago. The retreat of the ice at the end of the Pleistocene
Epoch – the thin sliver of the Holocene – marks the conventional beginning
of the human history of Canada. Joseph Graham, William Newman, and
John Stacy, *The Geologic Time Spiral: A Path to the Past,* US Geological Survey
General Information Product 58, 2008

NATURE AND NATION

———

Graeme Wynn

HAROLD INNIS, AN IMPORTANT early twentieth-century Canadian intellectual, famously claimed that Canada "emerged not in spite of geography but because of it." This assertion rested on Innis's remarkable study of the fur trade in Canada. The statement was intended to emphasize that the country occupied a broad swath of territory – extending northward from the St. Lawrence–Great Lakes axis and the forty-ninth parallel to wrap around Hudson Bay – where the fur trade had developed most fully. In this view, Confederation, and the transcontinental nation that followed, was the political reflection of a logic imposed by river systems (access routes) and the rock, forest, and muskeg (beaver-friendly habitat) of the Canadian Shield.

There is something uncanny about Innis's insight in the way that it floats easily between the mundane and the miraculous. It gives new significance to the inescapable fact that three of the five great North American drainage basins east of the Great Divide (which follows the crest of the Rocky Mountains) are almost entirely Canadian. It also makes obvious the not-entirely-self-evident conclusion that beaver from the boreal forests yielded heavier and better pelts than those from more southern climes. More than this, Innis's claim did important political and nationalist work in its day. In particular, it suggested – in defiance of arguments that the

The major drainage basins of North America.
Drainage patterns buttress the claim that Canada emerged
"because of geography." Cartography by Eric Leinberger

country was a fragile political anomaly, doomed by its attempt to straddle
the north-south grain of the continent – that the east-west nation rested
on robust, natural foundations.

Innis's provocative adage opened a new vista on the Canadian past, but
it intrigued and tantalized rather than altered how historians wrote. Innis

himself never fully explored its implications, although he had a more capacious view of the historian's task than most of his contemporaries. His work on the fur trade was unusual in that it paid attention to the biological characteristics and life history of the beaver. Memorably, he pointed out that the beaver is an animal that "migrates very little and travels over land very slowly."

But Innis was also a product of his times. His histories turned on the migration of Europeans to rich resource frontiers. They focused on the links between economic activity and political development, cultures and empires. He took the vast expanse of thin soil and exposed bedrock that encircled Hudson Bay – and the rivers that ran through it (upon which the fur trade was centred) – for granted. His book essentially ignored the eons of geological processes, climatic fluctuations, and biophysical changes that had brought these features into existence. It paid scant attention to the particular characteristics of the north country and offered little detail about their influence on Canadian development. For Innis, as for others in the years between the world wars, everything had a past, but not everything was grist for the historian's mill.

Today, rising anxieties about global climate change and other "environmental problems" have expanded horizons of concern, for both historians and the public at large. We are all now aware of the dynamic qualities of Earth systems and the complex reciprocal relationships that bind humans and nature together. So, it's important to return to Innis's assertion to rethink the bounds of Canadian history and develop a more expansive account of the past. Bringing history and geography together in this way means paying attention to the movements of mountains, the migrations of continents, the waxing and waning of deserts and swamps, and the advances and retreats of glaciers, plants, and animals. These processes open certain possibilities for human existence in some places and foreclose them in others. They create the (un)inhabitable earth. In other words, humans live in material settings produced by physical processes – and their capacity to amend and transform their surroundings is, and always has been, highly variable. Everywhere, however, lands and lives are shaped by the reciprocal interplay of humans and their environments. This is the central insight of environmental history and a source of endless fascination.

In Canada, ancient and continuing physical processes underpinned the development of a nation across the vast expanse of northern North America. So we need to think anew about the "deep past," which extends beyond the furthest reaches of human time, and the few millennia in which people have inhabited this ancient territory so recently named Canada. To look backward across this span is to contemplate a world in motion. Much of this movement was propelled by biogeophysical (or, broadly, earth) processes. Sometimes they were infinitesimally slow, sometimes they occurred at rates discernible only over the course of a human lifetime, and sometimes they were so rapid they were catastrophic. Humans came late to this place and story, and here and there, and with increasing potency, they added their agency to the forces of nature. Yet the very survival and prosperity of migrants to this world – which was at once old and new – rested on foundations laid down millennia before. At the same time, these people depended on their own resilience, ingenuity, and perseverance to adapt to circumstances and utilize nature's endowments.

Scientific and popular interpretations of the natural world have evolved through time, as have the words we use to describe it. This means that we need to pay attention to how knowledge is constructed. Only by doing so can we hope to understand nature's role in shaping human lives, people's individual and shared prospects and, ultimately, even intangible and elusive ideas such as nationhood. For example, the terms *pre-Cambrian* and *Canadian Shield* trip so easily from twenty-first-century tongues that it is easy to forget that both are recent coinages. The science of geology, to which these words "belong," only emerged in the late eighteenth and early nineteenth centuries. Not until 1835 was the name *Cambrian* applied to the earliest known fossil-bearing strata (in Wales and now dated to between 541 and 485 million years ago). Earlier so-called primitive rocks then became pre-Cambrian by implication, but they were also known until 1900 as Azoic (or lifeless) rocks.

When British North American geologists claimed, in 1863, to have discovered a primitive fossil, christened *Eozoön canadense*, in ancient (metamorphosed) limestone from the Ottawa Valley, they believed they had made a revolutionary discovery that challenged the Azoic paradigm. But they located their find in so-called Laurentian rocks, a local nomenclature that was applied (as *Laurentien*) in 1845 by François-Xavier Garneau, a French Canadian nationalist historian, to the mountains north of the St. Lawrence River. The term was subsequently conferred upon the larger Laurentian Plateau and the Laurentide Ice Sheet that covered it during the Pleistocene glaciation. The Canadian Shield only came into terminological being in the 1880s. Its name combines two ideas. The first was colonial politician Thomas D'Arcy McGee's vision, articulated in 1860, of "one great nationality bound, like the shield of Achilles, by the blue rim of ocean" encompassing "the Western mountains and the crests of Eastern waves" as well as the rivers and valleys between. The second was the strong nationalist sentiment of influential Canadian imperialists in the quarter century after Confederation.

Comprising over half the area of present-day Canada, the 8 million square kilometres of pre-Cambrian "shield" is the exposed portion of the ancient geological core of North America. Radiometric dating and other recent techniques have revealed that parts of it are 4 billion years old and that the whole is made up of various fragments of material, which erupted from hundreds of now-extinct volcanoes that coalesced and amalgamated between 2.45 and 1.24 billion years ago. But such a fine-grained understanding was beyond scientific reach until it became possible, in the latter part of the twentieth century, to determine the age of rocks by calibrating decay in their radioactive elements.

Scholars were skeptical when the German scientist Alfred Wegener suggested, in 1912, that the continents were in motion. He came to this conclusion in an effort to account for the presence of warm-climate fossils in Arctic rocks and to explain why continental edges seemed to fit together like pieces in a puzzle (think of Brazil and West Africa). Despite the intuitive logic of Wegener's idea, the notion of continental drift seemed largely fanciful until the 1950s. In that decade, studies of paleomagnetism (which reveal the intensity and orientation of Earth's magnetic field locked into ancient rocks at the time of their formation) showed that the Indian subcontinent had once been in the southern hemisphere. Within a few years, scientists had refined the idea of continental drift (or wandering continents, to use South African geologist Alex du Toit's felicitous 1937 phrase) into a theory of plate tectonics and had added a driving mechanism to explain the outwardly improbable. Simply put, the theory envisaged convection currents in the earth's mantle causing convergent and divergent movement of several plates comprising the earth's surface. Proceeding at between 250 to 1,500 millimetres a year, these movements are now understood to have caused the formation, breakup, and migration of continents over time.

Through the millions of years of these movements, the shield formed the nucleus around which geological processes built the North American continent. It shaped the configuration of the continent, differentiated its topography, and moulded its potential (or otherwise) for settlement and development by humans eons into the future. Two examples suffice to make the point. First, about 2 billion years ago, the Flin Flon greenstone belt of central Manitoba and east central Saskatchewan was formed by volcanic activity. Approximately 45 kilometres wide and five times as long, it is one of the richest mining areas on the globe. Since 1916, more than twenty mines have extracted copper, zinc, and related metals from this area, and three others have produced gold and silver. Second, some

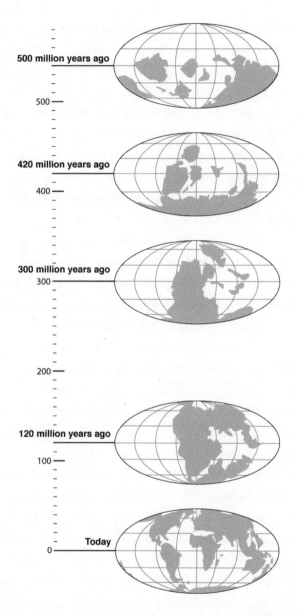

Changing configurations of land and water through half a billion years.
Met with skepticism early in the twentieth century, the idea of "wandering
continents," or that continents are in motion, now offers a robust explanation
for many aspects of Earth history. Cartography by Eric Leinberger

1.85 billion years ago, a giant meteorite struck the Nuna (or Columbia) supercontinent, from which later plate configurations evolved. The resulting crater, the second largest in the world, filled with magma that contained nickel, copper, platinum, gold, palladium, and other metals. Unsuspected and undetected until the decade before Confederation, these deposits made the Sudbury Basin of Ontario one of the world's most productive mining areas. Early this century, it produced half of the $10 billion generated annually by mining in Ontario. It also accounted for an eighth of the $40 billion that the 370,000 Canadians directly employed in mining contributed to Canada's GDP.

Through the ages, winds, rain, and ice eroded the shield's soaring mountains (some of them thousands of metres higher than present-day Everest) down to a low plateau of rolling hills. Vast quantities of sediment were deposited, layer after layer, in the shallow waters surrounding the plateau. Over time, they formed sandstones and shales, interleaved with limestones formed in clearer waters. Today, the land between the shield and the St. Lawrence Valley produced by these processes (the country north of Belleville in present-day Ontario) is a region of bare limestone plains, thin soils, and abandoned farms. This, wrote poet Al Purdy in a memorable phrase that echoed the tribulations of those who had tried to settle there in the nineteenth century, was "the country of our defeat."

Another vestige is the vast Western Canada Sedimentary Basin, the lower reaches of which are made up of limestone-dolomite rich in evaporite minerals, including potash. As the Laurasia (Laurentia and Eurasia) Plate, with the shield at its heart, traced its gradual course across the globe through tropical and subtropical latitudes during the Carboniferous and Cretaceous periods, lush vegetation flourished, died, and decomposed. It turned, eventually, into rich coal and oil and gas deposits in what we now call the Atlantic provinces, the central Plains, and British Columbia. At much the same time, an eastward-moving oceanic plate slid beneath the continental land

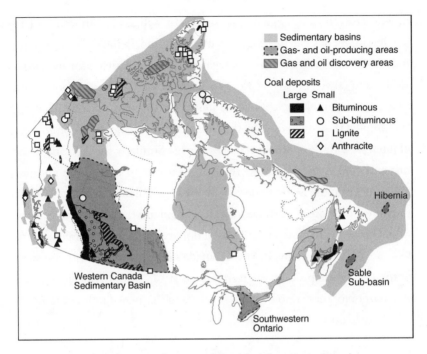

Legend:
- Sedimentary basins
- Gas- and oil-producing areas
- Gas and oil discovery areas

Coal deposits
Large Small
- ▲ Bituminous
- ○ Sub-bituminous
- □ Lignite
- ◇ Anthracite

Hibernia

Western Canada
Sedimentary Basin

Sable
Sub-basin

Southwestern
Ontario

Major sedimentary basins and fossil fuel deposits in Canada.
Encircling the pre-Cambrian shield, Canada's sedimentary basins hold most
of the country's reserves of fossil fuels. Cartography by Eric Leinberger

mass off the Pacific Coast. New terranes or continental fragments were accreted to the western margin of the continent. These processes raised up the cordilleran mountains and produced a spate of tectonic activity that created important deposits of copper, lead, zinc, gold, silver, and other minerals.

Much of Canada's modern development has turned on these ancient foundations. For all the importance that Innis attached to geography, Suzanne Zeller, a historian of science, argues that geology (as well as meteorology and botany) was crucial in bringing British North Americans to contemplate the idea of a transcontinental nation. In her view, the mid-nineteenth-century geological surveys of William Logan were vital to the development of an ideology of nation building. In the wake of Britain's industrialization, when coal was regarded as a prerequisite for industrial wealth and power, Logan's report of a dearth of coal in central Canada and its abundance in Nova Scotia was a significant impetus to Confederation. It prompted those who lived by the Great Lakes to recognize a "community of interest" with those who dwelled by the sea. Similarly, the gold and other mineral rushes that brought remote locations in the North and the Cordillera into the world trade system, fired Canadian imaginations about the value of the great Northwest and promoted interest in these territories. Mines continue to generate billions of dollars for the Canadian economy. Oil and gas do the same. In 2013, Canada's oil exports, about two-thirds of total domestic production, were valued at $75 billion. But the uneven distribution of these resources has shaped and sharpened political tensions within the country.

For all the antiquity of the country's geological core, the landscape of Canada is among the most youthful in the world. About twenty thousand years ago, most of the country was covered by ice. In the last of a series of great glaciations that began some 2 million years ago (in what geologists call the Quaternary Period), glaciers and ice sheets up to four kilometres thick scoured the surface of the land. Only the northern Yukon, parts of the Northwest Territories, the highest peaks of the western mountains, and a few areas of the Prairies, such as the Cypress Hills, escaped. Elsewhere, glaciers worked, in the words of American conservationist Peter Farb, as a "monumental plow upon the land, scooping out depressions in the earth and grinding boulders down to pebbles." Ice movement carved deep U-shaped valleys in mountains, scraped bare the bedrock of the shield, and deposited vast quantities of material beneath and beyond the ice.

When the ice began to melt, about eighteen thousand years ago, it left behind a forbidding, disorganized landscape. Vast areas were covered by deep deposits of unconsolidated clay, silt, sand, pebbles, and boulders known as glacial till. Moraines (usually long linear ridges of poorly sorted clay, sand, and stone) and eskers (long winding ridges of sand and gravel deposited by streams beneath the ice) snaked across and atop this till surface. Low, elongated tear-drop–shaped hills, often compared to inverted spoons in appearance, were formed under the ice and exposed by its retreat. These features, known as drumlins, are often found clustered together and aligned in the same direction. They form striking, distinctive landscapes, exemplified by the 900-square-kilometre drumlin field near Peterborough, Ontario.

The newly exposed land surface was in flux. Torrents of meltwater ran from the receding ice, eroding recently deposited materials and accumulating in vast lakes, the configurations of which were ever-changing. Lake Agassiz extended in a great arc around the southern edge of the retreating Laurentide Ice Sheet. At times more extensive than all the current Great Lakes combined, it spread variously over much of Manitoba and parts of Saskatchewan, Ontario, North and South Dakota, and Minnesota. Its remnants include numerous lakes, large and small, as well as numerous beach terraces that can be traced in the landscape from Riding Mountain, Manitoba, to Rosholt, South Dakota, to Dryden, Ontario. It drained periodically (and more or less catastrophically) into the Mississippi, Lake Superior, and Mackenzie drainage systems before the ice barrier breached. Then, when Lake Agassiz finally drained through Hudson Bay about 8,500 years ago, it raised global sea levels between 0.8 and 2.8 metres, disrupted the oceanic circulation system, and cooled the climate markedly.

By the mid-twentieth century, the legacies of the last glaciation – the panorama of low, rounded hills, lake-filled depressions, and wide exposures of ice-sculpted volcanic bedrock – were central to the iconography of Canadian nationhood. Espousing the view that direct contact with nature would yield a distinctively Canadian style of painting, Tom Thomson and other painters in the Group of Seven turned the southern edge of the shield into a symbolic landscape. Their astonishing sequence of canvases, portraying the area as pristine and essentially untouched by humans, struck a responsive chord across much of the nation. In 1995, Canada Post issued a set of ten stamps, each depicting a work by a member of the group or one of its associates. Almost two decades later, the Royal Canadian Mint issued commemorative silver coins featuring the group's work.

Other more prosaic but materially more significant legacies of the last glaciation include the large lakes of southern Manitoba (Winnipeg, Winnipegosis, Manitoba); Lake of the Woods; the rich, fertile soils of the Red River Basin; the Oak Ridges Moraine of southern Ontario; countless lakes and waterfalls that subsequently became valuable to the development of water power and hydroelectricity; and vast deposits of sand and gravel important to the construction of modern Canada.

As the ice sheets retreated, the earth's crust, formerly depressed by the sheer weight of ice, began to rise. This process of isostatic rebound was rapid at first but then proceeded slowly (at approximately one centimetre a year) and unevenly. It continues today. The consequences of this rebound have been dramatic. The magnificent Torngat Mountains in Labrador, which rise more than 1,500 metres above sea level, are the product of uplift and tectonic processes that elevated and tilted the ancient glaciated rocks. In 2008, they were designated Canada's forty-second National Park. The southeastern shores of Hudson Bay are now at least 285 metres above their level eight thousand years ago. Different rates of rebound in different places tripled the size and doubled the volume of Lake of the Woods and shifted it some fifty kilometres south between nine thousand and six thousand years ago. Today, the lake continues to deepen by a few centimetres a century at its southern end. Slow though they appear on human time scales, these changes complicate the distribution and movement of water in vast sections of northern Canada, where drainage patterns among innumerable rivers and lakes are still evolving.

Anyone who has visited or seen images of far northern tundra or the snout of a mountain glacier can readily envisage the appearance of the landscape as the ice sheets retreated across Canada. Lakes, bogs, low temperatures, bare rock, unconsolidated outwash deposits, frozen sediment, and shifting streams are not conducive to vegetation. At best, an impoverished flora of lichens and a few vascular plants trailed the hither edge of the retreating ice. Beyond, low mosses, herbs, saxifrage, arctic willow, and Cassiope appeared. Beyond this grew Labrador tea, black spruce, and scrub birch. Ten thousand years ago, a forest somewhat akin to today's boreal (spruce, balsam fir, jack pine, and birch) occupied southern Ontario. North of the Ottawa River and extending through present-day southern New Brunswick and Nova Scotia, dwarf spruce, willow, birch, wormwood, and ragweed grew.

Vegetation patterns evolved rapidly as the climate warmed. Seeds dispersed, carried on the wind or by birds and animals, and established themselves where soil and climate conditions were favourable. Maple and chestnut trees marched into southern Ontario from the mouth of the Mississippi; hemlock and white pine came from the eastern slopes of the Appalachians. On average, pine advanced three times faster than the chestnut, which made about one hundred metres of northward progress a year. Borne on strong southeasterly winds, white spruce seeds reached the shores of the Beaufort Sea nine thousand years ago, travelling at the rate of three kilometres a year, a thousand times faster than they were able to move against prevailing winds from Pennsylvania to Labrador. Compounded over time, different rates of migration made for an ever-changing vegetation mix. Although they started out together, pine took root in Ontario a thousand years before the hemlock, which requires shade and richer, moister soils for propagation.

Seven thousand years ago, the vegetation map of Canada broadly re-sembled that of today. Three thousand years on, continuing climate warming allowed lichen woodland (or taiga) to extend to Ungava Bay and the boreal forest to extend across present-day Quebec to fifty-five degrees north. Deciduous forest covered most of southern Ontario. In the west, grassland and parkland areas also expanded and extended northward. Then the climate cooled again, and one thousand years or so ago vegetation zones reverted to something approaching their present form.

Remote in time and difficult to trace in space though they are, these changes shaped habitats and possibilities for Indigenous peoples long before Europeans arrived on the continent. Indigenous peoples claim to have been in North America since time began, and on the scale of human history, this makes sense. Few people regard the French or the English as immigrants in their own countries, even though Celtic, Frankish, and other tribes oc-cupied Gaul, and Celts, Saxons, Angles, Romans, Vikings, and Picts colonized Britain much more recently than Indigenous peoples came into the spacious expanse of present-day Canada. Still, the long-standing view of Western scholarship is that Indigenous peoples crossed the Bering land bridge between Siberia and Alaska about thirteen thousand years ago and then made their way south when an ice-free corridor opened up between the Laurentian and Cordilleran Ice Sheets. Within a couple of thousand years, these Paleoindians had left archeological evidence (in the form of distinct-ively fluted Clovis projectile points, named after the New Mexico site of their first identification) from Florida to California to Nova Scotia. In broad terms, they colonized most of central and eastern Canada from the south as the ice retreated. But there are increasing doubts about this unitary model. Some posit alternative and earlier water-borne migrations that followed the outer shores of the continent. Others argue, on the basis of

DNA evidence, that the first North Americans arrived thirty thousand to forty thousand years ago.

The Paleoindians who first ranged into the territory of present-day eastern Canada about ten thousand years ago faced harsh conditions. Journeying towards the ice, they came in small groups to hunt caribou, mastodon, and mammoth, and they encountered cold temperatures and sparse vegetation dominated by scrubby spruce. As the land warmed and as a closed coniferous forest grew, the large mammoths either moved north or became extinct. The people developed a more diversified suite of stone tools, broadened their subsistence base, utilized smaller territories, and began to trade with others. About three thousand years ago, the use of rudimentary pottery marked the transition from the Archaic to the Woodland culture complex. By 500 BCE, many Woodland peoples lived in relatively permanent village sites. In northwestern Ontario, once-nomadic hunting, fishing, and gathering peoples settled and built large burial mounds along a three-kilometre stretch of the Rainy River, now designated the Kay-Nah-Chi-Wah-Nung National Historic Site.

A millennium or so later, some groups began to adopt the plants and techniques of shifting cultivation from the south, and between 750 and 500 years ago, agriculture became a major component of subsistence among the Wendat (Huron) peoples near Georgian Bay. Although they probably adopted maize and beans later than the Wendat, Maliseet people successfully cultivated these crops, along with ground nuts (*Apios americana*) and sunchokes on the banks of the Wəlastəkw (St. John) River through the climatically harsh years of the seventeenth century. On the West Coast, Indigenous peoples set controlled fires to enhance the production of berries and camas bulbs. They built rock-walled beach terraces or clam gardens to quadruple yields of some species and double those of others. And they erected sophisticated fish traps in estuaries. These innovations and adaptations reflect the remarkable environmental knowledge and resilience and ingenuity of

Indigenous peoples forced to cope with ceaseless, albeit gradual, shifts in climate and environment.

Shorter-term environmental disruptions often had dramatic effects. The brief extension of Norse settlement from Greenland to L'Anse aux Meadows in Newfoundland occurred during, and benefitted from, the Medieval Warm Period between 950 and 1250 CE. Early in the seventeenth century, explorers found ice strong enough to bear their weight on the north shore of Lake Superior in June, reminding us that early European engagements with Canada occurred in abnormally cool conditions. Approximately 250 years after that, botanist John Macoun, who was part of a CPR expedition surveying the West at a time of unusually high rainfall, declared even Palliser's Triangle, the most arid corner of the prairie, suitable for agricultural settlement. This snap judgment helped to justify the railway's choice of a southern route to the Pacific. A few years earlier, Henry Youle Hind had identified a vast "Fertile Belt" extending from Lake of the Woods to the Rocky Mountains. Together, Macoun and Hind laid the groundwork for "imaginative idealizations" celebrating the "Promise of Eden" in the West and set the stage for years of struggle by settlers who took their assessments at face value.

Disasters immediate and remote also impinged on Canadian lives. When a landslide (possibly triggered by an earthquake) blocked the Fraser River between 1,200 and 1,000 years ago, it disrupted salmon spawning, which very likely led to the abandonment of large, well-established pithouse villages and the cultural collapse of Indigenous societies upstream of Texas Creek in south central British Columbia. The distant but cataclysmic volcanic eruption of Mount Tambora in the Dutch East Indies in 1815 shrouded the earth with ash and caused agricultural crisis in northeastern America in 1816, "the year without a summer." Equally unpredictable events with more local effects included floods, fires, and violent weather – the "bad blows and big storms" that battered communities throughout the decades.

Over the last five hundred years or so, human agency has combined, ever more potently, with the work of nature to change the face of Canada. Indigenous peoples cleared forests for fields and then, when soil fertility declined, abandoned them. These clearings provided rich forage for deer and allowed their numbers to increase. European newcomers set cascading ecological consequences in motion (often without understanding that they were doing so) as they depleted stocks of beaver and cod, turned eastern Canada into Great Britain's woodyard, destroyed vast areas of forest to establish farms, dammed rivers to power mills, and plowed prairie sod.

Europeans also introduced a veritable ark of animals and plants into Canada. Various breeds of cattle, sheep, horses, poultry, cats, and dogs came ashore with newcomers, who also imported numerous varieties of trees, grains, pulses, birds, fish, and fruits and vegetables. These introductions were made for economic, aesthetic, and psychological reasons. When English-born Elizabeth Hale said that her newly acquired seigneury on the St. Lawrence, Sainte-Anne-de-la-Pérade, resembled "the Thames towards Putney," she spoke prospectively as well as metaphorically. Her work there included planting oaks (for "the honor of [her] native country"), orchards, flowerbeds, and hedges to "neatify" the estate.

Efforts to domesticate the material landscape found their intellectual counterparts in the works of cartographers and natural historians. Their sketches and descriptions of Canadian nature served to strengthen the newcomers' sense of wonder at, familiarity with, and attachment to the developing country. They also hinted, on occasion, at the settlers' collective transformation of the land. Catharine Parr Traill, sister of Susanna Moodie and a prolific author throughout her sixty-seven years of residence in Ontario, spliced nature and nation when she enjoined the "Mothers of

Purple Trillium.
One of the four thousand or so plants "native" to
Canada, this (and other wildflowers) seemed, to nature-
loving Catharine Parr Traill, to be vulnerable to the march
of settlement in the middle of the nineteenth century.
Painting by Agnes Fitzgibbon, in C.P. Traill, *Canadian
Wild Flowers* (1868). Courtesy of Thomas Fisher Rare
Book Library, University of Toronto

Canada" to teach their children to "know and love the wild flowers spring-
ing in their path" to ensure that their hearts and minds would in future
"turn back with loving reverence to the land of their birth: to that dear
country, endeared to them by the remembrance of the wild flowers which
they plucked in the happy days of childhood."

Humankind's utilitarian and intellectual efforts to transform and sub-jugate the landscape were both compounded and confounded by the work of nature. Species migrate, whether with the connivance of humans or without. Trial and error, science and luck, and basic climatic consideration influenced the survival and spread of most plant introductions. Collectively, they remade the settled countryside. Some introduced plants even escaped into the wilds beyond the farms and gardens to which they had been brought. Today, Canada has about 4,000 native species of vascular plants; another 1,225 or so alien (or introduced) species now reproduce beyond cultivation. Almost 475 of these alien species are considered invasive, which is to say that they threaten the environment, the economy, or society. Fewer than 50 were established in Canada before 1800, but that number more than quadrupled in the nineteenth century. Almost half of the invasives belong, in lay terms, to the daisy, grass, mustard, pea, and mint families. About 80 percent of them are from western Europe; China and Japan form the next most significant source area. For the 245 invasives for which path-ways can be established, over half were deliberate introductions. Of the remainder, about 70 percent arrived as contaminants in imported seed, forage, or garden supplies, and slightly less than 30 percent came along with livestock or as ship's ballast. Among the first pieces of (unsuccessful) environmental legislation introduced in several of the colonies were acts to stop the spread of thistles. This prickly, injurious weed came ashore from Europe, but as it spread into the United States it became known, inaccurately and unfortunately, as the Canada Thistle.

Newcomers also brought pests and pathogens to Canada. Introduced inadvertently, they wreaked more or less insidious havoc across varying spans of space and time. Undoubtedly the most catastrophic were the viral diseases that decimated Indigenous populations across the continent. Less tragically, the Beech scale insect was introduced from Europe through Halifax late in the nineteenth century and killed many trees as it spread through the forests of the Maritimes and into Ontario. The better-known

Dutch elm disease, a fungus of Asian origin spread by bark beetles, reached the United States in a shipment of wood from the Netherlands in the 1920s, spread to eastern Canada in the 1940s, and reached Ontario in 1967. It has since killed over 80 percent of the elms in Toronto, Montreal, Ottawa, and Quebec City. In the nineteenth century, grain crops were ravaged by the Hessian fly and the wheat blossom midge. The former, a gall midge, was introduced to North America in the straw bedding of German (that is, Hessian) soldiers during the American Revolution. In the 1790s, it was identified in Lower Canada. As settlement and cultivation expanded, it spread vigorously and did great damage to crops in the 1840s. The blossom midge appeared mysteriously near Quebec City in 1819. By 1834 it was causing severe damage near Montreal and, spreading at a rate of fourteen kilometres a year, it reached the north shore of Lake Ontario by 1849. First noticed in New Brunswick in the early 1840s, it spread across the province and into Nova Scotia, which reported severe crop losses in 1854. Two years later, losses of $2.5 million were attributed to the blossom midge in the Canadas.

Then as now, the economic losses stemming from particular weed and insect species are difficult to judge. And they are only a part of the story. Ecosystem diversity, structure, and function may also be threatened by introduced species. As a broad measure of impacts, however, some studies suggest that 99 percent of yield losses and herbicide costs borne by Prairie grain farms today are attributable to alien plant species. By one account, the cost to wheat, barley, and canola producers is over $1 billion a year. More broadly and more astonishingly, the hidden cost of reduced production in Canadian forestry, fisheries, and agriculture attributable to invasive species has been estimated recently at between $16.6 and $34.5 billion dollars a year.

Emphasizing the environmental transformations wrought by newcomers and their accompanying biota, some have called European settlers ecological revolutionaries. So they were. But their capacity to impose a new order on the world was forever challenged and limited by nature. Although pioneer farmers attacked the forests with a dedication that suggested a hatred of trees, they struggled to vanquish their vegetative enemy. Newly opened fields were soon reclaimed by fireweed and blueberry, by chokecherry and wild raspberry, and by saplings seeded from the surrounding forest. Little-understood and difficult-to-control infestations made people anxious and left them and their crops and animals vulnerable, as did unpredictable storms and inexplicable shifts in the onset and intensity of the seasons. When those selfsame late nineteenth-century nationalists who gave the Canadian Shield its name insisted that the country's cold winters would give rise to a hardy, intelligent, resilient people – "northmen of the New World," given to tossing pine trees about in their glee – they were making the best of harsh circumstances. But by affording nature a role in the shaping of their society, they unintentionally acknowledged the shifting fusion of people, place, and nature that gave (and continues to give) shape and substance to the country.

REFERENCES AND FURTHER READING

Harold A. Innis's "not in spite of geography" and the slow-migrating beaver observation are from *The Fur Trade in Canada: An Introduction to Canadian Economic History* (Toronto: University of Toronto Press, 1956 [1930]), 392–93 and 4. For assessments of Innis's historical contributions, see Carl Berger, *The Writing of Canadian History: Aspects of English-Canadian Historical Writing since 1900* (Toronto: University of Toronto Press, 1986), Chap. 4, and John Watson, *Marginal Man: The Dark Vision of Harold Innis* (Toronto: University of Toronto Press, 2006). Libby Robin's *How a Continent Created a Nation* (Sydney: UNSW Press, 2007) and Eric Kaufmann's "'Naturalizing the Nation': The Rise of Naturalistic Nationalism in Canada and the United States," *Comparative Studies in Society and History* 40 (1998): 666–95, add depth to the landscape-nationhood argument. The geological history of the Canadian Shield is treated in a lavishly illustrated book by Nicholas Eyles, *Canadian Shield: The Rocks That Made Canada* (Toronto: Fitzhenry and Whiteside, 2011), and in his *Ontario Rocks: Three Billion Years of Environmental Change* (Toronto: Fitzhenry and Whiteside, 2002), which has more on plate movements.

Essays by Charles F. O'Brien, "Eozoön Canadense: 'The Dawn Animal of Canada,'" *Isis* 61, 2 (1970): 206–23, and by Julie Adelman, "Eozoön: Debunking the Dawn Animal," *Endeavour* 31, 3 (September 2007): 94–98, discuss the purported Eozoön fossil. McGee's invocation of the "shield of Achilles" is from W.L. Morton, ed., *The Shield of Achilles: Aspects of Canada in the Victorian Age* (Toronto: McClelland and Stewart, 1968). The best starting point for plate tectonics is Naomi Oreskes, *Plate Tectonics: An Insider's History of the Modern Theory of the Earth* (Boulder: Westview Press, 2003), and her earlier *The Rejection of Continental Drift: Theory and Method in American Earth Science* (New York: Oxford University Press, 1999) is also helpful in this context. A book and similarly titled video by C.J. Yorath, *Where Terranes Collide* (Victoria: Orca Book Publishers, 1990) and *Where Terranes Collide: The Geology of Western Canada,* produced and edited by Gord More (Victoria: Quadra Productions for Geological Survey of Canada, 1992), offer the best account of terranes. The development of geology and the push to understand the earth is treated very well in Martin J.S. Rudwick, *Bursting the Limits of Time: The Reconstruction of Geohistory in the Age of Revolution* (Chicago: University of Chicago Press, 2005). The "country of our defeat" is from Al Purdy, "The Country North of Belleville," in *Beyond Remembering: The Collected Poems of Al Purdy* (Madeira Park, BC: Harbour Publishing, 2000). For the idea that coal contributed to Confederation, see Suzanne Zeller, *Inventing Canada: Early Victorian Science and the Idea of a Transcontinental Nation* (Toronto: University of Toronto Press, 1987).

Peter Farb's characterization of glaciers as plows comes from his *Face of North America: The Natural History of a Continent* (New York: Harper and Row, 1963), 12. See also Donald Worster, "Ice, Worms, and Dirt: The Power of Nature in North American History," in *Method and Meaning in Canadian Environmental*

History, edited by Alan MacEachern and William J. Turkel (Toronto: Nelson, 2009), 25.

James T. Teller and Lee Clayton's "Glacial Lake Agassiz" (Special Paper 26, Geological Association of Canada, Department of Geology, Memorial University of Newfoundland, St. John's, Newfoundland, 1983) provides an early, broad account of Lake Agassiz, but there has been much recent refinement and reinterpretation in which Garry Clarke has played an important role. See Garry K.C. Clarke, Andrew B.G. Bush, and John W.M. Bush, "Freshwater Discharge, Sediment Transport, and Modeled Climate Impacts of the Final Drainage of Glacial Lake Agassiz," *Journal of Climate* 22, 8 (2009): 2161–80. Bill Redekop provides an accessible treatment in *Lake Agassiz: The Rise and Demise of the World's Greatest Lake* (Winnipeg: Heartland Associates, 2017).

Further details about the last glaciation, vegetation patterns, the debate over the arrival of people in North America, and Indigenous lives and livelihoods before European contact can be found in Graeme Wynn, *Canada and Arctic North America: An Environmental History* (Santa Barbara, CA: ABC Clio, 2007). *The Historical Atlas of Canada*, vol. 1, *From the Beginning*, edited by R. Cole Harris (Toronto: University of Toronto Press, 1987) includes several informative plates dealing with these matters and others. See also E. Chris Pielou, *After the Ice Age: The Return of Life to Glaciated North America* (Chicago: University of Chicago Press, 1991).

Peter Storck's memoir, *Journey to the Ice: Discovering an Ancient World* (Vancouver: UBC Press, 2006), offers an accessible discussion of the archaeology of Paleoindian, Archaic, and Woodland peoples. Conrad Heidenreich's *Huronia: A History and Geography of the Huron Indians, 1600–1650* (Toronto: McClelland and Stewart, 1971) and Bruce G. Trigger's *People of Aataentsic: A History of the Huron People to 1660* (Montreal and Kingston: McGill-Queen's University Press, 1976) are informative guides to the Wendat. For Indigenous cultivation, see Heidenreich, *Huronia;* Jason Hall, "Maliseet Cultivation and Climatic Resilience on the Wǝlastǝkw/St. John River during the Little Ice Age," *Acadiensis* 44, 2 (2015):

3–25; A.S. Groesbeck, K. Rowell, D. Lepofsky, and A.K. Salomon, "Ancient Clam Gardens Increased Shellfish Production: Adaptive Strategies from the Past Can Inform Food Security Today," *PLoS ONE* 9, 3 (2014): https://doi.org/10.1371/journal.pone.0091235; and Nancy A. Greene, David C. McGee, and Roderick J. Heitzmann, "The Comox Harbour Fish Trap Complex: A Large-Scale, Technologically Sophisticated Intertidal Fishery from British Columbia," *Canadian Journal of Archeology* 39, 2 (2015): 161–212.

The best route into the Texas Creek landslide story is Bryan Hayden and June Ryder's "Cultural Collapse in the Northwest: A Reply to Ian Kuitj," *American Antiquity* 68, 1 (2003): 157–60, which clarifies the issues and cites the relevant literature. There are now several books on the Tambora eruption and its consequences: see, in particular, Gillen D'Arcy Wood, *Tambora: The Eruption That Changed the World* (Princeton: Princeton University Press, 2014). I borrow the phrase "bad blows and big storms" from David F. Duke and Allan J. MacDonald, in *Land and Sea: Environmental History in Atlantic Canada*, edited by Claire Campbell and Robert Summerby-Murray, 181–99 (Fredericton: Acadiensis Press, 2013).

Elizabeth Hales's invocation of the Thames is treated in detail in Colin M. Coates, *The Metamorphoses of Landscape and Community in Early Quebec* (Montreal and Kingston: McGill-Queen's University Press, 2000). The Catharine Parr Traill quotation is from her *Studies of Plant Life in Canada: Gleanings from Forest, Lake, and Plain* (Ottawa: A.S. Woodburn, 1885), ii, and is cited in Angela Byrne, "Catharine Parr Traill's Natural Histories," *Journal of Literature and Science* 8 (2015): 86–101. One of the first studies to consider the consequences of the movement of plants and animals into Canada was E.W. Claypole's "On the Migration of Plants from Europe to North America, with an Attempt to Explain Certain Phenomena Connected Therewith," in *Third Report of the Montreal Horticultural Society and Fruit Growers Association of the Province of Québec ... for the Year 1877*, 70–91 (Montreal: Witness Printing House, 1878). For a more recent and more general view, see Patrick Nantel, Renata Claudi, and Elizabeth Muckle-Jeffs, *Alien Invaders in Canada's Waters, Wetlands and Forests* (Ottawa: Canadian

Forest Service, Science Branch, 2002). The hidden costs of invasive species are estimated in R.I. Colautti, S.A. Bailey, C.D. van Overdijk, K. Amundsen, and H.J. MacIsaac, "Characterised and Projected Costs of Nonindigenous Species in Canada," *Biological Invasions* 8, 1 (2006): 45–59. J. David Wood uses the "ecological revolutionaries" phrase in *Making Ontario: Agricultural Colonization and Landscape Re-creation before the Railway* (Montreal and Kingston: McGill-Queen's University Press, 2000), xxvii. For Canadian nationalist sentiment in the late nineteenth century, see Carl Berger, *The Sense of Power: Studies in the Ideas of Canadian Imperialism, 1867–1914* (Toronto: University of Toronto Press, 1970).

These timeless figures, from Bonnie Devine's *Battle for the Woodlands* installation, are intended to remind us of the enduring presence of Indigenous peoples "here on the land." The three basket-weave figures represent those alive today from Devine's Serpent River First Nation; from Walpole Island, where Tecumseh, the great orator and defender of Indian lands in the American Northwest is believed to have been buried; and from the Mississaugas of New Credit, whose lands were included in the Toronto Purchase agreements of 1787 and 1805.

Bonnie Devine, *Anishinaabitude*, 2014–15, twigs, seagrass, Kraft paper, 2015, Collection of the Art Gallery of Ontario. Photo by Bonnie Devine

PAINTING THE MAP RED

—

Graeme Wynn

C ANADIANS HAVE HAD COMPLEX, changing and, in the end, curiously ambiguous relationships with nature, a notion that is, in itself,
curiously complex and ambiguous. Consider three maps of the Great
Lakes–St. Lawrence drainage and adjacent seas. The first, published in 1613,
was derived from Samuel de Champlain's epic early voyages and information about the interior provided to him by Indigenous people. It offers a
window onto early sixteenth-century European perceptions of the territory,
its inhabitants, and nature, and it sets the scene for a brief characterization
of the ways in which successive waves of newcomers engaged and interacted with the environments and peoples of the northern part of the continent. The second, a pictorial map painted by Grant Tigner in 1954 to mark
the beginning of work on the St. Lawrence Seaway and Power Project,
embodies very different views of the natural world and conceptions of the
human place in the ecosphere. It signals the culmination of a view, nascent
in Champlain's time and increasingly strong throughout the nineteenth
and early twentieth centuries, of nature as a commodity and Canada as a
storehouse of resources. The third, an installation at the Art Gallery of
Ontario by Anishinaabe (Ojibwa) artist Bonnie Devine, re-presents an early
nineteenth-century map to reinterpret the long history of colonial incursions into Indigenous territories and invites us to think anew about the

past. Three facets of this recalibration are particularly important. The first concerns the nature of interactions among humans and environments in this space we call Canada. The second invites reflection upon the long-term consequences of current behaviours. The third addresses the need to reshape attitudes and assumptions towards Indigenous peoples and nature that underpin many of the challenges that confront Canadians early in the third millennium.

The *Carte geographique de la Nouvelle France,* like other maps of its time, reflects a fascinating mix of careful observation, Indigenous knowledge, practical purpose, and whimsical fancy. Its depiction of the northeastern foreland of the continent is immediately recognizable. Indeed, the map, produced when navigation and map-making were still rudimentary arts, is remarkable for its advance, in scope and accuracy, over earlier maps (although it omits Prince Edward Island). Yet Champlain, to this point, had only travelled as far as the Lachine Rapids and a short distance along the Richelieu River. In other words, all of the information the map provides about the territory north of the St. Lawrence and west of Hochelaga (the Iroquois village on the site of latter-day Montreal) came from Indigenous informants.

Champlain's map clearly symbolizes the European ethos of discovery. In this spirit, explorers set off to uncover and document (what was to them, at least) the unknown. Early cartography, like early natural history, was essentially descriptive. Characterizing and cataloguing were first steps in making sense of unfamiliar terrain. To this end, explorers and map-makers strove to provide those who gazed upon their works with accurate information about the territory that they mapped and described. Yet culture shapes how people view themselves and their world. Expectations and experience coloured interpretations of all that the explorers encountered and recorded.

Champlain was fascinated by America. He described the people, flora, fauna, and other features he came across on his journeys in considerable detail. Close examination of the 1613 map reveals a fastidious mix of careful documentation and cautious invention tempered by cartographic convention. Otherwise blank oceans are decorated with depictions of European sailing vessels and more-or-less identifiable sea creatures. Here, too, Champlain finds room for the calipers that signal the cartographer's commitment to measuring and scribing the face of the earth. Landward, there are indications of hills, sketches of a bear and a beaver, and stylized depictions of trees, clustered in twos and threes and, in what seems peculiar to modern eyes, plantations. Among the trees, Champlain records the presence of Indigenous peoples by name ("montaignais"; "C[ontree] des algonnequins") through stylized drawings of clustered dwellings and in a sketch showing "la forme des cabannes almouchicois." Where the river broadens into lakes, there are depictions of Indigenous inhabitants in canoes. A cartouche shows two men and two women with various accoutrements. Although Champlain characterized these peoples as "montaignais" and "almouchicois," the precise identity of these St. Lawrence Algonquians remains unclear.

The "Almouchicois" woman carries corn and squash, and the plant growing tall between her and her partner is a species of sunflower, probably a Jerusalem artichoke (*Helianthus tuberosus*), also called a sunchoke. Beneath her, Champlain illustrates several more plants used by Indigenous peoples, including what may be wild ginger ("astemara") and "pisque penay" (Indian potato or ground nuts).

Of course, Champlain saw all of this and more with European eyes (and some have found resemblances to Greco-Roman statuary in the figures in the cartouche). Yet more than Jacques Cartier (who preceded him by the proverbial threescore years and ten), Champlain understood the value of Indigenous knowledge, depended upon Indigenous help, and worked hard to build trust with the people he met. He was adaptable and flexible in his

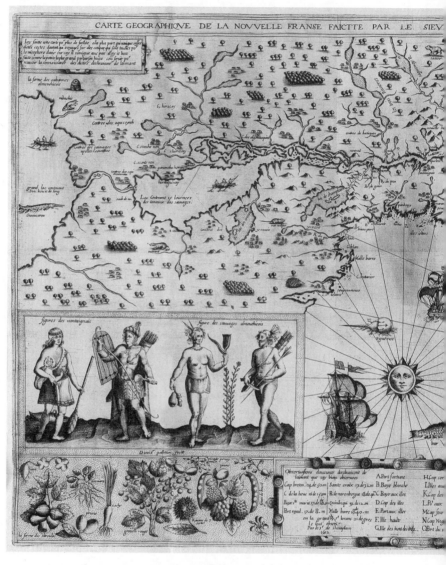

This engraving of Champlain's first detailed map
of New France was produced in Paris in 1612 and published as an
appendix to his *Voyages*, the 1613 account of his explorations since 1603.

Carte geographique de la Nouvelle Franse faictte par le sieur de Champlain,
Saint Tongois, cappitaine ordinaire pour le roy en la marine, faict len 1612
(Champlain Map, 1613), Library and Archives Canada (LAC), HMC 6327

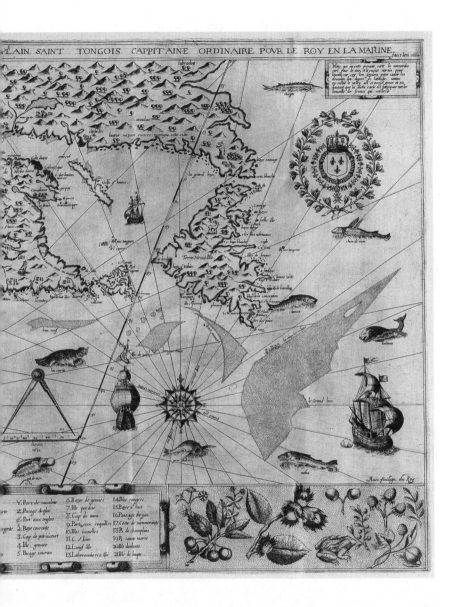

views. He was open, in short, to what we might call a kind of imaginative *métissage*. Early seventeenth-century New France was unfamiliar to early European visitors, but given their dependence on the skills, knowledge, and friendship of Indigenous inhabitants, they knew that it was not empty territory.

Later seventeenth-century depictions of New France, including Pierre Boucher's *Histoire véritable et naturelle des moeurs et productions du pays de la Nouvelle France vulgairement dite le Canada* (1664) and Louis Nicolas's *Codex canadensis*, added detail to Champlain's reconnaissance without eschewing the marvelous and the fanciful. The *Codex* – a hand-drawn,

Indigenous people of New France. Cartouche from
Carte geographique de la Nouvelle France. LAC, HMC 6327

Cartouche from *Carte geographique de la Nouvelle France*,
showing names of places identified on the main map, some plants
used by Indigenous peoples, and a frog. LAC, HMC 6327

hand-written document from 1700 or thereabouts (but published only recently) – includes 180 drawings of Indigenous peoples and the flora and fauna of New France. Detailed sketches portray people (and their appurtenances, from tattoos to canoes and snowshoes) from fifteen different

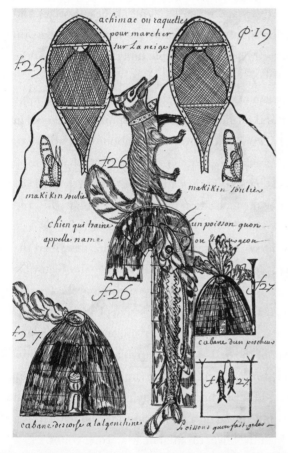

Louis Nicolas, *Codex canadensis*, ca. 1700. The seventy-nine-page *Codex* includes nineteen pages depicting Indigenous peoples and their dwelling types, modes of subsistence, and means of transportation that together form a remarkable ethnographic record. Courtesy of the Gilcrease Museum of Tulsa, Oklahoma.

Indigenous groups. Similar illustrations show 18 plants, more than 120 mammals and birds, 33 fish, and about 10 reptiles, batrachians, and insects. Blending observation, European understanding, and the products of a lively imagination, these efforts to come to grips with the exotic realities of the Americas are of great ethnographic and cultural value, despite their distortions – the appearance of tigers and unicorns alongside bears, wolves, and a moose and the inclusion of "an extraordinary plant called the passion fruit, whose parts," observed Nicolas, "resemble different symbols of the passion of Christ."

In general, early European newcomers to the continent expressed some mix of fascination, fear, and enthusiasm in their responses to Canadian nature. They celebrated its bounties and worried about their ability to survive the challenges it presented. Jacques Cartier carried what he took to be gold and diamonds back to France after his third voyage in 1541 only to be disappointed by the realization that they were iron pyrites and quartz.

Nicolas Denys, a seventeenth-century settler of Acadia, described the abundant codfish off the coast of Newfoundland as "a kind of inexhaustible manna." Champlain wrote of the "Utilitez du Pays de la Nouvelle-France." Pierre Boucher thought New France a "good country" replete with "a good portion of all that can be wished for." But Cartier also and famously characterized the north shore of the St. Lawrence near Blanc Sablon, with its vegetation of moss and stunted shrubs, as the land God gave to Cain. Champlain likewise noted that Indigenous people sometimes endured "great extremity, on account of the great cold and snow," which led "the animal and fowls on which they live [to] migrate to warmer countries."

Early modern Europeans were also intrigued by the differences between new world and old, or (as they often characterized it) the contrasts between wilderness and civilization. This often led them to regard Indigenous ways of life as inferior to their own. Many took Indigenous peoples' dependence on nature, especially their existence as mobile hunters and gatherers, as evidence that they belonged to an earlier, more primitive, stage of society. Yet most agreed that Indigenous societies and peoples had the potential to evolve. This had consequences. First, although early negotiations between newcomers and Indigenous peoples incorporated protocols rooted in Indigenous notions of trade and alliances, Europeans generally discounted Indigenous forms of government and religious belief as missionaries and others set about the task of Christianizing and "civilizing" them. Indigenous peoples' ways of understanding time and the past were also commonly disregarded.

Second, legal scholars in early modern Europe, influenced by Aristotle's doctrine of natural servitude, developed the principle that migratory peoples who lacked a king, faith, and law ("sans roi, sans foi et sans loi") held no ownership over lands where they lived and hunted. John Locke gave formal and influential English expression to this idea late in the seventeenth century with his labour theory of property. This doctrine held that the work people invested in acquiring things legitimated their claim to them. Conversely, thought Locke, it denied property rights in land to those who merely wandered over that land. Together, these developments paved the way for European colonization and Indigenous dispossession.

A century before Champlain mapped the St. Lawrence, there were between four hundred thousand and five hundred thousand Indigenous peoples in the territory we now call Canada. Inhabiting diverse ecological settings, they had developed deep and particular knowledge of the natural environments in which they had flourished over thousands of years before the arrival of Europeans. Theirs was predominantly local knowledge, finely attuned to the rhythms of the seasons and the specific characteristics of particular habitats. Dependent on the flora, fauna, birds, and marine creatures of their immediate surroundings, Indigenous peoples necessarily came to understand their milieus and treat their component parts with a measure of reverence and respect largely unfamiliar to those who came later to the continent. Origin stories traced collective genealogies to fish or animals and told of histories shaped by the interventions of various creatures, sometimes characterized as nonhuman people. All of this served to animate and enchant the natural world. Unlike their European counterparts, Indigenous peoples generally saw themselves as part of nature and developed elaborate protocols to govern relations with their environs.

The incursion of European settlers into this Indigenous space began relatively slowly. A century and a half after the first settlement at Quebec (in 1608), only sixty thousand non-Indigenous people lived along the lower St. Lawrence River, despite considerable efforts to encourage colonization. French-speaking Acadians settled around the Bay of Fundy numbered no more than twelve thousand before they were dispersed in 1755. Beyond the St. Lawrence Valley and Acadia, explorers, missionaries, and traders were more common than settlers until the 1760s.

Surveyors continued to fill out and refine their maps of Canada, often with Indigenous help. In Nova Scotia in the summer of 1770, for instance, one surveyor learned from "a number of Indians ... that there are no less than sixteen lakes and seventeen carrying places from the head of LaHave River to Annapolis Royal." In Cape Breton a few years later, another reported that the otherwise peaceable Mi'kmaq "seemed dissatisfied at the lake being surveyed, saying we had discovered now all their private haunts, which the French never attempted to do." The cartographic juggernaut had a relentless momentum, the consequences of which the We'koqma'q Mi'kmaq might have sensed but could hardly have understood. Across the country, Indigenous peoples' local geographical expertise was incorporated into the universal language of newcomer maps and texts, depriving Indigenous people of the power that knowledge confers and opening the way to massive changes in the patterns and forms of their existence. Across the country, treaties and other arrangements transferred land from those who had occupied it from the beginning of memory to settlers who coveted it; they opened the way for the amorphous forces of capital to exploit trees, minerals, and other resources as commodities of trade.

As the land was ordered and claimed by European and then Canadian governments, newcomers came to occupy it. Late in the eighteenth century, they arrived from New England, the newly independent United States, Scotland, the Palatinate states of the Rhine, and England and Ireland. But their numbers were relatively small. In 1800, barely three hundred thousand people of European descent lived in the vast territory east of Detroit. Immigration from Britain quickened after the Napoleonic Wars came to an end in 1815. It brought growing numbers of people up the St. Lawrence and into the eastern (seaboard) colonies. Relatively high rates of natural increase also contributed to population growth. At Confederation, the settler population of the new Dominion was approximately 3.5 million. Indigenous peoples were less well enumerated, but their numbers were in sharp decline: estimates of their population in 1870 barely topped one hundred thousand.

By 1910, the population of Canadians had doubled, driven upward by high rates of natural increase and a sustained influx of newcomers to the Prairie West and British Columbia after 1896. Then it doubled twice more over the next eighty years, to 14 million in 1951 and 28 million in 1991. The 1991 census (based on cultural origins or ancestry) reported an Indigenous population of just over 1 million. A contemporaneous survey conducted by Statistics Canada found 720,000 people who identified as "Aboriginal," as defined in the 1982 Constitution Act. At the census of 2016, there were about ten times as many Canadians as there were in 1867, in a much-enlarged country. Indigenous people accounted for just under 5 percent of this total (about 1.675 million, among whom almost 60 percent were First Nations, almost 30 percent were Métis, and less than 5 percent were Inuit). Taken together, these population figures are useful benchmarks, charting the decline and rebound of Indigenous peoples as their territories were occupied by newcomers. They also provide a rough metric of the environmental effects of a rising settler population armed with increasingly powerful technologies.

Because relatively few early settlers were literate, and most were heavily preoccupied with establishing themselves, we will never grasp the full range and complexity of newcomer responses to Canadian nature. Certainly, the sense of exoticism found in reports of seventeenth-century encounters declined with growing knowledge of and familiarity with northern North America. Still, interest in nature qua nature remained high and probably reached a popular peak in the middle decades of the nineteenth century, when natural history – devoted to the collection, description, and classification of plants, animals, birds, fish, and insects – had its heyday. Pursued and promoted by individuals (amateur and professional), governments and, above all, local societies, natural history was an accessible, inventorial form of science. Field naturalist, horticultural, ornithological, entomological, and other groups organized excursions to observe and experience nature. Many held long evening meetings during which enthusiasts listened to presentations on subjects as diverse as butterflies, mosses, changes in the colour of the North American hare, and the process of smoking Digby herring. Catharine Parr Traill, the author of *Canadian Wild Flowers* (published in 1868 and beautifully illustrated by her niece Agnes Fitzgibbon, the daughter of Susanna Moodie), noted that nature study offered relief "from the home-longings that always arise in the heart of the exile."

Many found more than this in their contemplation of nature. Discovering a peculiar mole-like animal during his work with the British North American Boundary Commission, John Keast Lord took this "grotesque and strangely-formed little creature" to be yet "another missing link in the great chain of Nature" and felt "God's power and omnipresence" in the western mountains. Careful observation of natural phenomena was always, and remains, tinged with other social, religious, and political implications.

Among others who set down their reactions, poets, painters, novelists, and songwriters were typically deeply conflicted in their engagements with the environment. This ambiguity often reflected interests "born of wonder and nurtured by greed" (as historian Carl Berger once characterized the interests of natural history enthusiasts). Landscapes might present grand vistas and stunning scenes, river valleys or rocky defiles might inspire picturesque musings or provoke awe, but even the artist's gaze was drawn, more often than not, to the actual or potential value of the land's resources. Most seventeenth- and eighteenth-century depictions of the St. Lawrence Valley, in prose or on canvas, emphasized the accessibility and commercial potential of Montreal, Quebec City, and other towns. Not until the nineteenth century did artists paint winter conditions with any great frequency – a move that reached its apogee in the popular works of the prolific Cornelius Krieghoff, whose fondness for bright colours and the stark whiteness of snow was regularly displayed in *paysannerie* genre paintings.

Likewise, early prairie scenes were often viewed "through a filter of Victorian optimism." They conveyed what geographer Ronald Rees once described as "an unforbidding, even cheerful image of the West." Even in the wildest parts of the prairie, Paul Kane painted grass "trimmed like English greensward." Upon this lush expanse, "lithe graceful horses ... sired by some highly bred blood strain" formed a "wonderful tableau" purported to be a buffalo hunt. Early in the twentieth century, the Group of Seven would portray and celebrate the granitic landscapes of the Canadian Shield for their intrinsic aesthetic appeal, but Robert Stead tapped into an older, prominent strain of Canadian art and letters when he celebrated the human dominance of nature in the Prairie West:

> For here on the edge of creation.
> Lies, far as the vision can fling,
> A kingdom that's fit for a nation –
> A kingdom – and I am the king.

Vigorous enthusiasm for the potential of the Canadian plains
lasted half a century and more. This poster envisages yet more opportunities
for prosperous futures beyond the North Saskatchewan River, echoing the
boosterish conclusions of a report on explorations of the new Northwest by
Frank P.J. Crean in 1908–09. *Courtesy of Canada's History Magazine*

In the main, British North America/Canada was a development project. Most migrants came to this place to get ahead. Sometimes this impetus had a conservative quality, as when people whose lives had been disrupted by change in Britain crossed the Atlantic in hope of holding on to the family-centred independence they had once known at home. Others, fleeing English industrial slums, the clearance of people from Scottish hillsides to make way for sheep, or famine in Ireland, simply came to better their circumstances. Armed with a collective metaphorical warrant to civilize the wilderness, almost all of these newcomers worked assiduously at immediate and mundane tasks such as felling trees, draining swamps, plowing prairie sod, and establishing homes, fences, barns, fields, and roads. Some extracted wealth from unlikely places: the sandbars of the Fraser River, the hard rock of the Canadian Shield, the high peaks of the Cordillera, and the sedimentary basins of Nova Scotia and the Cordilleran foothills, which yielded fossil fuels. Few gave much thought to the people who had lived in and around these places and were increasingly being confined to reserves or pushed to the margins of the most productive territories. If those engaged in turning "waste lands" into productive acres and large rocks into small fortunes had a loftier commitment in mind, it was almost always to the future. The idea of progress drove Victorian society forward. In Canada, where the idea became material, it was rarely questioned. But occasionally it was. In late nineteenth-century Ontario, for example, a few scientists and politicians grew concerned about the overclearing of land. Similarly, in the years of frenetic development before the First World War, the rapacious plunder of continental resources spawned the American conservation movement and Canada's bureaucratic response, the Commission of Conservation. In these and a small handful of similar cases, however, environmental concerns were overwhelmed, in short order, by the development impetus.

The development trajectory peaked in the boom years after the Second World War, and the construction of the St. Lawrence Seaway and Power Project was one of its high points. Although the St. Lawrence waterway portrayed on Champlain's map (and others) seems to slice, knife-like, into the heart of the continent, the natural channel of the river carved a more complicated path. Falls and rapids interrupted the river's course, and islands and outcrops deflected its flow. Largely invisible and continuous processes of erosion and deposition moved banks and shallows. Nineteenth-century engineers built and enlarged canals around the Lachine Rapids and Niagara Falls to facilitate commerce. Vessels grounded periodically on unseen shoals, but most were rescued by rising tides and seamen's wiles. As freight traffic increased and the vessels that carried it grew larger in the twentieth century, however, the river's quirks vexed those who craved greater economic efficiency. In the 1950s several factors coalesced to turn commercial frustration into a powerful dream. Among them were a developing geopolitical sense that improvement and development of the waterway would knit Canada and the United States closer together during the Cold War; the growing capacity of engineers to harness ever-more-powerful brute-force technologies to realize their designs; and the increasingly common high modernist conviction that human control over the environment would make the world a better place. Imaginations, expertise, and millions of dollars were turned to the task of converting the great river into a flowage basin – a navigation system and electricity-producing scheme that would transform the continent.

Hailed as one of the greatest megaprojects in history, the St. Lawrence Seaway and Power Project was frequently described in excited, even hyperbolic, terms as it was moved to completion between 1954 and 1959. Books and pamphlets remarked on the tens of thousands of people who had been employed and enumerated the number (all in the hundreds) of trucks, bulldozers, shovels, and draglines deployed on the project. They marvelled at the hundreds of millions of tons of rock and earth moved to eliminate islands, cut channels, and build dikes, and they noted in awe the staggering amounts of concrete poured to create dams and canals. Even the eleven thousand hectares or so of land, farms, and villages inundated by the lake (which formed above the Moses-Saunders Dam to generate almost two thousand megawatts of power for Canada and the United States) were incorporated into this eccentric accounting as a "matter of modern progress and international prosperity." In the end, the seaway and its Great Lakes extension allowed massive vessels (the length of two football fields, drawing almost eight metres below the waterline) to travel 3,700 kilometres from the Gulf of St. Lawrence to Duluth, Minnesota, 185 metres above sea level. It quickly became "the greatest construction show on earth," forming what one children's book described as "the tallest water staircase west of China."

Grant Tigner's pictorial map quite wonderfully illustrates prevailing opinion that the St. Lawrence Seaway and Power Project would crown four centuries of human endeavour along the river and set the scene for things to come. Commissioned by the Montreal distillers Seagrams Limited for their 1954 annual report, this remarkable work clearly echoed the views of company chairman, Samuel Bronfman. Unprecedented in scale, the soon-to-be-implemented project would have monumental effects. "Never before in the history of mankind," enthused Bronfman, "has a single engineering scheme embraced within a single grand design so many interlocking parts of a continent's life."

In producing his dramatic panorama, Tigner, an American-born illustrator and landscape painter recently relocated to Montreal, tapped into a flourishing and innovative American cartographic tradition. Pictorial maps, as works of this type are known, are conspicuous for their bold designs, bright colors, and lively detail and for combining fact and fancy in ways reminiscent of medieval and early modern map-making. Tigner's remarkable oblique or bird's-eye view carries the gaze northward from Cape Cod and Illinois, across the Great Lakes and St. Lawrence, and into the heart of the Canadian Shield. The Seaway and Power Project ("Builder of Trade, Commerce and Industry") teems with activity. Steamships crowd the lakes and sail through the Gulf of St. Lawrence amid cavorting whales and dolphins and the boats of fishermen hauling wealth from the waters. Hydroelectric power generators, upstream and down from Lake Ontario, send out powerful sparks, electrifying the atmosphere and symbolizing the ease with which so-called white gold could be distributed to power industry, homes, streetlights, and tramcars.

South of the international border, giant ears of corn, contented cows, and fat sows mark the productivity of American agriculture, but there are

Grant Tigner's *The St. Lawrence Seaway and Power Project.*
This marvelous pictorial map imagined a busy and prosperous future for the
Great Lakes–St. Lawrence corridor, portraying the St. Lawrence Seaway and
Power Project as the culmination of centuries of development and progress.
Courtesy of the Canadian Centre for Architecture and the family of Grant Tigner

thriving cities and industry here, too, in the blast furnaces of Ohio, the
steel plants of Gary, the assembly lines of Detroit, and the pulp mills of
Maine, all but the latter drawing obvious benefit from the seaway. North
of the border, farms soon give way to trees, but in this portrayal, Canada
is no northern fastness. Long, powerful trains bearing freight in box and
tanker cars seem drawn to the lakes as though by a magnet. Two appear
to stretch from the seemingly endless Canadian west as they converge on
the north shore of Lake Superior, only to be dwarfed by the enormous
grain elevators of Fort William and Port Arthur (twin cities later renamed
Thunder Bay).

THE ST. LAWRENCE SEAWAY
and POWER PROJECT
BUILDER of TRADE, COMMERCE and INDUSTRY

To the north and east, miners and loggers – giants among men – extract minerals from ancient rock and harvest the forests to feed the voracious appetites of the Sudbury nickel smelter, the Algoma steel plant, and the Chromium Mining and Smelting Corporation in Sault Ste. Marie, as well as dozens of pulp, paper, and lumber mills. Farther east, an enormous open pit north of the St. Lawrence marks the newly established Schefferville operations of the Iron Ore Company of Canada. Away to the west, the burgeoning petrochemical centre of Sarnia reveals the rising importance of oil and its derivatives in North American lives. And in the middle of it all, in a magnificent touch of whimsy, a Mountie stands on guard for Ottawa, his red tunic a beacon against the roll of paper spilling from the Gatineau mills and the world about him transformed by the relentless march of progress. A moose in Quebec and a deer in New Brunswick symbolize the call of the wild, but beyond them, all of Canadian nature has been turned into commodities. Of Indigenous people there is nary a sign.

All of this was remarkably prescient – and revealing. Five years after the publication of Tigner's map, in the first year of the seaway's operations, traffic on the St. Lawrence increased by two-thirds. In Toronto and Hamilton, overseas shipping rose by 150 percent and 700 percent, respectively. And in Kenosha and Duluth, shipping activity climbed twenty-fold and seventy-five-fold, respectively. Port authorities spent enormous sums on harbour improvements. Grain from the American Midwest and Canadian prairies soon accounted for more than a half of downstream freight. In the other direction, iron ore from the Labrador Trough left ports on the Lower North Shore of Quebec to replace declining yields from the Mesabi Ranges of Minnesota in the furnaces of old, established mills on the Great Lakes. Beyond grain and ore, the falling costs of moving dozens and dozens of other commodities to market greased the wheels of commerce. Producers and consumers in the Great Lakes Basin benefitted from wider market access and the greater availability of many goods. Land use and manufacturing patterns changed as people adapted to shifting circumstances. Coinciding with a period of increasing prosperity in North America, these developments spelled opportunity, economic progress, and the broadening of mass consumerism in the Great Lakes region through the 1960s. They gave substance to Tigner's bright vision of the area as a major engine of growth and development.

But there were losers as well as winners, and the good times did not last. Long-established grain-handling ports on Georgian Bay and Lake Huron were bypassed and fell into decline. Displaced residents of the "lost villages" flooded by the rising St. Lawrence River continued to grieve over well-loved farms and foreshores. When dredged sediments from the navigation channel were deposited on the edge of Lake Saint-Louis to form Tekakwitha Island, Mohawk residents of the Kahnawá:ke Reserve lost their traditional access to local waters. The long, narrow channel between island and foreshore, a couple of kilometres long and barely 250 metres wide, (ironically) named Recreation Bay, was soon subject to sedimentation, eutrophication, and declining water quality. Adding further to the deficit side of the ledger, by century's end many communities were battling the costly, pipe-clogging effects of zebra mussels inadvertently introduced into the Great Lakes ecosystem by seaway shipping.

Within a decade of the seaway's completion, the sun began to set on Great Lakes steel production as foreign factories undercut North American producers and the industrial heartland turned into the Rust Belt. In the quarter century after 1970, employment in manufacturing fell by almost a third across affected American states. The populations of Cleveland, Detroit, Buffalo, and Pittsburgh declined by about 45 percent between 1970 and 2006, leaving behind shuttered plants, abandoned homes, boarded-up businesses, and decaying infrastructure. Canada's manufacturing cities – Hamilton, Windsor, Brantford, Toronto – fared better, but growth slowed, and much industry was restructured. These difficulties combined with soaring interest rates and unanticipated operating costs to undermine the economic viability of the Seaway Authority. Late in the 1970s, its debts were restructured and assumed by Canada. In 1983, the Schefferville mine closed.

The self-confident conviction that underpinned megaprojects such as the St. Lawrence Seaway and Power Project – that humans had carte blanche to remake the world – has also withered in the last half century. Two of the many drivers of this change are especially pertinent: rising concern about the environment and growing recognition of the place of Indigenous peoples in the continuing development of Canada. Informed and inspired by Rachel Carson's 1962 blockbuster exposé, *Silent Spring*, people from all walks of life grew anxious about the harmful and often insidious effects of air and water pollution. In 1972, a book based on computer simulations and dotted with equations sparked widespread public debate about the limits to growth. Another, published a year later, envisaged "economics as if people mattered" and announced that "Small Is Beautiful." In 1973, a sudden price spike challenged Canadians' increasing dependence on oil for transport and domestic heating. At much the same time, widespread disaffection with the ethos of the corporate-industrial-military complex among North American youth spawned countercultural efforts to increase personal autonomy and to tread more lightly upon the earth. Environmentalism became a powerful and persistent force for change in the ways humans regard and use nature.

During the energy crisis of the 1970s, Prime Minister Pierre Trudeau faced strong economic arguments for the construction of a high-capacity, high-pressure gas pipeline from the Mackenzie River delta to Alberta (touted as the largest privately financed project in the history of free enterprise). He recognized the new realities by indicating that approval of the project could entail "no lowering of environmental standards or ... neglect of Indian rights and interests." The Mackenzie Valley Pipeline Inquiry, led by Justice Thomas Berger, famously gave voice to the concerns of Indigenous people and reported that Canadians should honour "above all else ... the legitimate claims of the native people" of the North. Such sentiments were strengthened by the entrenchment, in 1982, of Aboriginal and treaty rights in the Canadian Constitution. They were also endorsed by the United Nations' Brundtland Commission report, *Our Common Future*, which insisted, in 1987, that local communities should be involved in decisions governing the use of resources in their territories. These developments spawned various forms of consultation, participatory decision making, and project comanagement involving Indigenous communities, governments, and industry. Many criticize such arrangements, finding them incommensurate with Indigenous worldviews and concluding that they perpetuate the imbalances of colonial power. At their most trenchant, such critiques dismiss community hearings as theatre scripted to privilege concepts deeply ingrained in the Western tradition, such as progress, truth, evidence, and private property, while marginalizing or misinterpreting the traditional and conceptual foundations of Indigenous knowledge. Still, it is now clear, and the Supreme Court of Canada has affirmed, that the Crown has a duty to consult with and accommodate Indigenous peoples on decisions that may affect their rights and title to land.

The legacies of colonialism still shape relationships among peoples and nature in Canada, but they are being renegotiated apace and in striking, unforeseen ways – as in Bonnie Devine's *Battle for the Woodlands*. Invited in 2014 to create an installation for the Canadian Wing of the Art Gallery of Ontario, Devine, the founding chair of Ontario College of Art and Design University's Indigenous Visual Culture program, centred her work in an alcove created for an earlier exhibition titled *Constructing Canada*. There, a map taken from W.H. Bartlett's immensely popular *Canadian Scenery Illustrated*, published in London in 1842, had been enlarged to cover an entire wall. It provided both inspiration and a framework for the powerful statement that Devine would make by inserting another story atop an old colonial map.

Devine "wanted to talk about the transitions that occurred as Europeans landed here and then moved westward through this territory; the political ambiguities that they left behind and that we still contend with as Indigenous people." To open this narrative, she painted three sailing vessels on the wall to the "east" of the map. Carrying soldiers and settlers across the Atlantic, these vessels are freighted with meaning as they symbolize the arrival of newcomers and the beginnings of Indigenous dispossession.

Devine built the next chapter of her story around her realization that when explorers and Europeans came into the continent, they "saw the water as a means of getting some place, as a conveyance and as a commodity

Devine's installation in its (almost) full splendour.
Bartlett's overpainted map is on the far wall behind *Anishinaabitude.*
The Great Lakes, red and transformed, spill beyond Bartlett's Upper Canada to
the left; birds and animals flee across the Mississippi River from the near-empty
woodlands; and three cloaks await the return of warriors. Sailing vessels bearing
newcomers are barely visible on the right-hand edge of the photograph.
Bonnie Devine, *Battle for the Woodlands,* 2014–15, mixed media installation,
Collection of the Art Gallery of Ontario. Photo by Bonnie Devine

perhaps." Anishinaabe have a different view. To capture something of this, she painted the rivers of Bartlett's map red, calling to mind both Indigenous peoples' widespread use of red ochre to symbolize the life force and the spiritual connections between Indigenous peoples and water, "the blood-line to Mother Earth and to us." In a similar vein, she overpainted each of the Great Lakes, imagining and rendering them as the mythical animals Bison, Otter, Turtle, and Mishepishu (the Water Panther), and the rabbit or trickster figure Nanabozho (Nanabush). These (re)presentations of the lakes reference Anishinaabe pictorial and mythological traditions and reveal

Bison, Otter, Turtle, Mishepishu, and Nanabozho (Nanabush) take the shapes and shift the meaning of Lakes Superior, Michigan, Huron, Erie, and Ontario. Bonnie Devine, detail from *Battle for the Woodlands* installation, 2014–15, acrylic and mixed media on gallery wall, Collection of the Art Gallery of Ontario. Courtesy of Bonnie Devine. Photo by Dean Tomlinson. © 2017 Art Gallery of Ontario

the Anishinaabe's distinctive sense of their place in the environment. They recollect rock-painting sites "where sky, earth, water, underground and underwater" met and where medicine people and manitous (shape-shifting, other-than-human beings) could pass back and forth into each other's worlds. Devine reminds viewers of her installation that, for Anishinaabe, the lakes "aren't just bodies of water. They are beings who are cohabiting with us in this space right now. They are living. We are in a relationship with them. We have been for many hundreds of years."

Strips of brightly coloured, beaded fabric are looped across and over the place names on Bartlett's map. These treaty belts trace the border of "Indian Territory," defined in the Royal Proclamation of 1763. Vignettes

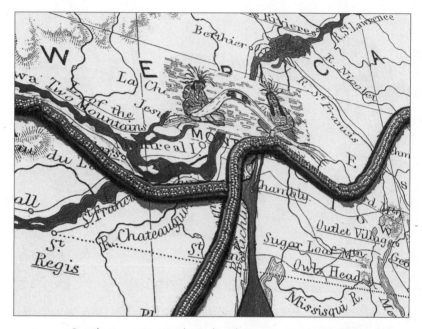

Detail commemorating the Dish with One Spoon agreement
and the Great Peace of Montreal, 1701. Bartlett's view of the Canadas in
1842, with superimposed treaty belts and overpaints of Indigenous people to
signal some of the changes produced by the influx of newcomers. Bonnie Devine,
Battle for the Woodlands, 2014–15, mixed media, felt, and nickel and brass beads,
Collection of the Art Gallery of Ontario. Photo by Janet Rogers. Courtesy of
CanadaLand, Janet Rogers, and Bonnie Devine

depicting Indigenous people engaged in various activities reassert an
Indigenous presence, missing from the original map. Other drawings denote
the violence of (dis)possession by showing little red- and blue-coated soldiers
(British and American troops, mounted and on foot) and episodes of conflict
between Indigenous peoples and newcomers.

As colonization swept westward, the Woodlands were plundered and
destroyed "to make room for settlers' cabins, and farming, and industrialization." Catastrophic habitat loss ensued "not only for the Anishinaabe and
the woodland peoples but for the animals." Devine renders this ecological

disruption as a frantic westward flight of animals and birds across the Mississippi, a movement that emptied and impoverished the Eastern Woodlands, reducing their bounty for the Anishinaabe and marking the end of their liberty to traverse the territory as they pleased.

Land and environment lie at the heart of this story. They are the centre pivot of the installation, which inscribes Indigenous conceptions of land (and human-nature relations) on familiar European settler representations of space, to challenge the erasures, perceptions, marginalizations, and injustices inherent in those representations. Devine's strategy, in short, is to "trace the absence of Anishnaabek ... using the colonial mapping and claiming techniques that have strategically served to erase their history and the Indigenous methods of mark-making and mapping that reassert it." To mark the line of the Royal Proclamation of 1763 on Bartlett's map is to note the extent to which it had been transgressed by 1840. To reference – with an image of a chief and a priest holding a cross together – the great wampum belt documenting the Mi'kmaq Concordat signed by the Grand Council of the Mi'kmaq and the pope in 1610 (as Devine does in the right corner of her installation) is to acknowledge that the Mi'kmaq gained some religious autonomy by undertaking to protect priests and allow the construction of churches in their territory.

Referencing the Concordat also makes the point, in Devine's words, that "the idea behind that original treaty was that we would share the land. We would live here together ... It's not a land cession at all. It wasn't about surrendering land in exchange for anything else." In other words, history might have taken a different course. The reference points to Devine's desire "to talk about the land ... as a being with whom we are in a reciprocal relationship." Settlers, she notes, made marks on paper and canvas to assert ownership of territory; Indigenous peoples painted pictographs on rocks, on the land itself, to mark their presence. Devine's installation makes clear that the long, hard battle for the Woodlands has been fought in many registers and that the familiar triumphal account of its struggles as stepping stones to economic development and creative transformation can no longer obscure a darker contrapuntal story of human and ecological disruption and loss.

More than this, Devine makes two strategic interventions to remind Canadians that the battle is far from done. Three figures woven with traditional basketry techniques stand in the centre of *The Battle for the Woodlands*, forming a separate installation called *Anishinaabitude*. They represent those alive today from Devine's Serpent River First Nation, from Walpole Island (where Tecumseh, the great orator and defender of Indian lands in the American Northwest is believed to have been buried), and the Mississaugas of New Credit, whose lands were included in the Toronto Purchase agreements of 1787 and 1805. Living branches gathered from foliage in each of these locations were brought to the Art Gallery of Ontario to be sculpted into these timeless figures as reminders, Devine notes, of the "enduring presence" of Indigenous peoples "here on the land." Although the 250,000 acres (100,000 hectares) encompassed by the Toronto Purchase now house some 6 million residents of the Greater Toronto Area, and although Indigenous people account for barely 0.5 percent of this total, they are not to be ignored.

On the "western" wall of the installation, where birds and animals flee the Woodlands, hang three cloaks made from animal hides. These "Objects to Clothe the Warriors" honour three great Indigenous leaders: Pontiac, who led the struggle against newcomer settlement in the Great Lakes region in the 1760s; Tecumseh, who formed a multitribal confederacy and envisaged an independent Indian nation east of the Mississippi River early in the nineteenth century; and Crazy Horse, the Oglala Lakota warrior who resisted American incursions into the Plains in the third quarter of the nineteenth century. "They are hung," Devine explains, "to be easily accessible should these warriors return to join in the ongoing battle for the Woodlands." Devine's work, observes art historian and curator Ruth B. Phillips, makes important claims about the continuing presence of Indigenous people in Canada, their enduring resistance to the social and environmental injustices of colonialism, and the need to consider alternatives "to 'ownership' and the uncontrolled and destructive exploitation of land." It offers another version of the imaginative métissage that stood Champlain in good stead, fuelling his "dream" that a diverse, tolerant, inclusive, and peaceful society might emerge in northern North America.

REFERENCES AND FURTHER READING

From the substantial literature on Champlain and his maps, the following are the most useful: Conrad E. Heidenreich, "The Beginning of French Exploration Out of the St. Lawrence Valley: Motives, Methods and Changing Attitudes towards Native People," in *Decentring the Renaissance: Canada and Europe in Interdisciplinary Perspective, 1500–1700*, edited by Germaine Warkentin and Carolyn Podruchny, 236–51 (Toronto: University of Toronto Press, 2001), and Conrad E. Heidenreich, *Explorations and Mapping of Samuel de Champlain, 1603–1632*, Cartographica Monograph 17 (Toronto: B.V. Gutsell, 1976). The Cape Sable quotation is from W.L. Grant, *Voyages of Samuel de Champlain, 1604–1618* (New York: Barnes and Noble, 1946), 28–29, and the later quote about "great extremity" is from Samuel de Champlain, *The Works of Samuel de Champlain*, vol. 1, edited by Henry P. Biggar (Toronto: Champlain Society, 1922), 110, and in Réal Ouellet with Mylene Tremblay, "From the Good Savage to the Degenerate Indian: The Amerindian in the Accounts of Travel to America," Warkentin and Podruchny, *Decentring*, 159–70. Victoria Dickenson's "Cartier, Champlain, and the Fruits of the New World: Botanic Exchange in the 16th and 17th Centuries," *Scientia Canadensis* 31, 1–2 (2008): 27–47, has a helpful discussion of the details of the 1613 map, and Victoria Dickenson and Elsbeth Heaman's "Introduction: Natural Science in the New World – The Descriptive Enterprise," *Scientia Canadensis* 31, 2 (2008): 1–11, discusses the descriptive qualities of natural history and mapping.

The idea of imaginative *métissage* is developed from a reference to *métissage culturel* in Natalie Zemon Davis, "Polarities, Hybridities: What Strategies for Decentring," in Warkentin and Podruchny, *Decentring the Renaissance*, 19–32, and from comments in Gilles Thérien, "Memoria as the Place of Fabrication of the New World," also in *Decentring the Renaissance*, 68–84. In *Champlain's Dream: The European Founding of North America* (New York: Simon and Schuster, 2008), 7, David Hackett Fischer renders this point as the dream of "a place where people of different cultures could live together in amity and concord."

For one example of how culture shaped the European gaze, see Olive Patricia Dickason, *Myth of the Savage and the Beginnings of French Colonialism in the Americas* (Edmonton: University of Alberta Press, 1984). Pierre Boucher's *Histoire véritable et naturelle des moeurs et productions du pays de la Nouvelle-France vulgairement dite le Canada* (Montreal: E. Bastien and Cie., 1882), from which the "good country" quote is taken, is discussed in Lynn Berry, "The Delights of Nature in This New World: A Seventeenth-Century Canadian View of the Environment," in Warkentin and Podruchny, *Decentring the Renaissance*, 223–35. Nicolas's *Codex canadensis* was published under the editorship of Gagnon in 2011, but its illustrations are available at, and the quotes are drawn from, Library and Archives Canada's collection of the same name, https://www.collectionscanada.gc.ca/codex/026014 -1500-e.html. For more general ruminations on this theme, see G. Ramsay Cook, "Cabbages Not Kings: Towards an Ecological Interpretation of Early Canadian History," *Journal of Canadian Studies* 25, 4 (1990–91): 5–16, and Christopher M. Parsons, "Wildness without Wilderness: Biogeography and Empire in Seventeenth-Century French North America," *Environmental History* 22, 4 (October 2017): 643–67.

The phrase "inexhaustible manna" is from Nicolas Denys, *The Description and Natural History of the Coasts of North America (Acadia)*, translated and edited by W.F. Ganong (Toronto: Champlain Society, 1908 [1672]), 257. For an important commentary on the differences between Indigenous and European notions of time, history, and change, see Deborah Doxtator, "Inclusive and Exclusive

Perceptions of Difference: Native and Euro-based Concepts of Time, History, and Change," in Warkentin and Podruchny, *Decentring the Renaissance*, 33–47. For "sans roi, sans foi," see Olive Patricia Dickason, "The Sixteenth-Century French Vision of Empire: The Other Side of Self-Determination," also in *Decentring the Renaissance*, 87–109. For a discussion of the state of nature and the labour theory of value, see Graeme Wynn, "Strains of Liberalism," Foreword to David Calverley, *Who Controls the Hunt? First Nations, Treaty Rights, and Wildlife Conservation in Ontario, 1783–1939* (Vancouver: UBC Press, 2018). For a careful estimate of the precontact Indigenous population, see Arthur J. Ray, *I Have Lived Here since the World Began: An Illustrated History of Canada's Native People* (Montreal and Kingston: McGill-Queen's University Press, 2011). For an example of the concept of nonhuman people, see Robin Ridington, *Trail to Heaven: Knowledge and Narrative in a Northern Native Community* (Vancouver: Douglas and McIntyre, 1988), xi. The Nova Scotia surveyors are quoted in Stephen J. Hornsby, *Surveyors of Empire: Samuel Holland, J.F.W. Des Barres and the Making of the Atlantic Neptune* (Montreal and Kingston: McGill-Queen's University Press, 2011).

Catharine Parr Traill's relief from "home longings" is from her *Studies of Plant Life in Canada: Gleanings from Forest, Lake, and Plain* (Ottawa: A.S. Woodburn, 1885), 3. See also Elizabeth Thompson, "'With Axe and Fire': Catharine Traill's Ecological Vision," *Canadian Poetry: Studies/Documents/Reviews* 42 (Spring-Summer 1998): http://canadianpoetry.org/volumes/vol42/thompson.htm. John K. Lord's "missing link" is described in his *The Naturalist on Vancouver Island and in British Columbia* (London: R. Bentley, 1866), 345. The "born of wonder" quote is from Carl C. Berger, *Science, God, and Nature in Victorian Canada* (Toronto: University of Toronto Press, 1983), 3. The discussion of prairie scenes, the comments on Kane, and the quote from Stead are drawn from Ronald Rees's "Images of the Prairie: Landscape Painting and Perception in the Western Interior of Canada," *Canadian Geographer* 20 (1976): 259–78. Suzanne Zeller's *Land of Promise, Promised Land: The Culture of Victorian Science in Canada*, CHA Historical Booklet (Ottawa: Canadian Historical Association, 1996) and *Inventing Canada: Early Victorian*

81

Science and the Idea of a Transcontinental Nation (Toronto: University of Toronto Press, 1987) add to our understanding of mid-nineteenth-century science in Canada. For more on the Commission of Conservation, see David Wood, "Picturing Conservation in Canada: The Commission of 1909–1921," *Archivaria* 37 (Spring 1994): 64–74, and Michel F. Girard, "The Commission of Conservation as a Forerunner to the National Research Council, 1909–1921," *Scientia Canadensis* 15, 2 (1991): 19–40.

The Tigner map and the Bronfman quote appeared in Distillers Corporation–Seagrams Ltd., "The St. Lawrence Seaway and Power Project," in *The St. Lawrence Seaway: The Realization of a Mighty Dream* (Montreal: Distillers Corporation–Seagrams Ltd., 1954). For the St. Lawrence Seaway and Power Project, see Daniel Macfarlane, *Negotiating a River: Canada, the US, and the Creation of the St. Lawrence Seaway* (Vancouver: UBC Press, 2014), and Graeme Wynn, *Canada and Arctic North America: An Environmental History* (Santa Barbara, CA: ABC Clio, 2007), 284–91. The "matter of modern progress" quote is from Lowell Thomas, *The St. Lawrence Seaway Story* (New York: Henry Stewart, 1957), 20. Claire Puccia Parham, *The St. Lawrence Seaway and Power Project: An Oral History of the Greatest Construction Show on Earth* (Syracuse, NY: Syracuse University Press, 2009) gives us the "greatest construction show"; and the St. Lawrence Seaway Management Corporation, *Tommy Trent's ABCs of the Seaway* (Ottawa: 1988), yields "the tallest water staircase," https://www.seaway.dot.gov/publications/tommy-trent-abcs -seaway.

For the American pictorial map tradition, see Stephen J. Hornsby, *Picturing America: The Golden Age of Pictorial Maps* (Chicago: University of Chicago Press, 2016). Macfarlane discusses the "lost villages" in *Negotiating a River*. For Tekakwitha Island, see V. Koutitonsky and M. Pelletier, "Numerical Modeling of the Circulation and Mud Transport in Recreation Bay: Actual Conditions and Remediation Scenarios" (Hydrosoft SA Technical Report HTR-16-1, Kahnawake Environment Protection Office, Kahnawake, 2016), and for the Rust Belt, see Stephen High, *Industrial Sunset: The Making of North America's Rust Belt, 1969–1984* (Toronto: University of Toronto Press, 2003).

For the broader literature of the 1960s and 1970s, see Rachel Carson, *Silent Spring* (Boston: Houghton-Mifflin, 1962); Donella H. Meadows, Dennis L. Meadows, Jørgen Randers, and William W. Behrens III, *The Limits to Growth* (Falls Church: Potomac Associates, 1972); and E.F. Schumacher, *Small Is Beautiful: A Study of Economics as If People Mattered* (London: Blond and Briggs, 1973). The Berger Inquiry submitted its report as *Northern Frontier, Northern Homeland.*

Two short videos provide the best available depictions and accounts of the making of *Battle for the Woodlands:* see Art Gallery of Ontario, *Timelapse: Bonnie Devine's "Battle for the Woodlands,"* July 29, 2014, and Art Gallery of Ontario, *Bonnie Devine's Woodlands,* December 11, 2015. Except when noted, quotes from Devine come from my transcription of *Bonnie Devine's Woodlands.* Further discussion and contextualization of the installation can be found in Ruth B. Phillips, "Between Rocks and Hard Places: Indigenous Lands, Settler Art Histories and the 'Battle for the Woodlands'" (Vienna Working Papers in Canadian Studies 1, Centre for Canadian Studies, Universität Wien, 2016). She draws the "absence of Anishnaabek" quote from an artist's statement by Devine. On the power of rock-painting sites ("where sky, earth, water"), see Grace Rajnovitch, *Reading Rock Art: The Indian Rock Paintings of the Canadian Shield* (Toronto: Natural Heritage/Natural History, 1994), 159.

Annie Ned was awarded the Order of Canada in 2003,
in part for her contributions to documenting history in the southern
Yukon Territory. Photo by Norma McBean

LISTENING FOR DIFFERENT STORIES

Julie Cruikshank

A T A MODEST ONE-DAY conference on early human history in south-west Yukon, held in Haines Junction in 1982, scientists, historians, archaeologists, and members of local First Nations discussed the environmental factors affecting regional history. Late in the afternoon, Mrs. Annie Ned, then in her eighties, rose from her seat to ask, "Where do these people come from?" Having lived, hunted, fished, trapped, and raised children and grandchildren in the region, she regarded most of the participants as outsiders. "You people talk from paper," she said, "I want to talk from Grandpa." After sharing something of her experience, revealing radical differences between Indigenous and Western perspectives on the environment, she advised participants to "listen for different stories." This, she implied, required more attention, engagement, reflection, and curiosity than simply listening *to* stories.

Most of the Yukon women I worked with were born shortly before or just after 1900, and I expected to hear about the impacts of the Klondike gold rush, construction of the Alaska Highway, and the increasing intrusion of the state into family lives. The majority of the stories they asked me to record centred on an encounter between a human and an unexpected visitor who looks like an ordinary person but is soon revealed to be an animal in human guise. From the beginning, in these stories, it is clear that human hubris has prompted this meeting. Sometimes the human protagonist is described as "playing with" or "fooling around with" an animal, offending that species. This act sets the story in motion. The animal-person entices the human protagonist on a journey across an identifiable boundary (under a log, through a cave, beyond the horizon) to an unfamiliar world often described as a white or colourless wintry place. They reach a village in which everyone looks human, but they are soon revealed as other-than-human animals, recognizably "persons," but animals nevertheless.

The human visitor struggles to make sense of it all. When the visitor feels hungry and asks for something to eat, the hosts are shocked by the choice. In one story, a boy lured away by salmon asks for fish eggs but, for fish-people, it is unconscionably rude to think of this as food. In counterpoint, the visitor's kin would never eat the food offered by the hosts. Everything is strange. Confusion abounds. This is a world turned upside down. Gradually, the protagonist becomes accustomed to the new surroundings but at great risk that acculturation will transform him or her into a member of the host species, unable to return to the human world. The rest of the story traces the complications of return; if successful, the traveller brings back specialized knowledge of value to humans who depend on that species for sustenance.

These narratives never identify what we now call nature as a separate category. Beginning with the view that knowing one's environment is largely a matter of *overcoming* the boundary between self and the world, these stories mobilize a complex set of humans and nonhumans entangled in relationships characterized by transformation and mutual interdependence. Yet for all their initial strangeness, it gradually became clear to me that these were life histories, because they dramatized an ongoing concern about how humans should properly situate or comport themselves in relation to other sentient beings – beings that many non-Indigenous people might now consider part of "nature."

To elaborate this point, consider Mrs. Ned's conversation with a wildlife biologist about the substantial herds of caribou found in the southern Yukon Territory when she was young. Scientists knew that two subspecies, *Rangifer arcticus stonei* and *Rangifer arcticus osborni*, had once inhabited this region, and they were puzzled by their disappearance in the late nineteenth century. In response to the biologist's specific, thoughtful questions about these matters, Mrs. Ned volunteered a narrative about one of the last times caribou were seen in the region.

By Annie Ned's account, caribou once enticed a man gifted with shamanic powers to follow them. He simply disappeared. Sometime later, his kinsmen saw what appeared to be a single caribou on the lake ice, but when they heard the animal singing the shaman's song, they understood that he had been transformed, and they recognized their obligations. Gradually, and with difficulty, they coaxed him home and drew him back into the human world. The transition was alarmingly difficult, and his newly acquired powers prohibited him from ever hunting or eating caribou again.

Mrs. Ned's story was long and evocative, and as daylight faded, she sang the shaman's song in her powerful voice. For Mrs. Ned, knowing caribou meant understanding the reciprocal relationships that bind humans with the animals they hunt. Her story's human protagonist would have returned with privileged insights about the caribou's expectations governing responsible human hunting practices. If caribou left the region, she indicated, responsibility lay at the feet of humans. The biologist agreed on the last point and was intrigued by Mrs. Ned's apparent mixing of "nature" and "culture" but concluded that this sort of thing had no place in the "expert knowledge" his research required.

More than half a century ago, anthropologist Irving Hallowell confronted the same conundrum but came to a different conclusion. After a decade of conversations with Anishinaabe hunters living near the southern rim

Small herds of woodland caribou were common in what is
now the southern Yukon Territory during the late nineteenth century.
Photo by Dean Biggins, US Fish and Wildlife Service, Division of
Public Affairs, WO3772–023

of the eastern Canadian Subarctic, he argued that the foundational narratives told by these hunters closely reflected their lived experiences. Lives and stories were conceptually consistent because similar principles guided the everyday existence of both human and nonhuman persons. Hallowell had grown skeptical of social scientists' efforts to understand human organization from *a priori* models, and he worried that investigators would project their own theoretical categories onto the social arrangements of societies with which they were unfamiliar. Although acknowledging that members of all societies ponder the meaning of personhood, Hallowell insisted that this question was a primary preoccupation of the Anishinaabe – the "focal point" of their efforts to know the world.

One conventional critique of such an approach is that it flirts with essentialism by assuming tradition-bound, homogeneous, timeless, communities – but that seems too simple. "All systems leak," wrote linguist Edward Sapir. Much like others, Indigenous communities struggle daily with tough economic and political decisions that are debated, discussed, and revised on an ongoing basis. Conflicting views are experienced not just within communities but also by individuals nominated to represent members in adversarial negotiations with governing states. Rather than being essentialist, this approach brings us to contemplate the central dilemma: the relationship between humans and what some call nature. And it does so with all the prescience of Hallowell's ringing insistence that people schooled in the Western tradition must learn how others give meaning to concepts and frame the world.

Crucially, this approach reveals Euro-American modernity as but one way among many of looking at the world and offers potential for discussing other forms of being modern. A key feature of the modern tradition so heavily influenced by Descartes and other thinkers of the European Enlightenment has been to keep humans and nonhuman entities separate and to enshrine a series of related dichotomies: mind-body, subject-object, fact-belief, person-thing and, above all, nature-culture. Such dualism is at the root of the pervasive Euro-American belief that separates nature from culture, that abstracts knowledge from its social and relational context and even views nature as a passive object to be mastered and exploited with labour and technology. Similar themes preoccupied the sociologist Max Weber, who attributed the disenchantment of the world to scientific, secularized, bureaucratic society.

French anthropologist Claude Levi-Strauss famously argued that some natural phenomena are "good to think with" because they provide material stimuli for ordering the social and material worlds we inhabit. Listening for stories, I came to appreciate the First Nations concept of sentient landscapes, specifically the agency of glaciers. The Saint Elias Mountains separating the Gulf of Alaska from the high-country interior include some of

North America's highest peaks and provide scaffolding for the world's largest nonpolar ice fields. The Icefield Ranges include glaciers that surge, or advance, without warning after years of stability, sometimes for several kilometres. They frequently create ice-dammed lakes that build up and eventually disgorge when the ice thins. In the 1970s, the women I interviewed often included glacier narratives in their life-history accounts. In the accounts, these glaciers appear as wilful beings that respond directly and dramatically to human activity, often with catastrophic results.

One story from Indigenous oral tradition concerns the Lowell Glacier, which drains to the Alsek River. This glacier's name in Southern Tutchone language is Nàlùdi (Fish Stop) because it interrupted salmon migrations up the Alsek River. Nàlùdi was reportedly provoked to surge when a young boy travelling inland with coastal Tlingit traders recklessly joked about a balding inland shaman – comparing his head first to a stump, then to a knobby glacier. The aggrieved shaman withdrew to the top of a high bluff across the river from Nàlùdi and began to dream, summoning the glacier to advance. The glacier crossed the Alsek, reached this bluff, and walled off an upstream lake. Scientists estimate that the advancing Lowell Glacier created a two-hundred-metre-high ice dam that impounded Neoglacial Lake Alsek (100 kilometres long) in the mid-nineteenth century, as it had several times during the previous 2,800 years. When that dam eventually tunnelled, then fractured, the outburst discharged water through the Alsek Valley in an enormous flood, emptying the lake in one or two days, with devastating downstream consequences.

Human hubris and its consequences are consistent themes in these glacier narratives. Women narrators insist that strict rules apply to cooking near glaciers: food should be boiled, never fried, and no grease should escape from the cooking vessel lest the glacier (or glacier spirits) take offence. The refined grease – processed animal fat – used for cooking provides solid, white, high-quality lard. It liquefies when heated and melts,

The Lowell Glacier is remembered by the name Nàlùdi (Fish Stop)
in Southern Tutchone language. A surging glacier, it crossed the Alsek River
several times, most recently in the mid-nineteenth century.
Photo by Julie Cruikshank

crackling noisily when used to fry food, in ways that might be imagined as "mimicking" a glacier and causing a cacophonous, retributive surge. But surges, in turn, are interpreted by some as glaciers mimicking the offence of "cooking with grease" as they begin sliding over surfaces. Some Elders speak of enormous heat accompanying an angry surge.

Some forty kilometres north of Nàlùdi, two sheep hunters returned to their camp at the end of a long day in October 1921. At a pole bridge, the first man to cross the river was killed instantly by an explosion of ice from an outburst flood that erupted without warning on the Donjek Glacier. Though deeply distressed, the survivor attributed his companion's death to poor judgment. The victim had insisted on cooking bacon for breakfast that morning, despite warnings that he should not cook with grease near a glacier. Worse, he had joked that "a glacier has no nose" (hence no sense of smell). It was generally agreed that this act of hubris within the glacier's hearing contributed to this death.

Brazilian anthropologist Eduardo Viveiros de Castro maintains that although many people now speak and act as though everyone sees nature and culture as straightforward binary categories – with nature providing the universal and singular background inhabited by plural and particular cultures – this view is far from universal. Throughout the Americas, he insists, Indigenous peoples identify an original state in which humans and animals were able to communicate freely and shared a condition of humanity (not animality, as in our modern evolution narrative). In this view, which Viveiros calls Amerindian perspectivism, the world is inhabited by animals, humans, and sometimes landscape features that see the world in the same way but notice different things in it from their distinct vantage points. Viveiros would replace the concept of multiculturalism with multinaturalism, in which differing kinds of nature – humans, animals, rivers, trees, glaciers, and more are all immersed in relationships of exchange. This is not relativism (groups interpreting the same things differently because of diverse cultural traditions) but something more fundamental. Animals see themselves as humans living in their own homes, eating human food, and immersed in human relationships. But they also see humans as animals – either predators or prey. This is the conceptual unity identified by Hallowell and reflected in the recollection of Roger McDonnell, an anthropologist who conducted research in Ross River, Yukon, during the 1970s:

> One [Kaska] man invited me to consider a beaver we had been watching. What we were able to see was an animal swimming about, cleaning off its fur, and eating bark and twigs, etc., and as he pointed out, we would appear just as different and strange to

the beaver as it did to us. [My companion urged me] to imagine myself over with the beaver, to reduce the strangeness of all the material and sensible differences that separated us. The inference was that it was my vantage point that created the differences; were I able to shift this, then what had seemed strange and remote would become intimate and familiar, the inedible wood would become food to eat and so on. Kaska [people] believe it is not only possible but necessary to make such a move ...

This kind of thinking offers a direct challenge to ideas developed by European philosophers to order and simplify the seemingly chaotic world by creating such oppositional pairings as nature-culture, animal-human, and personal-impersonal. Spread across the globe by colonial expansion, these categories now shape how many people think. So "nature" has come to be seen as something distinct, providing the platform for human life, and science has been charged with "discovering" the laws by which "nature" performs.

By contrast Amerindian perspectivism makes relationships central: sentient beings are bound together by connections. Outward appearance is simply one incidental attribute of any being; all beings are bound by an enduring, shared inner structure (translated variously as "spirit" or "soul" – a concept that English renders poorly). According to this theory of multinaturalism, humans, animals, rivers, trees, glaciers, and more are immersed in relationships of exchange; all have points of view and all can choose to act, to react, or even to exchange perspectives with other beings in the world.

In South America, Indigenous organizations are reasserting the value of multinaturalist perspectives. As ecological crises reopen debates about peoples' place in the world, conceptions of Nature (Pachamama) as "resource" are shifting. In Peru, Ecuador, and Bolivia, Indigenous popular movements are invoking nonhuman actors – sentient beings that include mountains, water, and soil – into public political arenas. Indeed, the 2008 Constitution of Ecuador gives specific rights to nature and, in 2011, Bolivia announced plans to grant nature equal rights with humans. In these ways, multinaturalism brings nature into the human social equation and extends relations among people and things.

What, then, can we learn from all of this? Can these narratives and perspectives help to clarify issues that modern beliefs obfuscate? Might Indigenous knowledge unsettle modernist presumptions? How might our understanding of the world change if Indigenous knowledge were considered as an intrinsic and valuable whole rather than as data mine for Western scientific inquiry? Can the arguments raised here help us better manage our collective relations with the earth and one another? In listening to the stories recounted here (and to others), surely we must be attentive to their deployment and reception over the years and ask what we should be listening *for*. But first we should remember that modern science achieves its accomplishments by abstraction. Scientific observations gain authority by being removed from local contexts and combined in larger wholes (framed as "universal") that both travel and transgress boundaries of custom and tradition. Local knowledge, on the other hand, is rooted in place and practice. It is the product of familiarity and belief accumulated and handed down through generations. It is tacit knowledge embodied in life experience and reproduced in everyday behaviour and speech. It offers certain people a particular understanding of the relationships among living beings (including themselves) and with the environment.

Traditional-knowledge studies originated in collaborations among Indigenous peoples, anthropologists, and field scientists, in genuine efforts to establish that people who pursue land-based economies know things about nature. By the early 1990s, the terms *Indigenous knowledge* and *traditional knowledge* were widely used in northern Canada. A quarter of a century on, these categories have extended globally, and early in the third millennium, Indigenous knowledge (most commonly referred to as traditional ecological knowledge or TEK) holds a central place in two important and related Canadian debates: over its value to field sciences committed to discovering new knowledge, and over its role in regulatory science dedicated to policy making.

Aspiring to integrate local knowledge, conceptions, and perceptions into their projects, some scientists seek to quantify or otherwise translate the observations of land-based hunters into data to fit their modernist frameworks. Strong pressures are at work here. Twenty-first-century definitions of what constitutes knowledge are highly instrumental and turn on metrics such as knowledge transfer, performance indicators, and policy outcomes, all of which have become naturalized within universities, funding agencies, and research institutes.

The leaders of these institutions maintain a piercing eye on, and a narrow conception of, the "utility" of research and (more troublingly) knowledge. In this context, Indigenous knowledge is valuable only if it can be converted into discrete "informational inputs." And this is no easy task, as the wildlife biologist's somewhat puzzled reaction to Annie Ned's story about the last of the caribou in the southern Yukon reminds us. Indigenous knowledge grows from particular beliefs and values as well as from the complex social relations and institutions of Indigenous societies, and it is shaped by the practices and protocols of oral tradition. As the examples here demonstrate, it is knowledge that informs peoples' understanding of the world and their places in it, and it is not an object easily amenable to the calculations of Western science or conformable to modern Western conceptions of the universe.

Bureaucratic efforts to incorporate so-called traditional knowledge into regulatory science and resource management were given international impetus in 1987 by the United Nations' Brundtland Commission Report,

Our Common Future, which asserted that Indigenous communities are "the repositories of vast accumulations of traditional knowledge and experience that link humanity with its ancient origins. Their disappearance is a loss for the larger society which could learn a great deal from their traditional skills in sustainably managing very complex ecological systems." Thereafter, efforts surged in tandem with Indigenous claims to lands and to rights, often framed in response to aggressive oil, gas, and mineral exploration. Even the most isolated Indigenous communities in Canada are now tied to global markets and various forms of international exchange. Many northern hunters are more knowledgeable about neoliberal economic and management strategies than many other Canadians. Indigenous engagement in modern land claims requires their participation in environmental impact assessments of fossil fuel and pipeline development proposals. Community hearings mandated by government policies now smoothly incorporate concepts such as comanagement and TEK into official jargon. In these proceedings, First Nations must often resort to uncharacteristic ways of speaking to accommodate consultative frameworks designed by a modern bureaucratic state. This integrationist model of knowledge claims to respect cultural difference but apparently requires no corresponding shift in epistemological or moral stance by certified experts. Increasingly, tensions hover on the very axis Annie Ned identified: knowledge imposed from "outside" versus knowledge from "Grandpa."

Rather than asking how information from hunters might contribute to scientific models, we should recognize that there are insights aplenty – and possibilities for fruitful surprises – in stories that we may have to struggle to understand. What disappears when we turn away from (or seek to translate and remake) puzzling accounts that apparently fail to fit within official regimes of knowledge are the relationships through which entities in the world come into being, as well as the capacities we might gain if we could actually learn to think with such stories. The process of translating understanding into data, always selective, narrows the register of what knowledge is deemed to be.

I have been struck over the years by how contemporary narrative strategies (especially those shared with me by Yukon women) echoed those advocated by philosopher Walter Benjamin many decades earlier. Information, he observed, is static – useful when it is new, but then absorbed and gone: "A story is different. It does not expend itself. It preserves and concentrates its energy and is capable of releasing it after a long time." The enchantment that pervades a universe inhabited by a community of beings in constant communication and exchange offers a hopeful (and possibly necessary) vision. It deserves more space in our modern world. Such ideas could provide crucial insights to guide future actions, given the cracks developing in the modernist project. In thinking about the nature of Canada, we might well listen for different stories, as Annie Ned advised all those years ago, because her counsel captures both the possibilities and fissures that reverberate through contemporary discussions of Indigenous knowledge.

REFERENCES AND FURTHER READING

My early work in Yukon, with Annie Ned and others, is reported in Julie Cruikshank, in collaboration with Angela Sidney, Kitty Smith, and Annie Ned, *Life Lived Like a Story: Life Stories of Three Yukon Elders* (Lincoln: University of Nebraska Press, 1990), and the glacier stories are discussed in Julie Cruikshank, *Do Glaciers Listen? Local Knowledge, Colonial Encounters and Social Imagination* (Vancouver: UBC Press, 2005).

My discussion of Anishinaabe hunters is drawn from A. Irving Hallowell, "Ojibwa Ontology, Behavior and World View," in *Culture in History: Essays in Honour of Paul Radin*, edited by Stanley Diamond, 19–52 (New York: Columbia University Press, 1960). The "all systems leak" phrase is from anthropologist

Edward Sapir, cited in Katerina Clark and Michael Holquist, *Mikhail Bakhtin* (Cambridge: Harvard University Press, 1984), 14.

Claude Levi-Strauss's "good to think" quote comes from *Totemism*, translated by Rodney Needham (Boston: Beacon Press, 1962), 89.

The death on the Donjek Glacier was reported in the *Whitehorse Star*, November 25, 1921. Four decades later, anthropologist Catharine McClellan heard this story from Albert Isaac, then living at Aishihik. Another four decades on, I heard the story from Elders at Kluane Lake.

The discussion of Amerindian perspectivism comes from Eduardo Viveiros de Castro's "Cosmological Deixis and Amerindian Perspectivism," *Journal of the Royal Anthropological Institute* 4, 3 (1998): 469–88, and the Kaska view of the beaver is from Roger McDonnell, "Symbolic Orientations and Systematic Turmoil: Centering on the Kaska Symbol of Dene," *Canadian Journal of Anthropology/Revue canadienne d'anthropologie* 4, 1 (1984): 39–56. On efforts to incorporate traditional knowledge into science and resource management and the implications thereof, see Erin L. Bohensky and Yiheyis Maru, "Indigenous Knowledge, Science, and Resilience: What Have We Learned from a Decade of International Literature on 'Integration'?" *Ecology and Society* 16, 4 (2011): 6; Carly A. Dokis, *Where the Rivers Meet: Pipelines, Participatory Resource Management, and Aboriginal-State Relations in the Northwest Territories* (Vancouver: UBC Press, 2015); Stephen Ellis, "Meaningful Consultation? A Review of Traditional Knowledge in Environmental Decision Making," *Arctic* 58, 1 (2006): 66–77; Paul Nadasdy, "The Gift of the Animal: The Ontology of Hunting and Human-Animal Sociality," *American Ethnologist* 34, 1 (2007): 25–43; and Graham White, "Cultures in Collision: Traditional Knowledge and Euro-Canadian Government Processes in Northern Land-Claim Boards," *Arctic* 59, 4 (2006): 401–14. On science and the social order, see Sheila Jasanoff, *States of Knowledge: The Co-production of Science and Social Order* (London: Routledge, 2004). For the Brundtland Commission, see *Our Common Future* (New York: Oxford University Press, 1987), 114–17. The Walter Benjamin quote is from his *Illuminations*, edited by and with an introduction by Hannah Arendt (New York: Schocken, 1968 [1936]), 90. Rane Willersley provides an illuminating Siberian study of hunting, animism, and personhood in *Soul Hunters: Hunting, Animism and Personhood among the Siberian Yukagirs* (Berkeley: University of California Press, 2007).

Victor Crowley stands between two massive codfish in front
of the salt store in Battle Harbour, Labrador, in 1901. The photographer,
Robert Holloway, noted that the larger fish was five feet, five inches
(1.65 metres) long and weighed sixty pounds (27.2 kg). Courtesy of the Provincial
Archives Division, The Rooms Corporation of Newfoundland and Labrador, VA 21–18

ELDORADO NORTH?

Stephen J. Hornsby and Graeme Wynn

C OD FISH AND BEAVER pelts were among the most significant commodities of trade in the early modern world. The cod fishery was
northern North America's equivalent of Potosí and Zacatecas, the silver
mines of Bolivia and Mexico that returned great wealth to Europe. Journalist
Mark Kurlansky, who calls cod the "fish that changed the world," plays for
effect when he claims that cod lifted distant colonies of starving settlers to
international commercial importance. Yet he is right in pointing out what
generations of earlier scholars established: that it provided invaluable
protein in the diets of European peasants and Caribbean slaves. The fur
trade was economically less important than the fishery, yet historian Tim
Brook claims that the fur trade marked the dawn of the global world. This
landmark was reached a century earlier when Spanish galleons linked
China to America and Europe. Still, the quest for beaver pelts (from which
the best felt was made) pushed the tentacles of European commerce across
northern North America, from the shores of the Atlantic clear to the Pacific
and the Subarctic. Spurred by an almost insatiable European demand for
felt hats, it recast many aspects of Indigenous existence. A missionary reported that a "Montagnais" trapper, surprised by the strangers' interest in
this abundant animal, concluded that "the Beaver does everything perfectly
well" because "it makes kettles, hatchets, swords, knives, [and] bread."

The fish and fur trades were based on renewable resources that supported people for several centuries. Both were complex endeavours. They depended on local knowledge; required particular skills; turned on custom, trust, and obligation; and were shaped by international connections. Yet they were very different enterprises, and they traced different trajectories through time. One ended in collapse through a combination of human greed, weak regulations, and a failure of management; the other also suffered the effects of acute competition, limited ecological understanding, and fluctuating fortunes. But it survived – albeit at a reduced scale. In both ventures, governments ("the state") intervened to help people confronting the consequences of resource collapse, notably in Newfoundland after the 1992 moratorium on fishing for northern cod and in the continental interior after the Hudson's Bay Company withdrew credit and supplies from Indigenous traders in the late nineteenth and early twentieth centuries. In sum, fish and fur fuelled European interest in a seemingly bleak and forbidding territory, drew Europeans (few though they were initially) to settle it, recast Indigenous lives, and laid the foundations for further economic, demographic, and sociopolitical development. Canada might never have existed but for these staple trades. Their histories show us how different modes of understanding the world, shifts in authority and control, and changes in the scale and power of technology and the momentum of market forces have shaped the exploitation and management of Canadian nature.

John Cabot's report of his 1497 voyage described immense quantities of codfish in waters off a "new founde land" in the western Atlantic. This was impetus enough for French, Spanish Basque, and Portuguese fishermen to swing their vessels westward. The English, for whom Cabot sailed, were not much involved in the fishery off Newfoundland until the late sixteenth century, however. Then the Danes squeezed competitors from the Iceland fishery, and the English, victorious at sea over Spain in 1588, displaced

Spanish ships from the fishing banks. The English and the French struggled for control over the fishery for a long century thereafter. England's triumph, in 1713, established its claim to Newfoundland, but the French retained rights to dry their catch on particular shores until 1904, and the United States claimed a vital interest in the offshore fisheries until Canada extended its exclusive economic zone in the 1970s.

A competitive international enterprise, the cod fishery encompassed an immense area of the continental shelf between northern Labrador and Cape Cod and from the mouth of the St. Lawrence River to the eastern edge of the Grand Bank (or almost twenty degrees of latitude and longitude). In this area, warm waters of the northeast-flowing Gulf Stream converged with the frigid southwestern flow of the Labrador Current to create ideal conditions for the growth of plankton. On this biotic foundation, capelin, herring, mackerel, cod, Atlantic halibut (and a dozen other species), seals, walruses, and whales thrived. Europeans quickly eradicated walruses and had severely depleted whale stocks in southern Labrador by the early 1600s. But cod remained remarkably abundant and seemingly resilient. Separate stocks lived on the Nova Scotia banks, the Gulf of St. Lawrence shallows, and the Newfoundland banks. The most abundant, the northern cod, spawned on the outer banks in the spring and then moved inshore in pursuit of migrating capelin. Smaller inshore substocks swam in the coastal bays of Newfoundland.

The seasonal movement of cod sustained two distinct fisheries that together required a large workforce. One fishery focused on the offshore banks and employed ocean-going vessels based in European or northeastern American ports. Men fished from the decks of these vessels or, later, from small rowboats. The numbers involved were striking: possibly four hundred vessels by the end of the sixteenth century. In the eighteenth century, between fifteen thousand and twenty thousand fishermen from Britain and France worked the banks each year. They cleaned and filleted their catch onboard and preserved it in brine (hence the characterization "green" or "wet" fishery).

The green fishery.
Men working from a vessel stand in barrels and shelter from the
elements with canvas windbreaks. Duhamel du Monceau, *Traité général des pesches*,
1782, Part 2, Section 1, Plate 9, detail. Courtesy University of British Columbia
Library Digitization Centre and Tony J. Pitcher, UBC Fisheries Centre

The other, inshore, fishery used small boats within three miles of the
Newfoundland coast. It developed at the same time as the banks fishery,
and it was initially also a transitory enterprise; ships and crews came for
the summer. Then "over-winterers" stayed to tend the shore works. By 1670,
a few women had settled in the area, and permanent settlements were initiated. By the close of the eighteenth century, Newfoundland had about ten
thousand long-term residents of European origin, ten thousand over-
winterers, and twenty-five thousand summer sojourners. In the inshore

This cartouche is inset in Plate 7 of Herman Moll's famous atlas, *The World Described*, published in London in 1720. Commonly known as the "Codfish Map," it is formally titled "North America. To the Right Honourable John Lord Sommers, Baron of Evesham in ye county of Worcester, President of Her Majesty's most Honourable Privy Council &c., This Map of North America According to ye Newest and most Exact Observations is most Humbly Dedicated." The drawing offers a composite rendering of the various processes involved in fishing, curing, and drying cod. Library and Archives Canada (LAC), C–003686

fishery, the catch was landed at the end of each day, to be cleaned, filleted, and dried with salt and exposure to the air over many days on special structures called flakes (hence "dry fishery"). Well-cured, dehydrated cod could last many months and survive high humidity and hot temperatures before it started to spoil. Vast quantities were shipped over the years to markets in Catholic Europe and to Caribbean sugar plantations.

Although vessels and crews differed, cod-catching technology varied little from the early sixteenth to the mid-nineteenth century. Fishermen used one or two handlines with multiple hooks baited with capelin or herring. In the 1860s, fishers began using the bultow, a long line (often two hundred metres in length) with about one hundred baited hooks on short traces. Joined together, as many as ten bultows laid on the seabed by a couple of fishermen could cover large areas. Bultows were used both inshore and offshore. In the 1870s, inshore fishermen began using the cod trap, a net box fixed to the sea floor that could catch large numbers of fish without bait. It usually took two boats to empty one. These were passive forms of fishing that harvested rather than hunted fish. Success depended on knowing the right place to put gear and the right conditions in which to fish.

Fishermen managed the inshore on a quasi-territorial but informal basis. Now and then, when customary rights were infringed, violence broke out, and locals sometimes appealed to government officials for intervention. In 1865, incensed fishermen of Cape North, Cape Breton Island, petitioned the Nova Scotia government for redress after neighbours from nearby New Haven encroached on waters they claimed for their own. Residents of southwestern Cape Breton Island also complained to provincial authorities about the continual "disputes ... among the fishermen which often ended in disgraceful rows as to the location of the different bouys [sic]" marking the fishing grounds around Port Hood Island. They requested a "competent person" to adjudicate disagreements "so that order may be preserved and justice ensured for all." Widely dispersed and particularistic though it was, the fishery required some oversight by the still-embryonic state.

The annual cod catch in Newfoundland waters grew slowly and remained below three hundred thousand tonnes until the 1860s, even as growing numbers of fishermen exploited new areas. By the early nineteenth century, Trepassey and St. Mary's Bay, St. John's, Conception Bay, and Bonavista Bay were probably overfished, and few cod were taken deep in Trinity Bay, where the English fishery had once flourished. Activity moved to the headlands and to the tip of the Bonavista Peninsula. Fishermen then began to work the west coast, the Northern Peninsula (the old French Shore), the Strait of Belle Isle, and southern Labrador. By 1910, the inshore fishery had achieved its maximum spatial extent and productivity.

Cod drying on flakes in Newfoundland, showing stages, flakes, and the waterfront necessary to conduct the traditional inshore fishery. LAC, PA–139025

The catch increased dramatically late in the twentieth century and topped a million tonnes in the 1960s. It came from the offshore fishery, spawned by massive growth in the size of vessels and new fishing technologies. After 1950, wooden schooners gave way to wooden-hulled draggers (less than sixty-five feet in length) and larger steel-hulled stern trawlers that revolutionized the industry. Large European factory ships operated on the banks, sweeping up enormous catches and processing and freezing them on board. New technologies – such as sonar to locate fish, short-wave radio to communicate with other vessels (and thus concentrate fishing effort in good areas), fishing nets to exploit different depths of the sea, fish-processing machines, and freezing technology – all massively increased production.

Aware of declining groundfish yields such as cod and haddock and the massively expanding presence of foreign vessels on the banks, Canada extended its exclusive economic zone two hundred miles offshore in 1977. This confined foreign fishers to the Nose and Tail of the Grand Bank – but Canadian fishing effort expanded massively. There was, said a Department of Fisheries and Oceans official, a bonanza attitude: "It was El Dorado again. The Canadian offshore boys got into the fishery and ... the processing industry went right through the roof. It was fabulous. For two or three years." Chasing profits as well as fish, inshore fishermen built longliners to reach the middle fishing grounds. Deploying large bottom trawls, fishers disrupted the seabed and eliminated places for juvenile cod to hide from predators. Natural factors probably exacerbated the effects of frenzied overfishing. Exceptionally low ocean temperatures associated with the negative phase of the Atlantic Multidecadal Oscillation might have created conditions too cold for cod to spawn. Increasing seal populations (attributable to restrictions on the harp seal hunt) raised predation pressure on northern cod. Stock replenishment rates fell, and the federal government closed the Newfoundland cod fishery in 1992.

Scientists at the Department of Fisheries and Oceans who overestimated the fish stock and underestimated fish mortality have borne much of the blame for the collapse of the fishery, but European countries and Canadian fish companies who pressed for fishing to continue were equally responsible. Even before the fishing moratorium, inshore fishermen noticed that stocks were declining and that they were catching smaller fish. On the banks, many of the cod caught in the 1980s weighed about four or five pounds, minnows compared with the legendary 180-pound codfish hauled up from Georges Bank in 1838. But these observations had little impact as fishermen (especially inshore) and fisheries scientists spoke different languages: one was based in local knowledge, fine-grained, and dependent on generations of first-hand experience; the other was scientific, broad-based, and reliant on biological models. One group talked about winds, currents, tides, cycles of the moon, and ice conditions; the other talked about exploitable biomass, total allowable catch, and maximum sustainable yield.

Snow crab and northern shrimp have increased in abundance since 1992, probably as a result of changing oceanographic conditions and a reduction in predation by codfish. These species now yield more value than cod did in the 1980s. But their capture employs fewer people on sea and land. Since 1992, residents of dozens of villages, or outports, around the coasts of Newfoundland, for whom cod was not only a cash product but a subsistence food, have struggled to survive. Many have moved on, carrying little more than fond memories of places they had to leave. A way of life shaped by people working "their land and sea together in intimate understanding of the local ecology" is fast being lost.

French and English adventurers seeking pelts for both luxury clothing and felt hats established different lines of connection – the French along the St. Lawrence, the English along the Hudson River and, after 1670, through Hudson Bay – with Indigenous peoples who trapped and traded furs. By 1700, the trade reached west of Lake Winnipeg, south of Lake Michigan, and into the Appalachian Mountains. Most of the material for the 21 million hats and sizeable numbers of beaver pelts Britain exported between 1700 and 1770 came from this area. After the northern half of the continent fell under British control in 1763, competition, and the seemingly insatiable European demand for fur, drove fur traders onward. The exploits of Alexander Mackenzie, David Thompson, and Simon Fraser, who opened new territory for the Northwest Company of Montreal, are marked in the names of three of the great rivers of the West. Meanwhile, profits accrued to the Company of Adventurers of England trading into Hudson Bay and to a large handful of merchants in Montreal, whose successes helped the city rise to metropolitan pre-eminence and whose legacy included the establishment of McGill University.

For a business that spanned a continent, the fur trade brought remarkably few non-Indigenous people into the territory. In 1805–06, the Northwest Company counted fewer than 950 employees beyond Sault Ste. Marie; the Hudson's Bay Company had fewer than 450 at its trading posts on and inland from the bay. As competition between the two groups increased, more men were engaged in the trade. By 1820, the HBC's numbers had doubled. A year later, the two companies were forced into a merger to end their often violent rivalry. This gave the HBC a monopsony and allowed Governor George Simpson, who was much devoted to "system and economy," to rationalize the trade and place it on more sustainable foundations. Trading posts were reduced in number from 125 to 52, and the price of trade goods was raised.

Indigenous peoples did the vital first work of the trade, trapping beaver and other fur-bearers. Success depended "very much," as the author of a classic nineteenth-century study of the American beaver recognized, "upon the knowledge the trapper has of the habits and mode of life of the several animals he seeks to capture." Ingenious tactics and technologies (including steel traps from Europe after 1790) were used to capture animals during the winter. Beaver driven from their lodges took shelter in burrows, which were then closed by the hunter, who opened the burrows from above and hauled the beaver out with hooks. Elaborate palisades placed strategically beneath the ice and monitored carefully allowed trappers to drown beaver intent on replenishing their food supply. Traps placed near small breaches in the dam snapped fast on beaver drawn from the lodge to repair the damage.

When fur-trading posts were few, trappers often faced long journeys to trade their pelts. Using canoes, they could each bring about 150 pelts to market in a single trip. This technological constraint on production was eased as posts proliferated (over six hundred were established, though most did not last) and as multiple trips became possible. Rising prices for pelts also intensified trapping efforts. Although some HBC traders thought that "giving Indians a larger Price [for their furs] would occasion the Decrease of Trade," and although some scholars argue that Indigenous traders were unresponsive to the market-price mechanism because they were happy to satisfy their needs and unwilling to expend additional effort to meet "imaginary wants," recent analyses of the trade have complicated and challenged this interpretation. First, behaviour varied with circumstances. Recognizing that beaver dams stabilized water resources, Indigenous groups on the dry prairies limited the number of beaver they killed. Indigenous peoples on the Canadian Shield had fewer taboos against hunting beaver, and animal populations there plummeted in the nineteenth century. Second, when escalating European demand and competition from Montreal-based traders pushed fur prices upward at Fort Albany and York Factory in the 1740s, substantially more furs were brought in, and trappers acquired more "luxury" goods.

Analysis of the annual returns of beaver pelts brought to Fort Albany and York Factory in the eighteenth century suggests that the harvest levels in their hinterlands were sustainable through the 1730s. Then trapping began to exceed the biological optimum, and returns fell to unprecedented lows after 1750. In 1824, when George Simpson, the governor of the HBC, passed through the once fur-rich Nelson River District back of Fort York, he saw not "a solitary vestige of a beaver." Similar patterns were evident in the Petit Nord between Lakes Superior and Winnipeg and James Bay. In 1780, beaver were reportedly plentiful throughout this area. By 1800, they were abundant in a pear-shaped zone east of Lake Winnipeg and a much smaller area east of Lake of the Woods. Twenty years later, beaver were aplenty only in five small territories, all but one of them smaller in area than Lake of the Woods. Most of the area's fur-bearing and food animals were close to extirpation by 1840.

Recognizing in 1822 that "the country is without doubt in many parts exhausted in valuable furs," Simpson sought to nurture the trade by limiting trapping in overexploited districts and extending it to new areas by closing some posts and opening others. Aware that muskrat populations fluctuated widely, depending on hydrological conditions, traders diverted trapping from beaver to muskrat when conditions were propitious. The company refused beaver killed in the summer; restricted the use of steel traps, which Simpson regarded as "the scourge of the country" that "should have been prohibited long ago"; and in several districts limited annual beaver pelt purchases to levels below the norm. These measures had limited effect. In 1841, administrators of the HBC's Northern Department reported that "the Impoverishment of the Country in the article of Beaver is increasing to such an alarming extent that it becomes necessary to take effectual measures." Purchases of beaver all but ceased at some trading posts, and other posts offered a premium for furs other than beaver in the hope of deflecting hunting pressure. When populations began to rebound after three years, a restricted trade was reopened.

In the end, changes in taste had more effect on the fate of fur-bearing animals than the HBC's conservation measures. In Europe, "an extraordinary break of fashion" in the 1830s suddenly brought silk hats into vogue. The felt hat business never regained its former glory. As settlers and politicians in Canada West focused their nation-building aspirations on the western interior, the HBC agreed to surrender Rupert's Land – almost 8 million square kilometres – to the new Dominion of Canada in July 1870. It was a classic commercial-political manoeuvre. Prime Minister John A. Macdonald observed that "no explanation" had been given to those who lived there: "All these poor people know is that Canada has bought the country from the Hudson's Bay Company and that they are handed over like a flock of sheep to us." Between 1871 and 1876, Treaties 1 through 7 extinguished Indigenous claims to the grassland, parkland, and woodland of the southern Prairies.

By commodifying beaver (and muskrat, marten, and mink), the fur trade did more than reduce fur-bearing populations. Beaver are known as ecological engineers. Building dams along small slow-moving streams in relatively level terrain (fifteen to twenty dams per kilometre have been recorded), they alter local hydrology by raising the water table, dampening flow peaks, and reducing stream volume. Streamside burrows can cause bank slumping and tree tipping. Dams create ponds and lakes of different sizes, which act as settling basins for large amounts of sediment and organic matter. (It has been estimated that hundreds of billions of cubic metres of such sediments accumulated prior to European contact. According to another account, beaver ponds and wetlands probably covered more than

Disconcertingly humanoid beaver appeared in a cartouche on Nicolas de
Fer's decorative wall map of North and South America, *L'Amerique divisee
selon letendue de ses principales parties,* which was published in 1713.
The version of the cartouche shown here appeared on Plate 8, *A New and
Exact Map of the Dominions of the King of Great Britain on Ye Continent
of North America,* in Herman Moll's *The World Described* (1720).
Moll's version is a mirror image of Fer's but without the list of the
tasks performed by the beaver. LAC, C–016758

eighty-five thousand square miles – the surface area of Lakes Superior,
Michigan, Huron, and Ontario – of the United States in the fifteenth century.) Ponds provide excellent habitat for fish and insects, which, in turn,
help support larger bird and animal populations. Vegetation is also affected.
Two decades after beaver build a dam, there will be few trees within twenty
metres of the pond. Because they favour poplar, aspen, and willow, beaver
also change the species composition of forests.

A Revillon Frères Company trader buying white fox furs and other skins
from Inuit at the company's post in Cape Dufferin, Quebec, ca. 1908–14.
Revillon Frères was a French fur and luxury goods company with trading posts
across the European Arctic and stores in Paris, London, New York, and Montreal.
It began acquiring furs in northern Canada at the turn of the twentieth century.
It was incorporated in Canada as Revillon Frères Trading Company Ltd. in 1912.
The company financed Robert Flaherty's 1922 film *Nanook of the North*.
Courtesy Glenbow Archives, NA–1338–102

In the past, when trapping (and epizootics, or wildlife diseases) reduced
beaver populations, most of these effects were reversed. As abandoned dams
leaked and broke, fish and waterfowl lost habitat, stream incision increased,
once-clear waters became murky, and soils dried as water tables fell. Ponds
became wetlands or bogs, and as they, too, dried out, sedge and bluejoint
grass formed so-called beaver meadows, from which fortunate European
settlers might take up to eight tonnes of hay per hectare.

The scale of these cascading changes is not easily determined. American
journalist Jim Sterba, who refers to the fur trade as "a feeble euphemism

for the massacre of beavers," claims that North American beaver populations fell from 400 million to 100,000 between 1500 and 1900. More
considered estimates, such as that by writer, artist, and conservationist
Ernest Thompson Seton, suggest a peak of 50 to 90 million beaver. Numbers
certainly plummeted as the fur trade expanded. In 1938, Ontario banned
beaver trapping for a decade. For all the opposition in the English-speaking
world to wearing and using furs, however, and even with falling prices
for pelts, about three hundred thousand beaver were trapped annually in
Canada at the turn of the millennium. Although farms and cities have
destroyed much of their habitat, there are 20 to 30 million beaver in North
America today. This recovery has had its own ecological impact. The world's
beaver ponds release a sixth as much methane (a greenhouse gas) as all the
world's wild ruminants.

Long before they began to use the fish and fur-bearing animals of northern
North America, Europeans had developed a rich set of customs, rules, and
regulations to govern uses of agricultural land, wild animals, and other
resources. The New World posed new challenges. Vast spaces, the relative
scarcity of newcomers (who knew little of the places in which they found
themselves), the increasing commodification of nature, and the initial
weakness of authority meant that much had to be figured out in situ.

Over three centuries, the fur trade was shaped by cycles of competition
– among the English, the French, and the Dutch, between the Hudson's
Bay Company and the Northwest Company, between the HBC and
American traders on the Pacific Coast and Columbia River, and between
independent hunters and the HBC. Competition generally worked against
conservation. Indeed, HBC officials, challenged by American rivals and
anticipating that the area would likely fall to the Great Republic, ordered
aggressive overhunting of furs in southern parts of the Columbia District
in the 1820s and 1830s. Yet the HBC's monopoly of the trade in remote

locales allowed for a measure of control and maintenance of the resource. By exercising its centralized authority to reduce the numbers of beaver purchased in heavily exploited districts, by refusing furs taken in summer or with steel traps, and by shifting demand curves for different furs by adjusting prices, the company was able to stem, at least temporarily, the decline in beaver populations. In the end, however, the new fad for silk hats was probably decisive for the survival of beaver across much of northern North America.

The taste for cod never abated. Ultimately, the combination of sustained demand, new technologies that allowed fishing offshore on an industrial scale to proceed year-round, competition between offshore and inshore fishers, and reliance on a regulatory regime shaped by science that favoured the offshore fishery brought northern cod stocks to the brink of destruction. Might things have been different? In the wake of the cod moratorium, some have argued for the benefits of bottom-up rather than top-down administration of resources. In this view, the practical knowledge necessary for successful management depends on "exceptionally close and astute observation of the environment." Those using a resource are best placed and most likely to observe its fluctuations carefully and adjust their practices judiciously. Moreover, shared local knowledge is an invaluable "living oral reference library for observations, practices, and experiments." Had the fishery been under local control rather than management by the Department of Fisheries and Oceans, the argument runs, fishermen would have tapped this knowledge, drawn on their experience, and better regulated their fishing practices.

But this view reflects an ideological critique of the modern state and discounts the value of large-scale coordination of the sort attempted by the HBC. Based in London, the company combined careful statistical monitoring of the harvest with on-the-ground observation of hunting efforts, gathered through regular communication with Indigenous hunters and trappers. It used its extensive network of trading posts to administer (and, to a degree, conserve) the fur trade in Canada. Many critics of scientific resource management have argued that it is deeply flawed because it rests upon assumptions that simplify the world and reduce complex systems to mathematical models. So, they say, fisheries managers typically focus on a particular stock and pay too little attention to many of its ecological linkages. Because their function is to establish clear and simple rules for the most efficient and sustainable use of the resource, critics claim, these managers put too much faith in (often uncertain) numbers, are too confident in their ability to predict, and cannot escape the political and administrative priorities of those whom they serve. Indeed, some would insist that any impulse to model and manage the natural world is an act of hubris that fosters an often unwarranted confidence in the human capacity to control nature. There are valid points in these arguments, but taken as a whole they tend to undermine the authority of scientists and discount their capacity to reveal and analyze the workings of ecological systems. This is unfortunate – and inaccurate. Unbridled skepticism of science will serve little good as we recognize (often through the lens of science) that much has been (and continues to be) wrong with the world and humanity's place within it.

Property rights have also loomed large in debates about resource conservation. Fish are a classic common-property resource, owned by none until caught. These resources, runs the oft-made argument, will be subject to predatory depletion unless privatized in some way – the so-called tragedy of the commons. Similar arguments have been made about fur-bearing animals. As the story goes, in the Indigenous world there was "an overriding principle" – amid a range of property-rights regimes (none of which was absolute, but many of which encompassed loosely bound areas and lacked any firm conception of trespass) – "that no one can prevent a person from obtaining what he needs for his family's survival." This pervasive norm, essential to survival in the Subarctic, reduced the incentive to conserve animals when prices rose. By these lights, only regulation – by local custom, by strict limits on access or catch quotas in the fishery, or of the sort contemplated by the HBC when it considered assigning specific hunting territories to particular Indigenous bands or families – could prevent disaster.

But efforts to regulate and restrain were fallible in the face of uncertain knowledge, economic pressure, and lack of political resolve. Initially, the imperatives of emerging markets trumped nascent efforts to find a balance between the still poorly understood ecologies of fish and fur-bearers and exploitation of the resources. In the nineteenth and twentieth centuries, the challenge of living wisely on the earth was complicated further by technological innovations (that generally facilitated exploitation); the growing importance of production and profit as measures of success; and the marginalization of stakeholder voices by the widespread embrace of expert knowledge (itself a construct of the liberal capitalist order) in framing human choices. If there was a simplifying fiction behind the decline of the fishery and the fur trade it was that economics is more important than ecology.

REFERENCES AND FURTHER READING

Any study of fish and furs should begin with Harold Innis's books *The Fur Trade in Canada: An Introduction to Canadian Economic History* (Toronto: University of Toronto Press, 1977 [1930]) and *The Cod Fisheries: The History of an International Economy* (Toronto: Ryerson Press, 1940). They are usefully supplemented by several sections and plates in R. Cole Harris, ed., *The Historical Atlas of Canada*, vol. 1, *From the Beginning* (Toronto: University of Toronto Press, 1987) and Plates 8, 17, 18, 19, and 37 in R.L. Gentilcore, ed., *The Historical Atlas of Canada*, vol. 2, *The Land Transformed* (Toronto: University of Toronto Press, 1993). There has been a great deal of other work on both fish and fur. On fish, see C.G. Head, *Eighteenth-Century Newfoundland: A Geographer's Perspective* (Toronto: McClelland and Stewart, 1976); W.G. Handcock, *So Longe As There Comes Noe Women: Origins of English Settlement in Newfoundland* (St. John's: Breakwater Books, 1989); Sean

Cadigan, *Hope and Deception in Conception Bay: Merchant-Settler Relations in Newfoundland, 1785–1855* (Toronto: University of Toronto Press, 1995); and Jean-François Brière, *La pêche française en Amérique du Nord au XVIIIe siècle* (Quebec: Éditions Fides, 1990) (from which the estimates of numbers in the eighteenth-century wet fishery are drawn). W. Jeffrey Bolster's *The Mortal Sea: Fishing the Atlantic in the Age of Sail* (Cambridge: Belknap Press of Harvard University Press, 2012) offers a sound, accessible account of fishing in the North Atlantic. On fur, see Arthur J. Ray, *Indians in the Fur Trade: Their Role as Hunters, Trappers and Middlemen in the Lands Southwest of Hudson Bay, 1660–1870* (Toronto: University of Toronto Press, 1974); Michael Payne, *The Fur Trade in Canada: An Illustrated History* (Toronto: James Lorimer, 2004); and Sylvia Van Kirk, *Many Tender Ties: Women in Fur-Trade Society, 1670–1870* (Norman: University of Oklahoma Press, 1980).

For the nineteenth-century debate over new fishery technologies, see the insightful discussion in Sean Cadigan, "Moral Economy of the Commons: Ecology and Equity in the Newfoundland Cod Fishery, 1815–1855," *Labour/Le Travail* 43 (Spring 1999): 9–42, and "Failed Proposals for Fisheries Management and Conservation in Newfoundland, 1835–1880," in *Fishing Places, Fishing People: Traditions and Issues in Canadian Small-Scale Fisheries,* edited by Dianne Newell and Rosemary Ommer, 147–69 (Toronto: University of Toronto Press, 1999). The 1865 petitions from Cape Breton Island are in Stephen J. Hornsby, *Nineteenth-Century Cape Breton: A Historical Geography* (Montreal and Kingston: McGill-Queen's University Press, 1992), 157–59. For the post–Second World War fishery, see J.A. Hutchings and R. Myers, "The Biological Collapse of Atlantic Cod off Newfoundland and Labrador: An Exploration of Historical Changes in Exploitation, Harvesting Technology and Management," in *The North Atlantic Fisheries: Successes, Failures and Challenges,* edited by R. Arnason and L. Felt, 37–93 (Charlottetown: University of Prince Edward Island Press, 1995). The Eldorado quote is from Alan Christopher Finlayson, *Fishing for Truth: A Sociological Analysis of Northern Cod Stock Assessments from 1977–1990* (St. John's: Institute of Social and Economic Research, 1994), 26. The 138-pound cod is from Mark Kurlansky,

Cod: The Biography of a Fish That Changed the World (Toronto: Knopf Canada, 1997). G.A. Rose, *Fisheries Resources and Science in Newfoundland and Labrador: An Independent Assessment* (2003), available at http://www.gov.nl.ca/publicat/royalcomm/research/Rose.pdf, is a fine, accessible assessment of the late twentieth-century fishery crisis. The "land and sea together" quote is from Ommer, "Rosie's Cove: Settlement Morphology, History, Economy and Culture in a Newfoundland Outport," in Newell and Ommer, *Fishing Places, Fishing People*, 29.

Estimates of numbers employed in the fur trade are from Harris, *Historical Atlas of Canada*. A good discussion of Indigenous beaver-trapping techniques and the "habits and mode of life" quote can be found in Chapter 8 of L.H. Morgan's classic, *The American Beaver and His Works* (Philadelphia: J. B. Lippincott and Co., 1868), 438, which is a mine of information. The suggestion that Indigenous trappers were unresponsive to the price mechanism is made in E.E. Rich, "Trade Habits and Economic Motivation among the Indians of North America," *Canadian Journal of Economics and Political Science* 26, 1 (1960): 49 and 46, which also includes the HBC trader (Isham) who feared a "Decrease of trade" and Simpson's quote, "not a solitary vestige of a beaver." The counterargument alluded to through the York Factory–Fort Albany data is found in several articles by Ann M. Carlos and Frank D. Lewis, but their *Commerce by a Frozen Sea: Native Americans and the European Fur Trade* (Philadelphia: University of Pennsylvania Press, 2010) is a good place to begin. James Daschuk points to differences in Indigenous attitudes to the beaver in "A Dry Oasis: The Canadian Plains in Late Prehistory," *Prairie Forum* 34, 1 (2009): 1–29. The best discussion of HBC conservation measures is in Arthur J. Ray, "Some Conservation Schemes of the Hudson's Bay Company, 1821–1850: An Examination of the Problems of Resource Management in the Fur Trade," *Journal of Historical Geography* 1, 1 (1975): 49–68, where the "exhausted" (51), "scourge" (55), "Impoverishment" (64), and "break of fashion" (67) quotations appear. The Macdonald quote is from Donald G. Creighton, *The Old Chieftain* (Toronto: Macmillan Company of Canada, 1955), 46–47.

There is a large literature on beavers as ecological engineers. D.R. Butler has contributed a fair part of it, and although it deals with more than beavers, his

"Human-Induced Changes in Animal Populations and Distributions, and the Subsequent Effects on Fluvial Systems," *Geomorphology* 79 (2006): 448–59, includes a useful bibliography. The methane estimates are from Colin J. Whitfield, Helen M. Baulch, Kwok P. Chun, and Cherie J. Westbrook, "Beaver-Mediated Methane Emission: The Effects of Population Growth in Eurasia and the Americas," *Ambio* 44, 1 (2015): 7–15. Jim Sterba's account of the fur trade is in "America Gone Wild," *Wall Street Journal*, November 2, 2012; E.T. Seton's estimate is in *Life Histories of Northern Animals: An Account of the Mammals of Manitoba* (New York: C. Scribner's Sons, 1909).

For more on De Fer, see Edward H. Dahl, "The Original Beaver Map: De Fer's 1698 Wall Map of America," *Map Collector* 29 (1984): 22–26. There is a full discussion of Moll's atlas in John E. Crowley, "Herman Moll's *The World Described* (1720): Mapping Britain's Global and Imperial Interests," *Imago Mundi* 68, 1 (2016): 16–34. Stephen Hornsby's *British Atlantic, American Frontier: Spaces of Power in Early Modern British America* (Hanover: University Press of New England, 2005) offers a thoughtful Atlantic perspective on the two trades discussed here (and more).

The quotations in the "might things have been different?" paragraph are from James C. Scott, *Seeing Like a State: How Certain Schemes to Improve the Human Condition Have Failed* (New Haven: Yale University Press, 1998). The argument that follows is implied in that work and is applied energetically to the cod fishery in Dean Bavington, *Managed Annihilation: An Unnatural History of the Newfoundland Cod Collapse* (Vancouver: UBC Press, 2010). The property-rights discussion references G. Hardin, "Tragedy of the Commons," *Science* 162 (1968): 1243–48, and Scott Gordon, "The Economic Theory of a Common Property Resource: The Fishery," *Journal of Political Economy* 62 (1954): 124–52, and it draws the "overriding principle" quote from Fikret Berkes, David Feeny, Bonnie J. McCay, and James M. Acheson, "The Benefits of the Commons," *Nature* 340 (July 13, 1989): 91–93.

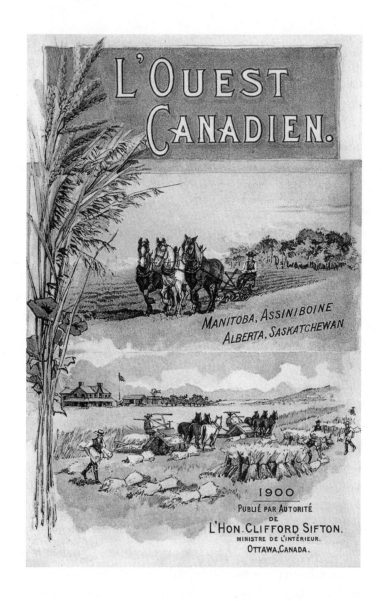

L'Ouest canadien, a publicity piece to attract French-speaking
settlers to the Canadian prairies, Department of the Interior, Ottawa, 1900.
This idealized view of a prairie farm focuses on extensive wheat fields,
sowed and harvested with the help of livestock and hired workers.

BACK TO THE LAND

——

Colin M. Coates

I N THE 1970S, WHEN young participants in the counterculture spoke of moving "back to nature," they defined "nature" in a fairly precise, though not necessarily obvious, way. A rare few, such as American writer Feenie Ziner's son Ben, headed for what some would term *wilderness,* living in the thick forest on a sparsely populated island off the British Columbia coast. But the vast majority of people who sought a counterculture lifestyle in nature left for the farm. They wanted to abandon urban sprawl and bustle and set up homesteads in rural areas. For them, a farm meant unmediated access to nature. In a wide range of places across Canada – such as Cape Breton, Prince Edward Island, Quebec's Eastern Townships, the Gaspé Peninsula, the Kootenays, and the islands in the Strait of Georgia – the postwar rural exodus had reduced the relative cost of rural properties, particularly on marginal agricultural lands. Here were bargains for young people with little cash. The government was at some distance from these locations, so one could even live off the grid. The hippies' back-to-nature dream involved a certain degree of self-sufficiency, which usually entailed small-scale farming. In ways that they might not have appreciated – though many read Thoreau's *Walden* (1854) for inspiration – agrarian independence had been a long-standing dream of many migrants to North America from the seventeenth century on.

As in the United States, agriculture had long formed the core of Canadian life. Historically, farming was the primary way in which Canadians of European descent experienced nature. Canada remained a rural country, in heart and body, until the decisive break that occurred around the time of the Second World War. Most Canadians lived in the countryside, in small towns, individual homesteads, or small resource-based communities. Until the 1960s, most dwelled in places with fewer than five thousand people. Generation by generation, since Europeans first came to the shores of the Bay of Fundy and the St. Lawrence River, people settled the land, carved farms from terrain that was as often reluctant as it was hospitable, and occasionally – even often – failed miserably in the process.

All of this meant that until fairly recently Canadians had direct connections with those who supplied their food, even if they did not produce it themselves. They were aware of the animals, the crops, and the vagaries of weather that governed their ability to survive through what was, in most parts of the country, a difficult and long winter. Through farming, they engaged directly with nonhuman nature.

Two millennia ago, in *De Natura Deorum*, Cicero wrote, "We sow corn [i.e., wheat], we plant trees, we fertilize the soil by irrigation, we dam the rivers and direct them where we want. In short, by means of our hands we try to create as it were a second nature within the natural world." In European settlements overseas, *second nature* had a doubled meaning as the phrase marked landscape changes quite as radical as those later produced by industry. Although they brought new practices, Europeans did not introduce agriculture to North America. Indigenous peoples practised several forms of farming. The Wendat and Haudenosaunee grew maize, squash, and beans (the three sisters), and the Wəlastəkw (Maliseet) extended maize cultivation into the northeast. People on the West Coast cultivated plant species such as camas bulbs, and they managed clam gardens. Despite the mistaken understandings of the newly arrived, Indigenous landscapes often reflected centuries of modification at human hands.

Iroquoian agriculture, from François du Creux,
Historiae canadensis (1664). Although Europeans did not tend to
acknowledge the comparability of their forms of food production,
many Indigenous peoples relied on different types of managed
agriculture long before the newcomers arrived on the continent.
Courtesy of Clara Thomas Archives and Special Collections, York University

For Europeans, however, *agriculture* meant domesticated plants, livestock, certain material technologies and, by the eighteenth century (at
least), a strong sense of property title. Newcomers often failed to recognize
Indigenous practices as agriculture. Colonial officials used Indigenous

peoples' different ways of occupying land to deny their claims. In the 1830s, Governor Francis Bond-Head of Upper Canada explained to the Odawa and Anishinaabe people that because they had not embraced farming as much as he deemed appropriate, their land was in danger from the influx of European settlers. They should, he said relocate to Manitoulin Island because "uncultivated land is like wild animals, and your Great Father [King William IV], who has hitherto protected you, has now great difficulty in securing it for you from the whites." However, in the first half of the nineteenth century, Anishinaabe in the Sarnia region who made considerable efforts to adopt agricultural practices similar to those of their neighbours were thwarted in almost every conceivable way. A few decades later, First Nations on the Prairies would face similar challenges as they attempted to adapt to the devastating decline in buffalo herds. Government agents forbade Indigenous farmers from using the same agricultural tools as their Euro-Canadian neighbours.

European styles of agriculture came to prevail in what is now Canada. French, English, Scots, and other newcomers adapted their farming traditions to local circumstances. Farmers in New France made grains of European origin the mainstay of their diets but planted maize ("Indian corn") alongside their fields of wheat, rye, barley, and oats. The South American potato came to British North America via Europe. Despite botanists' interest in indigenous species, Euro-Canadian farmers exploited few of them (although the syrup from maple trees has become an archetypically "Canadian" product). Writing in the 1720s, Father Pierre-François-Xavier de Charlevoix effused about how the ancients would have been delighted to see honey running from trees. Early French enthusiasm for the native Jerusalem artichoke (the sunchoke) dissipated fairly quickly when people recognized its flatulence-producing qualities. Non-Indigenous farmers on the West Coast never adopted the camas bulb.

In short, agriculture in areas inhabited by Euro-Canadians was based on exotics: introduced plants (grains and other garden plants), animals (livestock such as pigs, cows, horses, and sheep) and, of course, the weeds and pathogens that accompanied the plants and animals. Euro-Canadian agriculture took many different forms: a fairly sustainable mixed husbandry in many parts of eastern Canada, herding cattle in the Prairie West and attempts to herd bison in the Northwest Territories, orchards and vineyards in the Niagara Peninsula and the Annapolis and Okanagan Valleys, and large-scale grain monocultures on the Prairies. In many places, the second nature created by newcomers supplanted and replaced the second nature that Indigenous peoples had created. In this sense, going back to nature in Canada generally meant embracing a non-Indigenous, essentially European complex of species.

With its imported techniques and species, agrarian life came to epitomize the best and most worthy way of life in Canada. There was virtue in the farm, more than in the city or in resource-based industries such as forestry. When the character Jean Rivard in Antoine Gérin-Lajoie's eponymous 1862 utopian novel dreams of a future, it is an agricultural one, carved out of "first nature": "He imagined himself in the heart of a great forest. Suddenly men appeared armed with axes. Trees fell here and there under their blows. Soon the trees were replaced by rich harvests. Then orchards, gardens, flowers emerged as if by magic." Rivard follows this dream, leaving his rural home in the Trois-Rivières district and settling in a sparsely populated part of the Eastern Townships. He brings education, entrepreneurialism, and energy to the district, and the town that develops is eventually named Rivardville in his honour. Rivardville offers a moral landscape, far superior to the social hierarchies of Montreal, to which Rivard's good friend, an educated lawyer, had moved.

In much of Canadian literature, at least until after the Second World War, Canadians, French- or English-speaking, were proven wise to reject the siren songs of the city. That quintessential *roman du terroir*, Louis Hémon's *Maria Chapdelaine* (1913), presents the heroine of the story with three choices: an exciting life on the resource frontier with the compelling

Finnish settlers at Sointula, Malcolm Island, British Columbia, ca. 1902. Clearing land for agriculture was a back-breaking process in every forested region of what is now Canada, and immense West Coast trees made the work even more demanding. Many prospective farmers discovered that the soil was not always appropriate for large-scale agriculture. Courtesy of the Sointula Museum

François Paradis, a move to the bright lights of Boston with the oily Lorenzo Surprenant, or security on a Saguenay farmstead with the steadfast Eutrope Gagnon. The untimely death of Paradis means that Maria's decision to choose the farm becomes simpler. An *ex machina* voice informs her of the honourable timelessness of rural life: "In the country of Quebec nothing has changed ... we must remain in the province where our fathers have remained, and live as they lived." How many Maria Chapdelaines chose Eutrope Gagnons? Their Anne of Green Gables counterparts likely did the same. Not for Anne the temptations of Halifax or even Charlottetown but, rather, life in a country town. Although Lucy Maud Montgomery herself battled decades of depression as a country parson's wife, her best-selling novels still vaunted the superiority of rural life.

Social and religious elites continued to preach about the moral superiority of the countryside and the dangers of the city well into the twentieth century. Written in part by Charles Drury, the future leader of the United Farmers of Ontario and premier of the province, a series of resolutions from the Canadian Council of Agriculture exclaimed that "the greatest misfortune which can befall any country is to have its people huddled together in great centres of population." At Saint-Denis-de-Kamouraska, the sociologist Horace Miner heard the priest declaim to his parishioners in the 1930s: "You are farmers, not of the rich of the earth ... Don't envy those who run the streets until eleven o'clock at night going to theaters and cafés. They live low lives. In the cities there is no happiness. Love your land, the land of your fathers and your ancestors. Cultivate it; love it; love your humble calling."

Even as other countries industrialized at a faster pace, Canada attracted immigrants wishing to re-create older forms of agrarian life – crofters from Scotland in the Eastern Townships or Protestant Irish weavers in Mono Township in Upper Canada – that were increasingly difficult to maintain in their home countries. They wished to carve out some form of rural self-sufficiency. Likewise, city dwellers who had little prior agricultural experience seized the opportunity to homestead in the West. Soldiers returning from the Great War were offered farmlands, albeit in fairly marginal locations. Farming held the promise of a greater degree of independence, from landlords and the market and, as a result, generation after generation of Canadian immigrants and migrants embraced the agrarian dream.

Settlers were forced to confront the severe geographical and climatic limits of agriculture in Canada. Because of the northern latitudes at which they lived, the amount of sunlight varied considerably from winter to summer, and the continental climate that defines the weather patterns for much of the country brought frigid winters. As a result of these simple geographical and climatic facts, agrarian life followed seasonal patterns. In the eighteenth century, farmers near Quebec sowed their crops in early May and harvested as early as possible in late August or early September.

Canadian farmers in most places have likewise had to sow and harvest in an intense fashion. Through fall and winter, men could participate in complementary activities, including the fur trade and lumber camps. Later, scientific adaptations facilitated the expansion of agriculture in the Prairie West. In the late nineteenth and early twentieth centuries, the development of the Marquis strain of wheat, which could ripen in the region's short growing season, helped ensure large-scale agrarian settlement.

A late or an early frost could be devastating, as could other natural events. As early as 1640, Catholic authorities led public processions to stave off caterpillar and grasshopper outbreaks. In 1793, the bishop of Quebec allowed a rural priest to repeat prayers against a grasshopper infestation, but he wisely reminded him that such public scourges might not be relieved so long as any sinner remained in the parish. If the devastation did not end, the people had only themselves to blame. The distant explosion of Mount Tambora in what is now Indonesia had devastating consequences in eastern Canada, as it did globally, and 1816 was widely remembered as the "year without summer." In 1906, a bitterly frigid winter killed thousands of cattle and other livestock in the Prairie West. In that same region, dry-farming techniques for extensive wheat monocultures broke down the soil structure, making the Prairies particularly susceptible to dramatic consequences when dry conditions prevailed year after year in the early 1930s and winds blew the dry topsoil away. The Palliser's Triangle area on the border of southern Saskatchewan and Alberta was particularly hard hit. The propensity to spring flooding in the Red River Basin in southern Manitoba pitted lowland and highland farmers against one another over drainage issues. There are clear limits on the human ability to control agricultural conditions.

In general, the best agricultural lands were occupied within a few generations of European arrival in an area. French Canadian agrarian settlement in the St. Lawrence Valley peaked in the early nineteenth century. By the

1840s, French Canadians had already started to leave the farm for the growing factories of Montreal and New England. Agrarian settlement was even more rapid in Upper Canada, which Euro-Canadians began to farm in large numbers only in the 1790s. By the 1850s, farmers' children were departing the region for Michigan or other American states and territories. A few made the difficult journey to the rich soils of the Red River in present-day Manitoba. After the completion of the transcontinental railway in 1886, the Canadian west also filled in within a couple of generations. Most of the good farmland of Saskatchewan and Alberta was occupied by the 1920s. Still, state officials and other bodies such as the Catholic Church looked for new areas to homestead: the Peace River district, the Clay Belt of Northern Ontario, and the Abitibi-Témiskamingue district in northern Quebec attracted settlers as areas farther south filled and as property prices rose. Settlers and governments hoped that even the rocky soils of the Canadian Shield could support farming communities, but in areas such as Muskoka in Northern Ontario, tourism proved to be a much more lucrative activity for locals.

Overall, agriculture in Canada has been remarkably successful. Unlike all-too-frequent experiences in early modern Europe, farmers did not starve in Canada – there were no subsistence crises. Nonetheless, observers, particularly visitors from Europe, decried what they considered to be backward techniques among Canadian farmers: insufficient manuring by Nova Scotian Scots or French Canadians along the St. Lawrence, for instance. Such claims might have reflected professional aspirations and class biases as much as they were evaluations of practices on the ground. Trained agronomists such as Joseph-Xavier Perrault pleaded for the importation of superior European breeds of livestock in the 1860s. Some farmers embraced such views. The emotional and financial investment that some well-to-do farmers in Upper Canada made in their larger farm animals was reflected in the form of impressive portraits. Later critics believed that western

"Progressive" agriculturalists in the nineteenth century
paid increasing attention to the quality of livestock breeds. In this painting, titled
Good Friends, Ebenezer Birrell portrays a harmonious, well-fenced, and well-
stocked farm, full of horses, cattle, and sheep. Courtesy of the Art Gallery of Hamilton,
gift of Mrs. R.N. Steiner in memory of her mother, Mrs. L.C. Dillon, 1965

Canadian agriculture was not sustainable. French geographer André Siegfried castigated the western Canadian "miners of the land" because they did not love the soil: "When the prairies still existed in their natural state, the buffalo grass held the soil together. Now, after a few years of cultivation, if the crop is a failure, the soil pulverizes and is carried away by the wind in a storm of dust." Typically, critics wanted Canadian agriculture to be even more "European."

In an uncertain economic world and in regions with relatively small local markets, the appeal of agriculture lay in the promise of relative self-sufficiency. Upper Canadian journalist William Lyon Mackenzie, living in the town of York (later Toronto), articulated this goal in 1833 to prospective immigrants: "As to food, your own mutton and beef, and pork and veal, and butter and cheese, and potatoes and corn, and poultry, &c. raised at home, will render you as independent as King William IV." A participant in a back-to-the-land commune of the 1980s in the Bas-Saint-Laurent region explained his group's collective goals in a similarly lofty way: "It was a search for a healthy lifestyle, in contact with nature, for us collectively and individually, where work would regenerate us, and bodily and spiritual pleasures would have their place." Of course, farmers in Canada, and elsewhere, have never been entirely self-sufficient; they have always traded surpluses for goods that they could not furnish for themselves. But it required a shift in farming ideologies to produce almost exclusively for external markets – just as relatively reliable external markets were essential to any such trade.

From the beginning, farmers supplied urban markets, resource workers, and even markets beyond colonial borders. Ships carried wheat from New France to slave plantations in the Caribbean, and the large-scale agricultural settlement of what became Ontario was predicated on access to the rapidly expanding British market in the nineteenth century. Occasionally, the state encouraged production of crops for purposes other than human consumption. So colonial officials of the 1720s induced the farmers of Batiscan and other nearby seigneuries to grow and produce hemp for rope making. But the quality of the hemp and the expense of its production did not justify the effort, so local farmers soon returned to food crops. As populations grew and as relatively marginal agricultural areas came under the plow, farm families engaged in what historians call occupational pluralism; they participated in the fur trade or, later, the timber trade, although their main aim was to continue the agrarian lifestyle from generation to generation. Primary resource occupations did not carry the same moral weight as agriculture and, indeed, were often disparaged because of the dangers associated with them. In New Brunswick, writers derided the timber trade, notwithstanding its importance in generating economic wealth for the nineteenth-century colony, as an industry based on "adventitious transactions of precarious nature."

Canadian economic growth has long depended on the export of primary resources. But the family farm provided the essential basis upon which other resource trades could flourish. One justification for the establishment of permanent French agrarian settlements in the St. Lawrence Valley was the need to provide foodstuffs for French fur traders. The advantage of the family farm was that the family produced much of its own labour force. Children could contribute from an early age alongside their parents, by tending livestock, weeding gardens, assisting with housework, harvesting crops, fetching firewood, and procuring supplementary foods through fishing and hunting. In some locations, such as Upper Canada, work bees supplemented family labour. In others, such as the larger farms on the Prairies in the early twentieth century, harvests, which had to be completed fairly quickly, depended on a mobile and fairly inexpensive transient labour force. Fortunes, like those of Massey-Ferguson, came from supplying labour-saving machinery to farms in Canada and around the world.

The expansion of agriculture remained official government policy for many decades. Confederation promised solutions to some important political challenges in the 1860s, but the constitutional arrangement also held out a grander promise – the possibility of expanding agriculture to the West. George Brown, the leader of the Ontario-based Grit Party (the forerunners to today's Liberals), saw that the opening of Saskatchewan to agricultural settlement would allow the country to flourish. He was not averse to the exploitation of mineral or timber resources, but the family farm carried the greatest hope for him: "Our scheme is to establish a government that will seek to turn the tide of European emigration into this northern half of the American continent – that will strive to develop its great natural resources – and that will endeavour to maintain liberty, and justice, and Christianity throughout the land." Brown's vision of western settlement took some decades to reach full flight, but it happened quickly after 1896. Canada reached a high point of over 730,000 individual farm holdings in 1941, almost 300,000 of which were in the three Prairie provinces.

In their hubris, settlers sometimes imagined that they could influence, even improve, natural conditions through the expansion of agriculture. As writers attempted to explain the much colder winters (and often hotter and more humid summers) of the St. Lawrence Valley to readers situated on the same latitude in France, they blamed the winds from the north, the many watercourses and, most directly, the extensive forests for cooling the climate. Some writers thought removing the forests would effect a warming of the climate. When conditions did, indeed, warm from the late sixteenth-century Little Ice Age to the more temperate 1740s, scientists Jean-François Gaultier and Pehr Kalm attributed the trend to forest clearing. A century and a half later, despite warnings that large swaths of the western prairies would prove difficult for agriculture, government officials and some farmers chose to believe that rain would follow the plow. While the wetter conditions of the late nineteenth century seemed initially to confirm such beliefs, the particularly dry period of the 1930s exposed the challenges to prairie agriculture. A royal commission sounded the death knell of the agrarian vision of Canada: the "temporary retreat to the family homestead" could no longer suffice in times of economic depression. Henceforth, the Canadian government adopted welfare state approaches predicated on urban populations.

Over the course of three and a half centuries, the spread of European agriculture in all its forms had undeniable environmental and human consequences. Indigenous peoples lost access to land and resources that they believed their prior occupation and treaty rights ensured them. Farmers removed forest cover to plant their crops. This could simply involve burning the forest, a practice that scandalized some European visitors who were much less accustomed to seeing such vast expanses of trees. (Of course, farmers relied on the trees for their heating as well, and it was not in their interests to completely log the nearby forests.) By the First World War, over 90 percent of the mature woodland of southern Ontario had been removed. Farmers dug ditches to redirect water away from fields, and they had to ensure that beaver dams did not flood their crops. In the late nineteenth century, in a short space of time, hunters reduced the buffalo herds on the western Prairies to only a fraction of their earlier numbers. Introduced livestock diseases sometimes infected indigenous species, just as some exotic plants thrived in the new conditions. In northern Hudson's Bay Company forts, Euro-Canadian traders welcomed the dandelions they could consume, but these plants had hitchhiked passage to these new lands. Ultimately, most Canadians would be unable tell the difference between introduced plant and animal species and indigenous ones. Herds of feral horses now range free in British Columbia and Alberta and on Sable Island, in Nova Scotia. The European agricultural complex, to make a different play of words on the phrase, is now second nature to Canadians.

By placing agrarian life at the centre of Canadian environmental history, we can see that the choices made by Euro-Canadian settlers were revolutionary. They displaced Indigenous peoples, introduced exotic species, and removed forest cover and thick prairie grass to establish farms. In some parts of the country, the farming lifestyle remained sustainable for several generations. For a long time and for many people moving to or within "Canada," the future lay in farming, in escaping the city for a moral landscape where families could pursue dreams of self-sufficiency and profit. The youth of the counterculture of the 1970s and 1980s in Canada were not always aware of how much their moral choices about homesteading echoed the decisions of many generations in the past. Like them, they encountered a nature produced largely by the choices of European forebears.

This complex of animal and plant species, including many species of earthworms, was imported into North America and, like the immigrants themselves, many of the species found a new home on the soil of the continent. To understand this part of the nature of Canada, we must appreciate its relative novelty.

REFERENCES AND FURTHER READING

In their classic studies *Ecological Imperialism: The Biological Expansion of Europe, 900–1900*, 2nd ed. (Cambridge: Cambridge University Press, 2004) and *Changes in the Land: Indians, Colonists, and the Ecology of New England*, rev. ed. (New York: Hill and Wang, 2003), Alfred W. Crosby Jr. and William Cronon discuss the novelty of European agriculture in the Americas. Peter A. Russell's *How Agriculture Made Canada: Farming in the Nineteenth Century* (Montreal and Kingston: McGill-Queen's University Press, 2012) makes the case for the centrality of agriculture to Canadian history. R.W. Sandwell's *Canada's Rural Majority: Households, Environments and Economies, 1870–1940* (Toronto: University of Toronto Press, 2016) covers the persistence of varieties of rural lifestyles well into the twentieth century, as does the American study, Dona Brown's *Back to the Land: The Enduring Dream of Self-Sufficiency in Modern America* (Madison: University of Wisconsin, 2011).

The following are references to specific examples discussed in the essays. Feenie Ziner's memoir, *Within This Wilderness* (New York: W.W. Norton, 1978), describes her search for her son in an isolated region of BC. Various chapters in *Canadian Countercultures and the Environment*, edited by Colin M. Coates (Calgary: University of Calgary Press, 2016), deal with attitudes towards the environment among counterculture settlers in the 1970s and 1980s. The chapters in Douglas Deur and Nancy J. Turner's collection, *Keeping It Living: Traditions of Plant Use and Cultivation on the Northwest Coast of North America* (Vancouver: UBC Press, 2006) examine evidence for cultivation practices among nations in the Pacific

Northwest, and Jason Hall's "Maliseet Cultivation and Climatic Resilience on the Wəlastəkw/St. John River during the Little Ice Age," *Acadiensis* 44, 2 (2015): 3–25, discusses Indigenous agriculture on the East Coast. In "Seeing with Two Eyes: Colonial Policy, the Huron Tract Treaty and Changes in the Land in Lambton County, 1780–1867" (PhD diss., York University, 2015), Karen Travers looks at the difficulties faced by Anishinaabe farmers in the Sarnia region, while Sarah Carter, in "Two Acres and a Cow: 'Peasant' Farming for the Indians of the Northwest, 1889–97," *Canadian Historical Review* 70, 1 (1989): 27–52, reveals similar issues in the Prairie West in later decades. Thomas Wien's "'Les travaux pressants': Calendrier agricole, assolement et productivité au Canada au XVIIIe siècle," *Revue d'histoire de l'Amérique française* 43, 4 (1990): 535–58, discusses the agrarian calendar in New France. Father François-Xavier Charlevoix wrote enthusiastically about maple syrup in his natural history of the colony. See *Journal d'un voyage* (Paris: Chez Rollin Fils, 1744), 123. Victoria Dickenson, in "Cartier, Champlain, and the Fruits of the New World: Botanic Exchange in the 16th and 17th Centuries," *Scientia Canadensis* 31, 1–2 (2008): 27–47, recounts the shifting popularity of the sunchoke. John Sandlos's *Hunters at the Margin: Native People and Wildlife Conservation in the Northwest Territories* (Vancouver: UBC Press, 2007) deals with bison herding in the Northwest Territories. Scottish crofter and Irish Protestant immigration are covered in J.I. Little, *Crofters and Habitants: Settler Society, Economy, and Culture in a Quebec Township, 1848–1881* (Montreal and Kingston: McGill-Queen's University Press, 1991) and in R. Cole Harris, Pauline Roulston, and Chris de Freitas, "The Settlement of Mono Township," *Canadian Geographer* 19, 1 (1975): 1–17.

James Murton looks at post–First World War soldier resettlement in British Columbia in *Creating a Modern Countryside: Liberalism and Land Settlement in British Columbia* (Vancouver: UBC Press, 2007). The *Jesuit Relations and Allied Documents*, vol. 18, for 1640, edited by Reuben Gold Thwaites (Cleveland: Burrows Brothers, 1908), 83, mentions the procession against caterpillars and grasshoppers. The bishop's letter to priest Jean, Sainte-Geneviève parish, July 1, 1793, on the grasshopper infestation, is in the Archives de l'Archevêché du Québec, Registres des lettres, 210A, vol. 2, f. 60–61. Liza Piper looks at the localized impact of the Tambora eruption in "Colloquial Meteorology," in *Method and Meaning in Canadian Environmental History*, edited by Alan MacEachern and William J. Turkel, 102–23 (Toronto: Nelson Education, 2009). The implications of a low-lying drainage basin in southern Manitoba are examined by Shannon Stunden Bower in *Wet Prairie: People, Land, and Water in Agricultural Manitoba* (Vancouver: UBC Press, 2011).

For critiques of agriculture in Lower Canada and Nova Scotia, see Louise Dechêne, "Observations sur l'agriculture du Bas-Canada au début du XIXe siècle," in *Évolution et éclatement du monde rural: France Québec, XVIIe–XXe siècles*, edited by Joseph Goy and Jean-Pierre Wallot, 186–202 (Paris: Éditions de l'École des Hautes Études en Sciences Sociales et Presses de l'Université de Montréal, 1986), and Graeme Wynn, "Exciting a Spirit of Emulation among the 'Plodholes': Agricultural Reform in Pre-Confederation Nova Scotia," *Acadiensis* 20, 1 (1990): 5–51. I discuss hemp-growing subsidies in *The Metamorphoses of Landscape and Community in Early Québec* (Montreal and Kingston: McGill-Queen's University Press, 2000).

Various works show how people engaged in occupational pluralism in forestry and agriculture in the nineteenth century. For New Brunswick, see Graeme Wynn, *Timber Colony: A Historical Geography of Early Nineteenth-Century New Brunswick* (Toronto: University of Toronto Press, 1981), and for the Trois-Rivières region of Quebec, see René Hardy and Normand Séguin, *Forêt et société en Mauricie* (Montreal: Boréal Express, 1984). Catherine Anne Wilson examines "reciprocal work bees" in nineteenth-century Ontario in "Reciprocal Work Bees and the Meaning of Neighbourhood," *Canadian Historical Review* 82, 3 (2001): 431–64. Cecilia Danysk's *Hired Hands: Labour and the Development of Prairie Agriculture* (Toronto: University of Toronto Press, 1995) discusses the temporary labour force in western Canada. Dagomar Degroot and I explore the understanding of climate in New France in "'Les bois engendrent les frimas et les gelées':

Comprendre le climat en Nouvelle-France," *Revue d'histoire de l'Amérique française* 68, 3–4 (2015): 197–220. Doug Owram's *Promise of Eden: The Canadian Expansionist Movement and the Idea of the West, 1856–1900* (Toronto: University of Toronto Press, 1980) examines prevalent but changing images of the Prairie West for settlers in the second half of the nineteenth century. J. David Wood's study of Upper Canada, *Making Ontario: Agricultural Colonization and Landscape Re-creation before the Railway* (Montreal and Kingston: McGill-Queen's University Press, 2000) is sensitive to the revolutionary consequences of farm clearing. Liza Piper and John Sandlos extend the analysis that Crosby undertook for temperate areas into northern Canada in "A Broken Frontier: Ecological Imperialism in the Canadian North," *Environmental History* 12, 4 (2007): 759–95.

Quotations are from the following sources: Bond-Head's "like wild animals" is from Canada, *Indian Treaties and Surrenders from 1680 to 1890*, vol. 1 (Ottawa: S.E. Dawson, 1905), 112. The Antoine Gérin-Lajoie passage "as if by magic" is from *Jean Rivard*, translated by Vida Bruce (Toronto: McClelland and Stewart, 1977), 27. Louis Hémon wrote "nothing has changed" in *Maria Chapdelaine*, translated by Sir Andrew Macphail (Montreal: A.T. Chapman, 1921), 212–13. Drury's "the greatest misfortune" is from W.L. Morton, *The Progressive Party in Canada* (Toronto: University of Toronto Press, 1978), 298; Horace Miner, in *Saint-Denis: A French-Canadian Parish* (Chicago: University of Chicago Press, 1939), quotes the rural priest, "You are farmers," on page 96. André Siegfried, in *Canada: An International Power*, translated by Doris Hemming (New York: Duell, Sloan and Pearce, 1947), excoriated the "miners of the land" (150, 154). Mackenzie's encouragement that farmers in Upper Canada could be "as independent as King William IV" is in Michel Ducharme, *Le concept de liberté au Canada à l'époque des grandes révolutions atlantiques, 1776–1838* (Montreal and Kingston: McGill-Queen's University Press, 2010), 133. The quotation from the Québécois commune dweller, "search for a healthy lifestyle," is in Coates, *Canadian Countercultures*, 6–7. The critique of the New Brunswick timber trade, "adventitious transactions," comes from Graeme Wynn, "'Deplorably Dark and Demoralized Lumberers'? Rhetoric and Reality in Early Nineteenth-Century New Brunswick," *Journal of*

Forest History 24, 4 (1980): 171. Brown pronounced "our scheme" for Saskatchewan in *Confederation Debates in the Province of Canada, 1865*, 2nd ed., edited by P.B. Waite (Montreal and Kingston: McGill-Queen's University Press, 2006), 37. Figures on the number of farm holdings are from Statistics Canada, "Farm Holdings, Census Data, Canada and by Province, 1871 to 1971," http://www. statcan.gc.ca/pub/11–516-x/sectionm/M12_22-eng.csv. The quote from the royal commission is from *Rowell-Sirois Report: An Abridgement of Book 1 of the Royal Commission Report on Dominion-Provincial Relations*, edited by Donald V. Smiley (Toronto: McClelland and Stewart, 1963), 52.

Low-quality, crowded housing. Inferior water supplies.
Inadequate sanitation. Poverty. Limited understanding of both the causes
of disease and the ways in which they spread. During the nineteenth
and early twentieth centuries, all contributed to poor health and high
mortality rates in Canada's relatively fast-growing cities. In Henri Julien's
*Montreal's Night Mayor on His Ghastly Rounds (Dedicated to the Board
of Health)*, which appeared in the *Canadian Illustrated News,* June 5, 1875,
spectral miasmatic vapours rise from drains while crowded buildings
are the source of smallpox, typhus, dysentery, cholera, and fever.
McCord Museum M992X.5.82

NATURE WE CANNOT SEE

Graeme Wynn

M OST AUTHORS BETRAY SOME affection for, or sympathy towards, their subject. But it is challenging, if not impossible, to write posi- tively about pathogens. These disease-producing microorganisms include viruses, fungi, and bacteria. They are transmitted by various vectors, includ- ing inadvertent human action, and they debilitate and kill people and other species. When we tell stories about these pathogens, we do so not to recon- struct their histories in their own right but to explain their impact on humans. Still, it is worth noting that many of these pathogens originated in animals, including the livestock maintained by Eurasian agricultural societies, and that they have succeeded, as species, by reproducing quickly and effectively in human populations. Yet these successes are often associated with the improvements of modernity, particularly advances in transporta- tion, which facilitated the rapid movement of diseases. Pathogens have prospered by riding the rails of "progress."

A partial list of major epidemics only begins to chart this story: polio, tuberculosis, and HIV/AIDS took their toll in the twentieth century; cholera, typhoid, and typhus in the nineteenth; and smallpox, measles, and influ- enza from the seventeenth century onward. Influenza, measles, smallpox, chicken pox, German measles, and whooping cough are crowd diseases, associated with the rise of urban civilizations in Eurasia. All are acute or of short duration, infectious, and confined to human populations. Given sufficient numbers of people clustered together, these diseases become endemic, which is to say that they always exist in that population. For chicken pox, the endemicity threshold is 1,000, for smallpox and measles over 200,000. Because they provoke long-lasting immunity in those who contract them (though this protection is lessened for influenza by its propensity to mutate), endemic diseases typically affect only a small proportion of the population at any time, are relatively mild, and mainly infect the young. In places remote from these endemic hearths, or disease pools, where infections appear intermittently, there is less conferred immunity. In these settings, large numbers of people, including many adults, are afflicted, often severely, as the infection becomes epidemic. Over time, humans have managed to contain or even eradicate certain pathogens such as smallpox. Others, such as influenza, can have fairly mild effects in some contexts but epidemic consequences in others.

Until Columbus sailed the ocean blue, Indigenous peoples in the Americas lived with a limited disease suite, including tuberculosis, dysentery, pneumonia, strep and staph infections, and parasites such as hookworm and roundworm. But when Eurasian crowd diseases crossed the Atlantic, Indigenous peoples were tragically vulnerable to these hitherto unknown and invisible invaders. These diseases were, to adapt a phrase used by historian Alfred Crosby, the "shock troops" of the colonizers' advance, silent enemies that marched with "seven-league boots" and ranged across territory far in advance of the newcomers themselves.

In densely peopled Mexico and parts of the Caribbean, the effects were swift and devastating. Some estimate a 90 to 95 percent decline in Indigenous populations within a century. In the more sparsely settled North, numbers are harder to figure, but signs and suggestions of the havoc wrought by introduced diseases were everywhere. Early in the seventeenth century, a remarkable group of French missionaries in Acadia reported what they understood (through the baffles of language, unfamiliarity, and religious

conviction) to be the decimation of the Mi'kmaq population. One missionary reported that before Europeans came among them, these people
had not been "subject to diseases and knew nothing of fevers." Then a
"dangerous and deadly malady" reduced them to destitution and "sent
many to their graves." Indigenous people told missionaries that before their
"association and intercourse" with the French, their numbers had been
large, but they were now "dying fast" as "new diseases" thinned their population. One of the chroniclers speculated that this was perhaps attributable
to a change in diet, not disease, because the Mi'kmaq traded for "various
kinds of food not suitable to the inactivity of their lives." This seems unlikely,
but we will never know for sure.

From the seventeenth century, trade moved various illnesses through the
St. Lawrence corridor. Four epidemics devastated the Wendat of Huronia
(in present-day southern Ontario) and neighbouring peoples in the 1630s.
The first, in 1634–35, was probably measles; the second, in the fall of 1636,
influenza; a third, in 1637, possibly scarlet fever; and a fourth, in 1639, a
virulent smallpox outbreak that ravaged the St. Lawrence Valley. A century
later and half a continent away, James Isham, chief factor of the Hudson's
Bay Company post at Hayes River, noted "a very Remarkable Sickness and
Casualtys is very much [among] our Indn hunters this year."

The sickness that vexed James Isham was smallpox, which came among
the Homeguard Cree of York Factory during the summer of 1738. Brought
across the Atlantic to the American colonies, it travelled westward and was
carried to Hudson Bay by Indigenous fur traders from the interior. It ravaged
the inland population so severely that the number of Indigenous traders
arriving at the fort in 1739 fell by almost 40 percent, and in its wake
Anishinaabe (Ojibwe) people moved north into territory opened up by
high rates of mortality among the Cree. For a decade thereafter, introduced
diseases had little impact across the Petit Nord, that extensive area bordered
by Lake Winnipeg, Hudson Bay, and the western Great Lakes. Then smallpox, colds, dysentery, various acute respiratory diseases, and measles and

its associated secondary infections, including pneumonia, diarrhea, and encephalitis, took their tolls. In 1751, smallpox at Michipicoten killed 85 percent of the forty Indigenous people there. The remaining half dozen fled the fort, probably carrying the disease with them. In the next two decades, Hudson's Bay Company records are replete with reports of ill health among Indigenous peoples, different groups of whom were reported as being "very sickly" with "sore throats, violent coughs and difficulty breathing."

The smallpox outbreak of 1779–83 has been rightly described as "one of the most severe North American pandemics" to affect Indigenous people. It made its way northward from Mexico among equestrian hunting groups on the Great Plains and crossed the Missouri in 1781. By the end of that year, it had reached Cumberland House on the Saskatchewan River. From there, the rhythm of the fur trade shaped its diffusion through northern North America. When Indigenous peoples gathered with others at trading posts, they increased their chances of infection and heightened the possibility that disease would be carried into their home communities. Brigades of fur-bearing canoes also carried diseases along the waterways that linked the houses, posts, and forts of the fur-trading companies. In the fall or winter of 1782–83, smallpox again arrived in York Factory. In the summer of 1783, it plagued Fort Severn. At much the same time, smallpox moved from the Plains to the intermontane basin of the West, and then, among the Columbia River tribes, to Puget Sound and the Salish Sea (Strait of Georgia). Death rates can only be estimated. Some groups escaped infection. But half to three-quarters of the Anishinaabe living west of Grand Portage died. The Woodland Cree probably lost 75 percent of their number. When an intense La Niña event brought drought, harsh weather, and poor nutrition down upon the people of the western interior late in the 1780s, the effects of the pandemic were only made worse.

Disease outbreaks continued, and their incidence across the Western Interior increased in the nineteenth century as the region became better connected to the world. There were nine major disease events in the West between 1835 and 1850 and many more localized outbreaks. Influenza swept through the Hudson's Bay Company's Northern District six times in these fifteen years. Smallpox (1837), scarlet fever (1843), and measles (1846) also had widespread and severe impacts. Fur traders reckoned that the smallpox robbed the Assiniboine, Kainai (Blood), Tsuu T'ina (Sarcee), Piikani (Piegan), Siksika (Blackfoot), and Gros Ventre people of the Plains of up to three-quarters of their number. In 1843, Donald Ross of Norway House lamented that "every breeze from ... [the south] blows some foul disease or other amongst us." And in 1846, Chief Factor Nicol Finlayson, in transit to Rainy Lake, wrote that a recent outbreak of sickness in the Red River vicinity had "made such a ravage among the natives this summer, and the last," as to have "more the appearance of a pestilence than an epidemic." From near Kenora, in the same year, came another report that measles "accompanied by a Bloody Flux and Billious Complaints" had "made a havoc among the Natives."

Disease outbreaks affected many aspects of Indigenous societies. Along with guns and horses (which likewise came unevenly among interior peoples), introduced diseases shifted the distribution of power and remade the social, cultural, and political fabric of Indigenous lives. People relocated, often to occupy lands abandoned by others whose populations had been decimated. So Anishinaabe moved into the Red River Valley formerly occupied by Assiniboine and Cree. Survivors from different bands amalgamated to form new groups. All of this reshaped the landscapes of Indigenous life across the country. Some of this we can recover and reconstruct. The spiritual and psychological toll inflicted by these events and their consequences, from taboos abandoned to traditional beliefs weakened, will remain forever beyond our ken, however.

Overall mortality rates are impossible to ascertain. In some places they were catastrophically high. But diseases wax and wane, their impacts vary seasonally and regionally, and the health and cultural practices of affected populations shape outcomes. Moreover, inter-epidemic periods tend to be longer in small, scattered populations because, once they are infected, the number of susceptible individuals increases slowly. Among populations of northern hunter-gatherers, mortality rates were probably considerably lower than those documented in some Central American communities; among densely settled Indigenous populations in southwestern British Columbia, they might have approached Mexican levels.

As Captain George Vancouver and his crew approached and explored the coast of southern British Columbia in 1792, they found abandoned settlements from the Strait of Juan de Fuca to Desolation Sound. Near the sound, where the country presented "one desolate, rude and inhospitable aspect" to European eyes, they came upon "an extensive deserted village, computed to have been the residence of nearly three hundred persons." They had seen others, similarly abandoned, near the entrance of Puget Sound, where they noted also "the scull, limbs, ribs and back bones, or some other vestiges of the human body ... promiscuously scattered about the beach in great numbers." Most of the few Indigenous people they encountered bore the unmistakable marks of smallpox. But it was not "very easy," Vancouver wrote, "to draw any just conclusions on the true cause from which this havoc of the human race proceeded."

Survivors wrestling with the unfathomable catastrophe visited upon them developed their own explanations. In 1898 or 1899, when Ellen Webber of Vancouver thought to listen to Indigenous residents of nearby Keatsey in order to gather the history of a kitchen midden (a prehistoric refuse heap) on the site of a former "Kwanthum" village forty kilometres up the Fraser River, she learned that the people had enjoyed centuries of prosperity, punctuated by warfare with neighbouring groups. After one defeat, misfortune struck when the vanquished returned to their village. As they recovered strength, a fearful creature with eyes of fire and breath of steam awoke in a nearby swamp and breathed on the children: "Where his breath touched them sores broke out and they burned with heat ... and they died to feed this monster. And so the village was deserted."

Today, we doubt that smallpox was brought on by dragon's breath. But in the past, without alternative explanations for unspeakable tragedies, such stories offered a salve to grief, and they remind us that Europeans as well as Indigenous people long struggled to understand the origins of diseases and to mitigate their effects. Chinese medical practitioners produced immunity to smallpox a thousand years ago by blowing powdered smallpox scabs into patients' noses, and a form of prevention or variolation (inoculation) practised in parts of Africa, the Ottoman Empire, and India was known in England and New England as early as 1721. Not until 1796, however, did Edward Jenner, an English country doctor, develop an effective vaccination against smallpox based on cowpox. Similarly, it took almost three hundred years for the germ theory of disease, first advanced in the sixteenth century, to gain traction among scientists and medical practitioners in the English-speaking world. By and large, Europeans tended to associate diseases with miasmas and blamed environmental contexts. They were not entirely incorrect in some cases and utterly mistaken in others.

Cholera offers a case in point. Confined to India until 1817, the scourge reached England in 1831 and was anticipated with foreboding in British North America. At that time, medical doctors debated whether cholera was caused by foul air, contagion, or intemperance and immorality. No one understood the transmission of this virulent disease before the 1850s, when physician John Snow mapped cholera deaths around a water pump on Broad Street in London and concluded that the disease was a bacterial infection spread through fecal contamination of food and water supplies. But this view was only accepted gradually. After its rampage through Europe (it killed two hundred thousand in France), no one doubted that it would cross the Atlantic in the filthy, fetid, dark, and crowded holds of immigrant vessels. Limited in population and wealth, the colonies were already struggling to accommodate the rising tide of immigrants flooding into Quebec and other, lesser, ports. Acting on such advice as he could muster, Governor General Lord Aylmer established a quarantine station fifty kilometres downriver from Quebec City and created local boards of health to enforce rules of cleanliness.

Under these provisions, every vessel proceeding up the St. Lawrence was to be inspected at Grosse-Île. Those from cholera-infected ports or with cholera on board were quarantined for up to thirty days. While the vessel was purified, passengers were sent ashore, either to be hospitalized or to clean themselves and their baggage. Meanwhile, newly appointed health wardens set about improving sanitary conditions in the city of Quebec. They ordered that houses be cleaned and whitewashed and garbage carried away. Each warden was supposed to list all residents in his assigned area, visit every dwelling three times a week, and produce daily reports.

These were earnest but impractical measures. In 1832, four hundred ships and twenty-five thousand passengers reached Grosse-Île in May and early June. Hundreds of immigrants struggled for space and water to wash their belongings on the small island. Quarantine inspectors were overwhelmed, and vessels and people escaped their scrutiny. Among Quebec's twenty thousand people and three thousand dwelling places, fifteen wardens stood ready to repulse the scourge. But the numbers did not add up. Each of them would have had to inspect about one hundred properties a day to meet their mandate.

Cholera reached the St. Lawrence in late May, but it was not immediately acknowledged. It was reported in Grosse-Île on June 6. Three days later, doctors recognized several advanced cases in the Quebec Emigrant Hospital. The vessel that brought cholera into the city – "a pestilent steamer owned by speculators whose morality lay in profit" – had already gone on to Montreal. There, the first victim was reported on June 9. Three days later, the disease had claimed ninety-four victims in a city of about thirty thousand people.

Death was often swift and gruesome, marked by frequent, violent cramps, vomiting, diarrhoea, and dehydration so severe it thickened the blood and turned skin blue. Between June 15 and June 22, over one hundred people

THE

CHOLERA

B E A C O N,

BEING A TREATISE ON THE

EPIDEMIC CHOLERA

AS IT APPEARED IN

UPPER CANADA,

IN 1832—4:

WITH A PLAIN AND PRACTICAL DESCRIPTION OF THE

FIRST GRADE, OR

PREMONITORY SYMPTOMS,

AND THE VARIOUS FORMS OF ATTACK, BY WHICH THE DISEASE

MAY BE DETECTED IN ITS CURABLE STAGE ;

TOGETHER WITH DIRECTIONS FOR SUCCESSFUL TREATMENT.

DESIGNED FOR POPULAR INSTRUCTION.

By ELAM STIMSON, M. D.

LICENTIATE IN PHYSIC, SURGERY AND OBSTETRICS.

DUNDAS :

PRINTED BY G. H. HACKSTAFF.

1835.

Title page of *Cholera Beacon* (1835).
About one thousand people died in the Toronto cholera epidemics
of 1832 and 1834. In a city of barely ten thousand, few could have been
unaffected. Lawrence Bostwick wrote in a letter on August 15, 1834, "Dear
Grandmother: Your son is no more – My father was seized night before last with
the Cholera and in 14 hours was in his grave ... the times are truly awful –
our friends are dying all around us." Courtesy of Toronto Public Library

a day succumbed in Quebec City. In Montreal, shortly before the daily toll
peaked at 150, a local newspaper reported that one could see on every street
"women with terror in their countenances, and many of them weeping"
as coffin carts carrying four or five bodies trundled by. Business was paralyzed, and the entire citizenry seemed to have been seized by "a panic of
almost indescribable nature."

Cholera at Quebec City.
Painted in Romantic style by Joseph Légaré, a politician, painter, and member of the Quebec Board of Health, this depiction of the market place shows smudge pots burning in front of dwellings to fumigate against the plague. On the left, a man falls dramatically to the ground. Near the centre, the dead or dying are loaded onto a cart. To the right, a crowd follows a hearse. Joseph Légaré, *Cholera Plague, Quebec,* ca. 1832, oil on canvas, 82.2 × 111.4 cm. Courtesy of the National Gallery of Canada

Although the intensity of the outbreak diminished, it continued to spread along the routes of immigrant travel into Upper Canada and the United States and across the countryside as people fled the cities. The disease arrived in York (now Toronto) on June 19, and people were only "just beginning to breathe from the cholera" at the end of September. But the respite was short-lived. Cholera returned in 1834 and again in 1849, 1851, 1852, and 1854. The death tolls remain uncertain. In 1832, official records reported 5,820 deaths in Lower Canada and at least 1,000 more in Upper Canada, but some doubled those figures.

People tried everything to avert and alleviate these crises. They engaged in days of public fasting, humiliation, and prayer. They were bled by leeches and subjected themselves to bilious purging. They burned tar, pitch, and sulphur, and they ingested a concoction of ground maple charcoal, hogs' lard, and maple syrup. All their efforts failed. Baffled medics, distraught families, bewildered citizens, and anxious politicians did what they thought best. In the long run, their responses probably strengthened state and civil society, but when one in ten or one in twenty of the population died suddenly and seemingly at random, people confronted circumstances beyond their normal expectations and experience. They struggled to recognize what they were facing and how best to respond.

The situation was no different with poliomyelitis, now a distant memory for most Canadians but once among the most feared diseases of twentieth-century North America. Caused by a virus for which humans are the only natural host, polio had been known for centuries as an endemic and relatively harmless infection that only occasionally produced cases of infantile paralysis. But then it became highly infectious. Between 1880 and the 1960s, seemingly ever-more severe epidemics swept the industrialized world, and they were deeply disturbing. The disease mainly affected young children, it was more virulent in places where infant mortality rates were otherwise low, and it tended to burst forth in summer, especially in middle-class suburbs. In the 1950s, Canadian newspapers called the hottest months "polio season," and parents warned their children of "the grim terror" of that "fierce monster" polio.

Polio became epidemic in parts of Canada in 1910. Outbreaks occurred west to east through the 1920s and early 1930s, and in February 1949, polio left fourteen dead and thirty-nine paralyzed in Chesterfield Inlet, the Thule Inuit settlement or "place with a few houses" on Hudson Bay. In 1953, there were 8,878 cases in Canada, and Manitoba experienced a particularly acute epidemic: 2,300 people were infected (1,100 of them in August). Eighty-two died. In all, almost fifty thousand Canadians contracted polio between 1927 and 1962.

The physical, emotional, and financial effects on afflicted families were severe, and paranoia was common. Provincial governments provided convalescent serum, iron lungs, and standardized splints and frames, and they developed hospitalization and aftercare policies. Although they also funded research to either prevent the disease or cure its consequences, researchers struggled. "There is no disease over which the public is more apprehensive and in which both the laity and the medical profession feel so helpless," wrote a contributor to a Manitoba medical journal in 1936. Polio "paralyzed more than just muscles" and remained an enigma until Joseph Salk, with the important assistance of Andrew Rhodes of the Connaught Labs in Toronto, developed a vaccine in the mid-1950s. Early in the 1960s, a new oral vaccine further reduced the incidence of the disease, which today is endemic in just ten Asian and African countries that report fewer than one thousand cases a year. But polio's legacy remains. Post-polio syndrome – a chronic illness marked by weakness, fatigue, difficulty tolerating low or high temperatures, and troubles swallowing, breathing, or sleeping – continues to affect aging patients and place demands on contemporary society.

It gradually became clear that societies had unleashed the poliovirus upon themselves. Convinced that epidemic diseases were caused by poverty, pollution, poor hygiene, and poor sanitation, an emerging public health movement had worked to banish "dirt," flies, and pests from public and private spaces. Their success reduced the incidence of the everyday infections that immunized infants against the poliovirus. When children were later exposed to the virus in the schoolyard or playground, they were more vulnerable. Deeply committed to improving health standards and the promotion of personal hygiene, public health professionals grappled with the rise of nervous system infections and paralysis among those who had most assiduously lived up to their ideals. Ironically, prosperity and polio went hand in hand.

Fredericton's first polio clinic opened at Victoria Hospital in 1941,
but its deplorable conditions led to the construction of a new Clinic and Health
Centre in 1955. Some patients were bedridden for long periods, and many
lived out their lives dependent on crutches, wheelchairs, and orthopedic devices.
To assist with their rehabilitation, teachers, parents, relatives, military personnel,
and others joined health care workers in supportive communities. It has been
said that the sheer number of polio victims, their relative youthfulness, and
their visibility helped to change attitudes and win new rights and services
for the disabled. Provincial Archives of New Brunswick, Gillian Liebenberg
Polio Years, 1941–54, collection, P384–58

Influenza proved more difficult to understand and control than polio.
In the late nineteenth century, it was attributed to miasma and "unascertained atmospheric conditions" and was attacked with mustard plasters
and hot water vaporizers. Then a French researcher incorrectly identified
it as a bacteriological disease subject to control by quarantine. At the
end of the First World War, a flu outbreak on the battlefields of France
erupted into a worldwide pandemic when demobilized soldiers carried
the infection around the globe between 1918 and 1920. The so-called
Spanish Influenza has been described as "the greatest medical holocaust
in history" because it killed at least 50 million people worldwide and
claimed almost as many Canadian lives as the war itself: of the country's

8.3 million people, at least fifty thousand (of all socioeconomic classes and in all parts of the country) died. Until the viral nature of influenza was recognized in the 1930s, it remained a mysterious, dangerous, and enigmatic infection. Medical science has blunted its sting, and most of those afflicted today are temporarily debilitated rather than mortally threatened. Still, the virus evolves quickly. In 1957–58 and 1968–69, the so-called Asian and Hong Kong flu pandemics each claimed about 1 million lives worldwide. In Canada, where antibiotics helped to reduce the effects of secondary infections such as pneumonia, the toll was more muted; about 7,000 in the 1950s and 4,000 (of some 20 million) in the 1960s. New combinations of antigens (typically avian and human) occasionally produce virulent new strains of influenza that overwhelm vaccines and pre-existing immunity and escalate to pandemics.

Similar transfers across species barriers marked the origins of other diseases. Originating in Africa, where it was probably conveyed from simian to human populations by the consumption of "bushmeat" early in the twentieth century, HIV/AIDS reached North America in the 1960s and was identified in 1981. It is now a major and tragic pandemic. In the last three decades, 40 million people have died of the disease, and there are currently about the same number of cases worldwide. Rapidly increasing case numbers and high mortality rates in North America in the 1980s generated acute fear of AIDS, and because it was initially associated with gay men, those infected were widely stigmatized. When it became clear that anyone could contract HIV, general anxiety soared. Enormous effort was poured into HIV/AIDS research, and remarkable progress was made in developing antiretroviral treatments. As a result, in Canada today, where there are approximately 75,000 cases, HIV is widely regarded (in stark contrast to the situation in sub-Saharan Africa) as a manageable, chronic disease rather than an automatic death sentence. Still, patterns of HIV infection and successful treatment are shaped by socioeconomic factors. Risks are greatly elevated for those who are susceptible to malnutrition and illness or unable

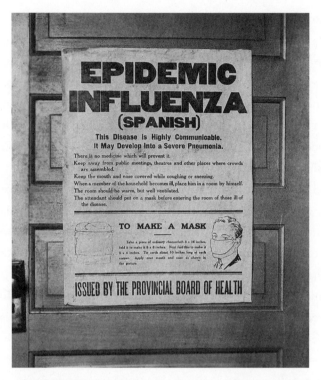

Public health authorities across Canada produced posters
such as this one from Alberta to inform people about the Spanish Flu,
the name given to the strain of influenza that caused a pandemic in 1918–20.
The simple admission that "there is no medicine which will prevent it" speaks
volumes about the anxieties induced by virulent disease outbreaks.
Courtesy Glenbow Archives, NA–4548–5

to access prophylaxis and drug therapy because of prejudice, social-psychological reasons, or economic circumstances. As a result, there are large differences in rates of HIV/AIDS infection among various segments of the population.

In November 2002, in China, a severe form of pneumonia crossed the species barrier probably from civets or raccoon dogs to humans. In mid-February 2003, the World Health Organization reported that five people had died of and that three hundred more had been afflicted by a mysterious respiratory disease in Guangdong Province. A week later, the Chinese Ministry of Health wrongly attributed the illness to a common bacterium, *Chlamydia pneumoniae*.

On February 23, the respiratory affliction reached Canada when a resident of Scarborough, Ontario, flew home from Hong Kong. The woman was one of a dozen people who had unknowingly been infected with the yet unnamed SARS virus by a Guangdong doctor staying in the same hotel. When she died, on March 5, her death was attributed to a heart attack. But then her son became ill. He was thought to have tuberculosis. Meanwhile, another guest from the Kowloon Hotel died in Hanoi and hospital workers there and in Hong Kong became ill. Only in mid-March, after the son of the March 5 patient died and tuberculosis was ruled out as a cause, were the rising number of atypical pneumonia cases linked back to Guangdong. Recognizing the highly contagious nature of the infection, which was produced by a coronavirus, Ontario health workers ramped up isolation and infection-control measures. In the last two weeks of March, public anxieties were heightened by the declaration of a health emergency and calls for people who might have been infected to quarantine themselves.

Between March 16 and 19, two, five, seven, then nine new people were classified as "probable" SARS patients each day. The numbers of suspect and probable cases peaked over three days in late March, and a week into April there were 91 probable and 135 suspected SARS cases in Canada. Ten people had died.

New incidences began to fall, only to resurge through mid- and late May. Ultimately, the efforts of front-line health care workers, astute researchers, and timely policy decisions contained the outbreak, even though many aspects of one of the most well-funded health care systems in the modern world proved seriously inadequate to the task at hand. In all, 438 "probable or suspect" SARS cases were identified in Canada between February and September 2003, and 44 people died.

Beyond Canada, modern medicine also limited the SARS outbreak in time and space. No cases have been reported since 2004, and only about eight thousand people (in twenty-nine countries) contracted SARS worldwide. Their mortality rate was approximately 10 percent. Yet public anxiety ran high. The World Health Organization listed Toronto among places to avoid, people took to wearing surgical masks in public, and falling tourism and hospitality industry revenues probably shaved a couple of billion dollars off the national GDP. In the assessment of a high-ranking public health official, the spring of 2003 was an "extremely frightening, extremely traumatic" time for Ontario health care workers and the general public alike.

Two years later, the crisis received its classic twenty-first-century denouement when an "emotional, medical and political thriller" showed the formerly healthy and hygienic city of Toronto reduced to "the pariah of the western world" by a dragon-like and lethal form of infection. In the made-for-TV movie *Plague City*, no one seems to know what is happening. Citizens and those who care for them succumb to an unidentified affliction. Without a firm diagnosis, it's difficult to treat and control the pestilence. As panic spreads more quickly than the virus, public places are abandoned, and travel into the city is restricted. The film was described as arresting (because it explored "one of the greatest fears stalking modern medicine," the diffusion of a deadly contagious virus) and illuminating (because it helped people gain perspective on a mysterious, threatening moment in their lives).

Like SARS, most of the disease outbreaks in Canadian history came among people unexpectedly or irresistibly, often from elsewhere, and they caused great anxiety as well as suffering and death. Each disease ran a different course, shaped by diverse considerations such as scientific and medical knowledge, communication technologies, the political and social organization of the societies and communities infected, and the complex interactions of pathogens and people, nature and culture. Microorganisms invisible to the naked eye drove these epidemics, but they did not do so alone. Human actions and reactions (and, indeed, human circumstances shaped by economic and social conditions) did much to shape the course and consequences of each and every epidemic. In the process, the markers and boundaries by which people made their ways through the world were blurred, taken-for-granted beliefs and assumptions were thrown into question, and uncertainty and anxiety grew. Epidemics were and are, emotional, psychological, and social, as well as medical, demographic, and political events.

Pathogens have played and continue to play an important role in the creation of contemporary Canada. Tagging along with those quintessential drivers of "progress" – trade and migration – diseases remind us that national boundaries are often of little significance for environmental forces. Recognizing as much in the wake of the SARS outbreak, the federal government established the Public Health Agency of Canada to promote and protect the health of Canadians. Taking advantage of the latest advances in medical science and communications technology, this agency has strengthened the Quarantine Act and improved surveillance to improve disease detection at Canadian borders. The agency has enhanced public health and laboratory capacity across the country, and it has ensured that the country's antiviral stockpile and vaccine capacities are at levels appropriate to the threat of pandemics. Canadians are now less vulnerable to the effects of infectious disease outbreaks than ever before. But complete safety is impossible to achieve. It is a chimera (which, incidentally but perhaps appropriately in this context, was the name given in Greek mythology to a fire-breathing monster).

Although the entanglements of pathogens and people have greatly affected the lives and destinies of Euro-Canadians, and although the future will continue to be shaped by them, the most striking legacy of this entwinement is the part that it played in opening the American continent to colonization. Introduced diseases undermined the physical, social, and emotional health of Indigenous peoples, reduced their numbers, and encouraged the view that North America was a relatively empty land. Misled by much-thinned populations, or perhaps unwilling to think of Indigenous peoples as capable of sustaining larger numbers, early scholars massively underestimated the Indigenous presence. Some claimed barely 200,000 precontact inhabitants for the entire country (with about 85,000 in British Columbia, 51,000 in the rest of the West, and 54,000 in eastern Canada). Today, we reckon that in 1600 there were between 400,000 and 500,000 Indigenous inhabitants in Canada. Low estimates fit well with eighteenth- and nineteenth-century narratives of progress and colonial achievement, in which there was little room for tales of failure, hardship, environmental despoliation, and other unfortunate consequences of the European encounter with the New World. More broadly, they also give substance to current critiques of earlier histories of colonialism, which have been described as exercises in justification and rationalization that distort, disfigure, and destroy the pasts of the colonized.

REFERENCES AND FURTHER READING

English historian Asa Briggs, in "Cholera and Society in the Nineteenth-Century," *Past and Present* 19 (1961): 76–96, and American Gerald E. Grob, in "The Social History of Medicine and Disease in America: Problems and Possibilities," *Journal of Social History* 10, 4 (1977): 390–409, seek to move beyond the study of epidemics as medical epidemiology by attending to what the latter calls the "complex relationship between disease patterns, social structures and environmental conditions" (392). For the argument that diseases are context-specific and context-determining, see also Charles E. Rosenberg, "Introduction: Framing Disease – Illness, Society and History," in *Framing Disease: Studies in Cultural History*, edited by Charles E. Rosenberg and Janet Golden, xiii–xxvi (New Brunswick: Rutgers University Press, 1992).

My discussion of disease and Indigenous populations draws especially from Paul A. Hackett, *"A Very Remarkable Sickness": Epidemics in the Petit Nord, 1670–1846* (Winnipeg: University of Manitoba Press, 2002). I borrow the idea of disease pools from him and depend upon his treatment for discussion of the Petit Nord. This book is the source for the Isham (71) and Finlayson (223) quotes and for the "sore throats" (87), "severe pandemic" (93), "every breeze" (155), and "Bloody Flux" (223) quotes. Two books by Alfred W. Crosby Jr., *The Columbian Exchange: Biological and Cultural Consequences of 1492* (Westport: Greenwood, 1972) and *Ecological Imperialism: The Biological Expansion of Europe, 900–1900* (New York: Cambridge University Press, 1986), are classic sources for this broad topic. The "seven-league boots" phrase is from *Ecological Imperialism,* 201. Crosby uses the term "shock troops" on page 295 to characterize Amerindian, Indigenous, and Māori first comers establishing beachheads in their respective territories. The Acadia descriptions of missionaries Pierre Biard, Nicholas Denys, and Chrestien LeClerq are available digitally and in translation, but they are conveniently summarized and discussed in Calvin Martin, *Keepers of the Game: Indian-Animal Relationships and the Fur Trade* (Berkeley: University of California Press, 1978), 43–55.

The smallpox epidemic of the 1780s has been much discussed, but Adam R. Hodge's "Vectors of Colonialism: The Smallpox Epidemic of 1780–82 and Northern Great Plains Indian Life" (master's thesis, Kent State University, 2009) is a useful contribution with an extensive bibliography. For the teleconnections between La Niña and disease, see Joelle J. Gergis and Anthony M. Fowler, "A History of ENSO Events since A.D. 1525: Implications for Future Climate Change," *Climatic Change* 92, 3 (2009): 343–87. The observations from George Vancouver's 1792 mapping expedition are in his *A Voyage of Discovery to the North Pacific Ocean, and Round the World...,* vol. 2, 111, 115, 230–32, available at https://archive.org/details/voyageofdiscover02vanc_0. And those relating to Puget Sound also feature in Elizabeth A. Fenn's popular history of the 1782 smallpox epidemic, *Pox Americana: The Great Smallpox Epidemic of 1775–82* (New York: Hill and Wang, 2001), 11. For further discussion on shifting power relations, disease, and so on in the western interior, see Arthur J. Ray, "Diffusion of Diseases in the Western Interior of Canada, 1830–1850," *Geographical Review* 66 (1976): 139–57; Jody F. Decker, "Tracing Historical Diffusion Patterns: The Case of the 1780–82

Smallpox Epidemic among the Indians of Western Canada," *Native Studies Review* 4, 1–2 (1988): 1–24; James Daschuk, *Clearing the Plains: Disease, Politics of Starvation and the Loss of Aboriginal Life* (Regina: University of Regina Press, 2013); and Theodore Binnema, *Common and Contested Ground: A Human and Environmental History of the Northwestern Plains* (Norman: University of Oklahoma Press, 2001). More detail on smallpox on the Northwest Coast is available in Robert T. Boyd's *The Coming of the Spirit of Pestilence: Introduced Infectious Diseases and Population Decline among Northwest Coast Indians, 1774–1874* (Vancouver: UBC Press, 1999); R. Cole Harris, "Voices of Disaster: Smallpox around the Strait of Georgia in 1782," *Ethnohistory* 41, 4 (1994): 591–626; and James R. Gibson, "Smallpox on the Northwest Coast, 1835–1838," *BC Studies* 56 (1982–83): 61–81. Little is known about Ellen R.C. Webber other than her article, "An Old Kwanthum Village: Its People and Its Fall," *American Antiquarian and Oriental Journal* 21, 5 (1899): 309–14. For discussions of measles on the Pacific littoral, see R.M. Galois, "Measles, 1847–1850: The First Modern Epidemic in British Columbia," *BC Studies* 109 (Spring 1996): 31–43.

Any discussion of cholera in Canada has to start with Geoffrey Bilson, *A Darkened House: Cholera in Nineteenth-Century Canada* (Toronto: University of Toronto Press, 1980). My treatment also draws from Louise Dechêne and Jean-Claude Robert, "Le choléra de 1832 dans le Bas-Canada: Mesure des inégalités devant la mort," in *Les grandes mortalités: Étude méthodologique des crises démographiques du passé*, edited by Hubert Charbonneau and André Larose, 229–56 (Liège: Editions Ordina, 1979); Walter Sendzik, "The 1832 Montreal Cholera Epidemic: A Study in State Formation" (master's thesis, McGill University, 1997); and Bettina Bradbury, *Wife to Widow: Lives, Laws, and Politics in Nineteenth-Century Montreal* (Vancouver: UBC Press, 2011). The "women with terror in their countenances" and "a panic of almost indescribable nature" quotes are from *Canadian Courant*, June 16, 1832, which includes a translation of an item in *La Minerve*, June 14, 1832, referenced by Sendzik and Bradbury. The "pestilent steamer" and "just beginning to breathe" quotes are from Marian A. Patterson, "The Cholera Epidemic of 1832 in York, Upper Canada," *Bulletin of the Medical Library Association*

46, 2 (1958): 170, 182. For John Snow, see *Snow on Cholera: Being a Reprint of Two Papers by John Snow, M.D.* (London: Oxford University Press, 1936) and Tom Koch, "The Map as Intent: Variations on the Theme of John Snow," *Cartographica* 39, 4 (2004): 1–14. In "'In Sable Garments of Mourning': Cholera Devastates Upper Canada, 1832," *The Beaver* 72, 2 (1992): 43–50, Chris Raible makes effective use of James Lesslie's diary to trace the impact of cholera in York.

My discussion of polio draws heavily from Christopher J. Rutty's "'A Grim Terror More Menacing, More Sinister Than Death Itself': Physicians, Poliomyelitis and the Popular Press in Early 20th-Century Ontario" (master's thesis, University of Western Ontario, 1990); from his "'Do Something! ... Do Anything!' Poliomyelitis in Canada, 1927–1962" (PhD diss., University of Toronto, 1995); and from the Health Heritage Research Services website. "Polio season," "grim terror," "fierce monster," and "apprehensive and ... helpless" are from Rutty's "The Middle-Class Plague: Epidemic Polio and the Canadian State, 1936–1937," *Canadian Bulletin of Medical History* 13 (1996): 278. The "paralyzed more than muscles" quotation is from "The History of Polio," http://www.healthheritage research.com/Polio-Vaccine/PV-comHistory.html. For a detailed study of the 1949 outbreak, see Liza Piper, "Chesterfield Inlet, 1949, and the Ecology of Epidemic Polio," *Environmental History* 20, 4 (2015): 671–98. For an excellent treatment of efforts to banish "dirt," see Dawn Day Biehler, *Pests in the City: Flies, Bedbugs, Cockroaches, and Rats* (Seattle: University of Washington Press, 2013). There is no Canadian counterpart of this work, although Mariana Valverde's *The Age of Light, Soap and Water: Moral Reform in English Canada, 1885–1925* (Toronto: McClelland and Stewart, 1991) brings discourse theory to bear on the moral reform movement in Canada.

For influenza, see Alfred W. Crosby, Jr., *America's Forgotten Pandemic: The Influenza of 1918* (Cambridge: Cambridge University Press, 1989). The "greatest medical holocaust" is in Theodore H. Tulchinsky and Elena A. Varavikova, *The New Public Health: An Introduction for the 21st Century* (San Diego: Academic Press, 2014), 28. "Unascertained atmospheric conditions" is from Mark Osborne Humphries, *The Last Plague: Spanish Influenza and the Politics of Public Health in*

Canada (Toronto: University of Toronto Press, 2013), 65. For the 1918–20 influenza epidemic in Canada, see Esyllt W. Jones, *Influenza: Disease, Death, and Struggle in Winnipeg* (Toronto: University of Toronto Press, 2007), and Magda Fahrni and Esyllt W. Jones, eds., *Epidemic Encounters: Influenza, Society, and Culture in Canada, 1918–20* (Vancouver: UBC Press, 2012).

On HIV/AIDS, see Randy Shilts's classic, *And the Band Played On: Politics, People and the AIDS Epidemic* (London: Souvenir Press, 2011), and Jacques Pepin, *The Origins of AIDS* (Cambridge: Cambridge University Press, 2011). Informative short summaries of the SARS crisis can be found in Public Health Agency of Canada, "SARS in Canada: Anatomy of an Outbreak," http://www.phac-aspc. gc.ca/publicat/sars-sras/pdf/chapter2-e.pdf, and in Bjug Borgundvaag, Howard Ovens, Brian Goldman, Michael Schull, Tim Rutledge, Kathy Boutis, Sharon Walmsley et al., "SARS Outbreak in the Greater Toronto Area: The Emergency Department Experience," *Canadian Medical Association Journal* 171, 11 (2004): 1342–44. The "frightening, traumatic" judgment is reported in Althea Manasan's "MERS Outbreak: 3 Lessons Canada Learned from SARS," *CBC News*, June 15, 2015. *Plague City* (2005) was directed by David Wu; the "greatest fear" quote is from the BBC Horizon production *SARS: The True Story*. For reflections on SARS and history, see Jacalyn Duffin and Arthur Sweetman, eds., *SARS in Context: Memory, History, and Policy* (Montreal and Kingston: McGill-Queen's University Press, 2006).

The lowest estimates of Indigenous populations are from James Mooney, "The Aboriginal Population of America North of Mexico," in *Smithsonian Miscellaneous Collections 80*, edited by John R. Swanton, 1–40 (1928). For a telling indication of how such numbers were reached, see the discussion in the archived content at Statistics Canada, *Census of Canada, 1871*, https://www150.statcan. gc.ca/n1/pub/98-187-x/4151278-eng.htm#part2.

Lafarge Cement Plant at Lac des Arcs, Exshaw, Alberta,
on the edge of Banff National Park. The industrial sublime,
the Canadian contradiction. Photo by Tina Loo

THE WEALTH OF WILDERNESS

———

Claire E. Campbell

E IGHTY YEARS OR SO ago, Stephen Leacock, a professor at McGill
University, noted Canadian humorist, and one of the English-speaking
world's best-known authors, was asked by a colleague whether he might
retire to England. He responded by writing a luminous essay that declared:
"I'll Stay in Canada." There were many reasons for his choice, among them
the affirmation that

> to all of us here, the vast unknown country of the North, reaching
> away to the polar seas, supplies a peculiar mental background.
> I like to think that in a few short hours in a train or car I can be
> in the primeval wilderness of the North; that if I like, from my
> summer home, an hour or two of flight will take me over the
> divide and down to the mournful shores of the James Bay,
> untenanted till yesterday, now haunted with its flock of airplanes
> hunting gold in the wilderness. I never have gone to the James
> Bay; I never go to it; I never shall. But somehow I'd feel lonely
> without it.

Having grown up in southern Ontario, I find Leacock's declaration both
familiar and natural: forest and lakes reaching north almost endlessly to a

Porcupine Vipond Gold Mine, 1915 – an example of Stephen Leacock's "hunting gold in the wilderness." The Canadian Shield as commodity frontier.
Library and Archives Canada (LAC), PA–030215

place that I will, probably, never see; the nationalist conceit that all that territory is my birthright. More than this, Leacock's improbable affinity for a vast and never-seen space conveys the reassuring message that Canadians – divided by geography, language, politics, and much else – share *something.*

Yet there is something unsettling about Leacock's essay. He wrote as a political economist rather than as a romantic nationalist. He was more interested in commodity production than wilderness identity. The "peculiar mental background" he treasured was not simply the freedom of northern air. In his view, the unfailing interest of Canadians in their country lay "in its vast development, its huge physical future." In the sixty years he had known the country, he noted, "we have filled it in and filled it in ... shovelling up mountains, floating in the sky to look for gold, and finding still the Star of Empire in the West." Here, the Canadian wilderness is a site of material progress, something *out of* which we build a nation.

Wilderness is a form of imaginative rhizome that sprouts in different forms – in politics, culture, identity, and other forums of Canadian public life. Art and literature are thus critically important to understanding the connection (or disconnection) between our sense of self as Canadians, the land we occupy, and our knowledge of how we have used that land. Since Confederation, Canadians have produced a gallery of wilderness images and a library of texts that characterize their country's vast expanse. These representations do two somewhat contradictory kinds of work. They aim to reassure us, as Leacock did, that the "great spaces" remain resilient even if they are not intact. At the same time, they seek to distract us from the industrial; they imbue economic investment with a noble cultural aura. Despite half a century of academic and artistic critique, our belief in the existence of pure wilderness survives quite healthily, because it has been successfully grafted into, diffused through, and constantly represented in popular culture and the language of protected places. Thus, we deceive ourselves into believing that we are more ecologically enlightened or empathetic than we are.

At a time when the living standards of most Canadians are among the highest in the world, many of us find perverse pleasure in the horrified reactions of early explorers confronting the new land. Recall Jacques Cartier at Labrador ("C'est la terre que Dieu donna à Caïn") or Samuel de Champlain between the Ottawa River and Georgian Bay ("un pays mal agreable ... désert, & sterile, & peu habité"). Think of English gentlewoman Susanna Moodie's account of *Roughing It in the Bush*, which has generally been read for its depiction of encounters with a nature that is daunting, terrifying, overwhelming. How far we have come, these examples seem to imply, now that a nice summer property where Champlain passed through Lake Nipissing will run you several hundred thousand dollars and a lakeside cottage near Moodie's Peterborough might set you back a million.

Of course, Indigenous peoples did not share the early Europeans' contempt for, or inability to read, the land. And even some nineteenth-century settlers were able to find the picturesque and the profitable in the backwoods. The settlement project required economic as well as ideological affirmation. Cheery Catherine Parr Traill, sister of Susanna Moodie, was determined to see the wilds as God's gift to British America, waiting to be unwrapped and understood. "There is something good and pretty to be found everywhere if people will but open their eyes to see it, and their hearts to enjoy the good things that God has so mercifully spread abroad for us and all his creatures to enjoy," Traill wrote. She continued, "Canada is really a fine country, and is fast becoming a great one." This little homily came in the middle of a children's story about a family of gray squirrels – Nimble-Foot and his sisters, Velvet-Paw and Silver-Nose – "gambolling about in the wild woods." Hardly "nature, red in tooth and claw" or the sort of forbidding forest that Moodie apparently saw as something to be suffered and endured.

Relentless optimism, coloured with a significant degree of bullishness, underpinned the confederation of Britain's North American colonies and Canada's claim to dominion over the northern half of the continent. But the gamble paid off, because, as survey parties began to confirm, the interior was a storehouse of riches. Seen from a distance and little understood, the wilderness encouraged a rhetoric of ambition, of potential, that could distract provinces from their distrust of one another and the new federal government. Canada's vast new expanse provided a geographical affirmation of sovereignty that looked particularly impressive on a map of the world (i.e., to other nation-states). And its very emptiness, its wilderness quality, implied future occupation without requiring it immediately, thus bestowing on a new and vulnerable country the grandest and most "natural" of destinies.

As the "First Daughter of the Empire," a status cherished by the country's Anglo-Celtic elites, the new nation envisaged a bright future based on the aesthetic value and resource wealth of its wilderness. Exhibitions of "industrial arts" showcased the profits "recovered from the wilderness and

Catharine Parr Traill's cottage on Stony Lake, Ontario, 1899.
Another, more palatable, vision of wilderness from the Canadian Shield
and for the people of southern Ontario. LAC, C–067353

added to the productive resources and the wealth of the Dominion" along-side dioramas that displayed the country's attractions for sportsmen. Canadian corporations certainly understood the value of sponsoring the wilderness arts. It was perfect advertising, promoting an image of respect-able, even heroic service to the new nation-state while displaying assets to investors. The Canadian Pacific Railway excelled at selling wilderness, sponsoring artists and writers to travel from eastern Canada through the Canadian Shield to the Rocky Mountains. While the trans-Canada route was celebrated as a technological triumph (by the CPR) and a territorial accomplishment (by Ottawa), images of mountain scenery provided evi-dence of the scale of that achievement as well as aesthetically pleasing material for a new spin-off industry – tourism.

Although most Canadian policy and much Canadian art was devoted to cultivating (literally) a settled, pastoral landscape, scenes of wilderness – reassuringly distant and recognizably different – also had particular political value. They appealed to metropolitan imperialists seeking a signature contribution to the Empire. They also drew the attention of an emerging Canadian group of northern nationalists seeking evidence of "a peculiar mental background" to deter American annexationists. Politicians and their outriders placed much store in historical connections to the territory claimed (however tenuously) by the new country. John A. Macdonald won the 1891 election by identifying himself with those who "gave up everything that men prize, and were content to begin life anew in the wilderness rather than forgo allegiance to their Sovereign" a century or so before. Sanctioned by history, a northern, transcontinental nation, spread far beyond the four original provinces, could appear preordained.

As the West was won – by relentless efforts to sell and settle this arable empire – agriculture's displacement of the fur trade endangered conceptions of the Northwest as wilderness. At precisely this moment, a loose group of male poets framed hymns to nature close to (their) homes, in the woods of New Brunswick, the marshlands of the Bay of Fundy, and "the lake region" and "winter uplands" of the Canadian Shield. Though their allegiances were regional, the so-called Confederation poets shared delight in the solitary experience of nature and made northern woods and winters the main themes of their work. So, for example, a collection of verse by New Brunswicker Bliss Carman, attached by its title, *Low Tide on Grand Pré*, to the pastoral shore of Nova Scotia, included "A Northern Vigil," written "by the gray north sea, / in the wintry heart of the wild."

Poems about Ontario's lake country redeemed the ancient and difficult territory that had defeated a generation of farmers at mid-century and continued to obstruct access to the West. In these works, the rocky, forbidding southern edge of the Canadian Shield was painlessly transmuted into a wilderness within convenient reach for those among the country's growing urban population who sought to get "back to nature." The spruce forest stretching beyond "the last portage and the height of land ... [in] the lonely north enlaced with lakes and streams" represented both a nation's claim to a vast territory and individual freedom. At scant remove from the "crowded southern land / With all the welter of the lives of men," wrote Duncan Campbell Scott, "here there is peace ... Here on the uplands where the air is clear." This poetry modelled and endorsed a burgeoning tourism industry in parts of Northern Ontario, Quebec, Nova Scotia, and New Brunswick, though tourists tended to prefer the summer face of such "wilderness." Its wintry heart was better left to poetry.

Early in the twentieth century, artists brought their paints to the same locations to seize the same motifs. Together, Tom Thomson and members of the Group of Seven developed a distinctive, vigorous artistic style to convey a striking vision of wilderness – the sweep of the northland, the boreal forest, the perspective of the solitary canoeist. Heavily promoted by many of the country's art institutions and patrons – including the National Gallery, which spent much of the 1920s promoting the group's view of Canada in London and Paris – these works rapidly achieved iconic status. Travelling exhibitions and associated publications spread their fame and reinforced in words what the group presented in images: that "the Canadian environment is the most potent stimulus to Canadian creative genius."

However, just as cultural arbiters embraced the southern edge of the Canadian Shield, industrial capitalists turned its boreal north – the recently acquired "New Ontario" – into the country's most active frontier of mineral exploration, pulp and paper production, and hydroelectric development. Paintings and company towns were both statements of ownership, of different kinds of new wealth that would bolster Canada's claim to the twentieth century. Art celebrated nature inviolate; industry envisaged nature transformed. But this rather substantial difference apart, they offered grand and safely complementary measures of the Canadian temperament. As Vincent Massey, who would go on to be governor general of Canada,

Associated with the Group of Seven, whose paintings would be widely reproduced as exemplars of Canadian wilderness, Tom Thomson often depicted the forests in Algonquin Park – a world away from "the crowded southern land" and yet still within easy reach of metropolitan Canada. Tom Thomson, *In the Northland*, 1915, oil on canvas, 101.7 × 114.5 cm. Courtesy of the Musée des Beaux-Arts de Montréal. Photo by Denis Farley

told the Royal Society of Canada in 1930, "In Canada it is peculiarly necessary to realize that the human imagination can express itself just as well in engineering and in business as in poetry ... Our Northern wilderness is, in a special sense, the scene of the poetry of action with its great treasure hunt conducted from the sky, its railways nosing their way through the forest to northern oceans, the harness which is being thrown on rapid and waterfall."

Massey embodied these two impulses to perfection. The chair of the Royal Commission on National Development in the Arts, Letters and Sciences (otherwise known as the Massey Commission, which sat from 1949 to 51), he was heir to a considerable fortune derived from the industrializing economy of southern Ontario, and as Canada's envoy to the United States, he served two masters with equally keen interest in the "great treasure hunt."

By mid-century, historians were the country's most eloquent voices for a national wilderness identity. Donald Creighton, Arthur Lower, and W.L. Morton crafted some of our most memorable claims to a *Dominion of the North* (as Creighton titled his 1944 history of Canada) and a wilderness nature. Their work appealed because it gave Canadians the best of both worlds, as Lower explained: "For nothing can eliminate our frontier, that vast land to the north there, just beyond our glance, a land which the airplane may fly over but will never subordinate. We Canadians will always have this northern window through which to let fresh air into our civilized room."

These historians did not ask Canadians to choose between industrial exploitation and spiritual equilibrium, between economic prosperity and cultural maturity. Rather, they suggested that one evolved out of the other. Typically, Morton asserted that the "alternate penetration of the wilderness and return to civilization is the basic rhythm of Canadian life, and forms the basic elements of Canadian character." Such a pattern allowed an eastern-based population to claim a remote space without requiring any permanent presence.

Implicit in this view of wilderness as a place of human impermanence was a strong sense of its resilience to industrial incursion. "This," wrote A.J.M. Smith, "is the beauty / of strength / broken by strength / and still strong." And Douglas LePan voiced similar sentiments in his 1948 poem "Canoe-Trip":

And then up to the foot of the blue pole star
A wilderness,
The pinelands whose limits seem distant as Thule ...
There are holes here and there for a gold-mine or a hydro-plant.
But the tartan of river and rock spreads undisturbed ...
Let whoever comes to tame this land, beware!

But was it nature's resilience or Canadian restraint? Americans "look to you as the one incorruptible guardian of virgin country," the editor of the *Atlantic Monthly* told members of the Empire Club of Canada in 1955. Americans might be tempted by the lure of new prosperity, "but with your respect for law and your love of the wilderness," he concluded (just a bit patronizingly), "I have faith that you will hold your own [with] the power and wealth of an untapped land and the feeling of destiny that goes with it."

The 1960s rejoiced in this same view of wilderness – a reservoir of wealth to be mined but never bankrupted – with little concern for this contradiction. While the federal government was busy completing a TransCanada pipeline and highway, and blasting open the St. Lawrence Seaway, the cultural sector was equally busy celebrating timeless wilderness as the wellspring of the national spirit. Anticipating and celebrating the centennial of Confederation, the National Film Board commissioned Gilles Vigneault's anthem "Mon Pays" (1965) and published the best-selling *Canada: A Year of the Land/Canada, du temps qui passe* (1967). It also released *Enduring Wilderness* (1968), which promoted national parks as "museums that we visit to gain knowledge of ourselves, to weigh the value of our civilization against the ageless splendour of the wilderness."

The rapid growth of the national parks system, the expansion of the environmental movement, and the tercentennial of the Hudson's Bay Company in 1970 produced an avalanche of romantic wilderness iconography. The lone canoeist was reinvented for a new generation by "wilderness artist" and conservationist Bill Mason and by Prime Minister Pierre Trudeau.

Mason's films and books were extremely popular in the 1970s, and Trudeau's essay "Exhaustion and Fulfillment: The Ascetic in a Canoe," inspired by a trip "more than a thousand miles by canoe, from Montreal to Hudson Bay," was first published in English in 1970. Ontario scholars such as Bruce Littlejohn, Bruce Hodgins, and John Wadland drew the wilderness narrative into the academy through the new fields of Canadian studies and environmental studies, insisting, exactly as the Group of Seven had done with art a half-century earlier, that "if there is one distinguishing element that sets Canadian literature apart from most other national literatures, it is the influence of the wild."

Something critical happened in the 1970s, however. New, diffuse, and broadly disapproving conceptions of wilderness joined the long-standing industrial and romantic visions, although they utterly failed to dislodge them. Three broad strands of critique intertwined. The first had its roots in ideas articulated in the 1950s and then revisited in the mid-1960s by the literary critic Northrop Frye, who noted a tone of deep terror in Canadian poetry and coined the phrase *garrison mentality* to describe the consequences, for Canadian settlers and writers, of the "huge, unthinking, menacing, and formidable" wild that he saw enveloping the soul and minds of those surrounded by "the vast unconsciousness of nature." Picked up and popularized by Margaret Atwood in *Survival* (which was named, she argued, for the central distinguishing feature of Canadian literature, whose protagonists seemingly and invariably adopted one or another variant of the victim position), these ideas subverted many of the positive values previously ascribed to the wilderness by holding it responsible for reducing the Canadian experience to "hanging on, staying alive" (albeit barely). Then postmodernist critics made the Group of Seven the easiest of targets, as totems always are, with dismissive indictments of their masculine bias, their *regional* bias, their elite patronage, the racial or racist superiority of the northern rhetoric to which they had contributed, and their role as handmaidens of governments intent on appropriating Indigenous lands.

Environmental historians, meanwhile, pointed out the implications of thinking about wilderness as something *out there,* beyond us, with "limits as distant as Thule," rather than recognizing it as a product and projection of civilization. Using terms such as *cultured, constructed,* and *manufactured,* academics drew back the veil of wilderness imagery to expose an inhabited and occupied space misleadingly presented as pristine.

Artists also began to recognize the imprint of technology and the limits of wilderness by peopling the wilderness even as they referenced the styles and subjects of the Group of Seven. John Hartman drew figures from local history onto the Georgian Bay shoreline; Jon Sasaki reinserted the artist's equipment into the scene of Tom Thomson's wilderness art. Jin-Me Yoon's *Souvenirs of the Self* (1991) and *Group of Sixty-Seven* (1996) were a greater departure: assembled portraits of Korean Canadians in front of paintings by Lawren Harris and Emily Carr, suggesting both an effort to "be Canadian" and a sense of distance from those very scenes. Most recently, Edward Burtynsky, who points out that he "was born a hundred years too late" to photograph pristine wilderness, has emerged as Canada's best-known landscape artist. His industrial scenes finally give precedence to the second strand of the Canadian cultural DNA: wilderness lain bare, exposed as an artifact of, not inspiration for, the imagination.

But is this so? Canadians may appreciate Burtynsky in a gallery and as an ecological critic, but few hang his work in their living rooms. Many read Roy MacGregor's folksy accounts of canoeing for pleasure, few engage with Northrop Frye's erudite criticism unless it is assigned in class. Images of a Shield wilderness and a quasi-wilderness lifestyle were too ubiquitous, too well-grafted onto public life, and too appealing to be overwritten by increasingly obscure academic voices. For many Canadians, especially those in southern Ontario, paintings by the Group of Seven are not artifacts of aesthetic or political power to be deconstructed and dismissed; they are reminders of the most desirable and the most privileged things about life in a northern country. In 2008, the Ballet Jorgen Company, inspired by the choreographer's favourite pastime of canoeing in Algonquin Park, premiered a version of *The Nutcracker* set against Group of Seven paintings. In 2009, the McMichael Gallery (the institutional beneficiary and defender of the Group) and the Department of Canadian Heritage launched *Footprints: Legacy of the Group of the Seven*, which recorded the efforts of a pair of outdoor enthusiasts who photographed the exact location of Group paintings and then encouraged others to do the same on their own canoe trips.

Affection for wilderness pervades Canadian media and popular culture as well. From *Due South* and *Nothing Too Good for a Cowboy*, from *North of 60* to *Arctic Air*, and in the annual parade of summer beer commercials, English Canadian television has developed a signature style of knowing, lightly satirical fondness towards Canada's wilderness. This encourages viewers to enjoy pristine visuals of the boreal forest even as they make fun of it with a knowing wink to demonstrate their sophistication. It's worth pointing out that these shows also tend to present a positive coexistence between Indigenous peoples and settlers – anticipating and projecting a reconciliation that has yet to materialize but is necessary if we are to think of such landscapes as pleasantly available. Thanks in part to such images, a generalized boreal wilderness remains the international signifier for Canada, the most successful national stereotype in the country's history (though perhaps dented early in the twenty-first century by growing criticism of Canada's weakened stance on climate change and environmental protection). For the Vancouver Olympics in 2010, the Hudson's Bay Company did their best to foster images of "a nation of pioneers, explorers, and dreamers" – albeit more stylishly outfitted than in the seventeenth century. Today, outfitting is key to rejuvenating our wilderness identity: it is something we shop for. Recreational wilderness is deceptively democratic; it celebrates the paddle over the motor, the lighter pack over the luxury item. Much of Canadian commerce sells the wilderness lifestyle – think of Mountain Equipment Co-op's elite hiking gear, Roots sweatshirts, and entire aisles of outdoor "stuff" in Canadian Tire stores.

This idea of wilderness remains strongest at its historical epicentre in southern Ontario, where investment in its nationalist symbolism has been greatest and where large numbers of people can afford access to the near-northern forest. In the 1960s and 1970s, Jill Ker Conway, an Australian-born, sometime University of Toronto historian, concluded that fishing camps and cottages on Georgian Bay and "a thousand glorious northern lakes" formed "the core of an Ontarian's sense of place."

But how, we must ask, does the wilderness myth sit with the innumerable cultural traditions of contemporary Toronto, the most multicultural city in the country? Many immigrants regard the romantic wilderness as entirely foreign, difficult to reach, and anachronistic, if not downright irrelevant. For all that, and despite its capricious attitude to environmental protection, the federal government presents an ability to identify with wilderness as a key Canadian trait. Parks Canada and the Department of Immigration supply new Canadians with "learn to camp" programs and free passes to national parks, seemingly in the belief that knowledge of these places is essential to proper Canadianness. Does contact with the land teach an af-finity for it? It may. In her installation speech as governor general in 1999, Adrienne Clarkson spoke of her family's immigration, as refugees, to Canada, where they gained "a country with lakes ... We became addicted to the wilderness."

The relationship between national identity and wilderness has been most actively nurtured (*and* successfully concealed) in Canada's national and provincial parks. These places are not wilderness; they are parcels of land designed to attract and accommodate human recreation. In order to ensure the democratic reach of wilderness as a national birthright, parks cater to a wide audience – and they have been markedly successful in teaching generations of southern Canadians to think of "wilderness" with affection and affinity. Since the late 1980s, intensified efforts to manage national parks for ecological integrity have produced mixed results for Parks Canada. At its centennial in 2011, it spent heavily on promotional materials celebrating its stewardship of wilderness lands *and* encouraging Canadians to visit them as much as possible.

This dichotomy is nothing new in the nature of Canada. The contradiction is bred in the bone. The year 2011 was full of rhapsodizing about national parks as wilderness, as national treasures – rhetoric that seemed to describe a different place, a different country, than the one simultaneously withdrawing from international climate change treaties and promoting transborder pipelines. At the same time, the federal minister of natural resources warned Canadians against radical environmental groups, backed by foreign funding, who, he said, were trying to obstruct the growth of the energy industry and, thus, the national interest. According to this fevered argument, construction of the Canadian Pacific Railway in the nineteenth century had demonstrated the "natural" Canadian impulse to *develop* the wilderness – and it was this impulse that environmentalists threatened to suppress.

Soon after, the Canadian oil company Cenovus launched an advertising campaign that portrayed oil sands technology as the latest in a long line of Canadian innovations, including the telephone and Canadarm. This is a Canada that Stephen Leacock and Vincent Massey would recognize – a place in which wilderness is a rich natural resource, the backbone of our economy as well as our imaginations, awaiting redemption by use and forever inexhaustible. We hunt oil more than gold now, but we still find absolution in the notion that wilderness can be at once peopled and empty, pristine and exploited.

REFERENCES AND FURTHER READING

It is telling that much of this essay about ideas of wilderness in modern Canada draws from writing – whether poetry, satire, politics, or autobiography – by well-educated, middle-class, white men living most of the year in Toronto or Ottawa. (That said, three of the women quoted – Traill, Conway, and Clarkson

– were immigrants to Canada, one a woman of colour, and they marvelled at and began to adopt the same sentiments.) Many of these writers operated as public intellectuals, moving between the spheres of academia, political life, and the arts, which amplified their voices. They also benefitted from sanction by and positions in certain institutions of authority, including the university (for Leacock and Conway and historians Morton and Lower); cultural institutions such as literary organizations, the Art Gallery of Toronto, and the Empire Club of Canada; and political office, whether the position be that of prime minister (Macdonald), governor general (Clarkson), or the minister of natural resources (Oliver).

This is not to suggest that this view of wilderness was insincere: the lyrics of Campbell, Lampman, and LePan as well as their resonance within popular culture are evidence of genuine sentiment and attachment. But we need to acknowledge that such a view of wilderness – as something central to the Canadian character, as northward boreal lake country, as a heroic "beauty of strength" (as in Smith's poem, "The Lonely Land") – aligns with and testifies to the national/ist agenda, material advantages, and sense of security of those in central Canada. (Al Purdy's characterization of the Canadian Shield as the "country of defeat" is a rare acknowledgment of the limits of settler hubris.)

Stephen Leacock's "I'll Stay in Canada" was published in *Funny Pieces* (New York: Dodd, Mead, 1936), 317–26. The "recovered from the wilderness" quote is from *Official Catalogue of the Canadian Section for the Colonial and Indian Exhibition; Published under the Authority of Sir Charles Tupper* (London, 1886). The "peculiar mental background" phrase is from Leacock's 1936 essay. Macdonald's quote "gave up everything" is from his 1891 election address. "The last portage and height of land" and "crowded southern land" are from Duncan Campbell Scott's "The Height of Land," published in *The Poems of Duncan Campbell Scott* (Toronto: McClelland, 1926), 46–47. The "potent stimulus" phrase is from the catalogue for the Group of Seven's first exhibition, as cited in Marylin J. Mckay, *Picturing the Land: Narrating Territories in Canadian Landscape Art, 1500–1950* (Montreal and Kingston: McGill-Queen's University Press, 2011), 177, which also has, on page 188, some discussion of the Massey quote from 1930.

Arthur R.M. Lower's "window" is in his autobiography, *Unconventional Voyages* (Toronto: Ryerson Press, 1953), viii. W.L. Morton's basic rhythm is in his *The Canadian Identity* (Madison: University of Wisconsin Press, 1961), 5. A.J.M. Smith's "is the beauty" is from "The Lonely Land," *McGill Fortnightly Review*, 1921. The speech by Edward Weeks, editor of the *Atlantic Monthly*, is available at http://speeches.empireclub.org/60403/data. The "distinguishing element" claim is in Bruce Littlejohn and Jon Pearce, eds., *Marked by the Wild: An Anthology of Literature Shaped by the Canadian Wilderness* (Toronto: McClelland and Stewart, 1973), 11. Frye's "huge, unthinking, menacing" quote is from his conclusion to the *Literary History of Canada: Canadian Literature in English*, edited by Alfred G. Bailey, Claude Bissell, Roy Daniells, Northrop Frye, and Desmond Pacey (Toronto: University of Toronto Press, 1965), 830. The phrase "limits as distant as Thule" is from Douglas LePan's poem "Canoe-Trip," published in *The Wounded Prince and Other Poems* (London: Chatto, 1948). Jill Ker Conway's appreciation of "a thousand glorious … lakes" appears in her *True North: A Memoir* (Toronto: Random House, 1994), 114. As historian William Cronon noted in a well-known essay, wilderness is very much the product of the very civilization that hopes to hold it apart. See "The Trouble with Wilderness: Or, Getting Back to the Wrong Nature," in *Uncommon Ground: Rethinking the Human Place in Nature*, edited by William Cronon (New York: W.W. Norton and Co., 1995). The romantic, expansive, imaginative, and consumer view of wilderness is part of, and bought with, the "wealth of the Dominion" touted in imperial London – and in Ottawa today. An economy predicated on the harvest of natural resources allowed Canada to prosper; a culture of wilderness offered a feeling of entitlement and belonging.

Calgary as "Vienna on the Bow."
Thomas Mawson's projection of a "city beautiful" in 1913.
Courtesy of the Thomas Mawson fonds, Canadian Architectural Archives,
Archives and Special Collections, University of Calgary

IMAGINING THE CITY

Michèle Dagenais

F EW CANADIANS ASSOCIATE CITIES with nature or think of them as
natural places. Canadians tend to locate their collective national identity
in iconic landscapes of conquest – of the North, the forest, and the countryside. Even today, almost a century after the majority of Canadians became
urban dwellers, our trademark images still reflect an economy heavily
dependent on natural resource extraction and a tourism sector that show-
cases large open spaces, outdoor adventure, and wilderness parks.

Until recently, most of those classed as urbanites by the Canadian census
lived in small agglomerations, settlements with more than one thousand
people but still small by today's standards. In 1921, only six Canadian cities
had more than one hundred thousand people, and only Montreal and
Toronto topped half a million residents. Today, more than half of all
Canadians (18 million people) live in the Windsor to Quebec City corridor.
In Ontario and British Columbia, seventeen of every twenty people (88
percent of the population) live in cities. In Newfoundland, fewer than one
in two (47 percent) do so. And in New Brunswick, the proportion is just
over half (52 percent). However, over half of those enumerated as urban
dwellers reside in low-density suburbs rather than downtown cores. Despite
these nuances, the metropolis has dominated our historical and spatial
understanding of the urban experience and city planning. But this paradox

does not reflect the actual places where Canadians lived. The city is an imagined environment, a discursive reality that does not always directly translate how people occupy space. Since the nineteenth century, Canadians have projected their values and social norms onto a series of idealized cities.

Following rapid urbanization and the rise of large cities at the turn of the twentieth century, successive dominant discourses on the city have provided a central narrative for understanding urban realities. The conceptions, images, and metaphors that reformers and planners used to characterize urban places contributed to the elaboration of schemes aimed at rationalizing urban change. In earlier times, as today, the main problems raised by urban growth were understood in practical, spatial terms. Planners have typically addressed questions about municipal road services, the distribution of drinkable water, the management of waste and public health, food provision, and access to green and leisure spaces in relation to territory rather than society. They have framed the debates as if the processes of urbanization were about the distribution of specific elements rather than matters of human interaction. Technical solutions have been elaborated in reference to the built and natural elements of the urban physical environment. Cities and their problems have been seen, simply, as products of a set of material characteristics.

Among the various models that inspired city planning and growth since the end of the nineteenth century, three are particularly emblematic. The garden city concept, developed in the context of rapid urbanization and industrialization, served as a response to the industrial city of the late nineteenth and early twentieth centuries. In the period following the Second World War, the suburb became the ideal form of urban development and offered salvation to ageing cities in need of improvement. Finally, since the 1960s, the sustainable city has emerged as an alternative to the urban sprawl that has dominated Canadian urban landscapes.

Even before the middle of the nineteenth century, as tens of thousands of immigrants looking for a better life disembarked on the docks of Montreal or Halifax, and as epidemics such as cholera and typhus threatened the lives of city dwellers, the novel character of urban growth generated a great deal of anxiety among political and medical elites in British North America. But it wasn't until the end of the century, when urban populations started to explode because of industrialization and large-scale immigration, that writers turned their energies to examining the phenomenon of the large Canadian city. The period also saw the emergence of a vast urban reform movement, intent on solving the most pressing urban problems of the day.

Canada's urban population grew by more than 60 percent in the first decade of the twentieth century. Many people were perturbed by the pace of expansion and felt that large cities were growing too quickly. Montreal, Toronto, Winnipeg, and Vancouver all housed more than one hundred thousand inhabitants in 1911. And the ethnic diversity of city dwellers exacerbated concerns, particularly in Winnipeg, where over half of residents in 1911 (55.9 percent) had been born outside the country. Some observers feared not only for the future of cities but also for the future of the nation.

Drawing on European and American examples, critics argued that large cities provided a particularly fertile soil for illnesses, crime, and poverty. Older neighbourhoods, in particular, raised the spectre of evil and provoked fears about the future. "The Ward" in Toronto, the "North End" in Winnipeg, "Chinatown" in Vancouver, and the "City Below the Hill" in Montreal, all inhabited by generally poor and immigrant populations, shared many characteristics. Located close to industrial sites or on the edges of waterways subject to seasonal flooding and polluted by toxic smoke from factory chimneys, these quarters had few accessible green spaces, and clean water was not always available. From the perspective of reformers, these working-class neighbourhoods were too densely populated and, consequently, subject to pollution and overcrowding.

The dense, urban grid in Canada's biggest city, Montreal, 1929.
Pont Jacques Cartier is being constructed in the distance.
Ville de Montréal, Section des archives VM97-3-01-028

Urban reformers tended to assume causal relationships between the environmental conditions experienced by the groups they studied and their social behaviours. Holding the milieu responsible for "deviant" behaviours, they concluded that urban environments had to be remade to improve the morals of the people. This agenda was given greater urgency by fears that poor neighbourhoods (and their pathologies) would multiply if nothing were done to eradicate them. As Charles Hastings, the medical officer of health for Toronto, stated eloquently: "If any part of the human body is cut off from or lies outside the due irrigation of the nutritive fluids of the body, that area becomes not only useless to the body, but prone to engender a putridity which will infect even the soundest part of the system.

Thus will the contamination of any one class of the people infect the rest of the social body."

Reflecting the conviction that congestion and excessive density caused problems of urban squalor and sickness, reformers proposed solutions to improve ventilation and water circulation. One after another, Canadian municipalities developed sanitation and public health services to address these issues. They constructed sewers and connected them to dwellings in order to remove sources of contagion. They collected and disposed of industrial and human refuse and introduced filtration technologies to ensure the safety of public water supplies.

Observers feared that rapid urban growth was disturbing the social equilibrium by increasing the gap between rich and poor and between town and countryside. In this context, rational management based on the principles of town planning appeared to be essential and quickly became the preferred response to most urban problems. In 1914, the president of the Commission of Conservation of Canada, Clifford Sifton, created a division of urban planning under the leadership of Scottish urbanist Thomas Adams. In a major study, *Rural Planning and Development,* Adams identified the existence of an imbalance resulting from the fact that "neither the city not the country has developed properly because of their neglect of each other." According to the famous planner, town and country should be considered in tandem to encourage the harmonious growth of the two settings. In this context, he adapted the concept of the garden city, developed by British reformer Ebenezer Howard, as an ideal locus for living. This model foresaw the creation of towns of modest size (with average populations of about thirty thousand), low densities, and many green spaces. Ideally, they would be surrounded by agricultural land. The solution relied on the beautification and improvement of living conditions. It aimed to combine the best of the city and the countryside by neutralizing the problems intrinsic to each of these spaces.

Canadian cities rarely adopted the model wholesale, but a few did. Following the Halifax Explosion of 1917, the Hydrostone neighbourhood was built on garden city principles, as were resource towns such as Temiscaming in Quebec and Iroquois Falls in Ontario. The ideal of the garden city also inspired the development of new neighbourhoods on the outskirts of cities. For the urban elites who proposed this solution, the best way to solve problems of congestion, overcrowding, and pollution was to move closer to nature, but not so far as to lose the professional opportunities afforded by the city. Municipalities zoned the new suburbs to provide green space and gardens, and they often maintained forests or other natural features that provided habitats for birds and animals. The elites who lived in these areas could enjoy popular open-air leisure activities such as rambling and birdwatching.

The suburb evolved further in the post–Second World War period. Affluence and the embrace of modernity stimulated rapid suburban growth. The change appeared to be even more rapid because urban development had slowed considerably during the Great Depression of the 1930s. Ageing housing stock and the almost complete cessation of construction during that decade created a housing crisis in many Canadian cities. The postwar baby boom made the situation even more critical. Earlier concerns about urban congestion were supplanted by disquiet about the problems of the decaying city. Urban renewal became the guiding mantra of urban planning, and in this spirit, large areas of Canadian cities were transformed in the 1950s and 1960s. Professional urbanists, who now numbered in the hundreds, replaced the reformers and dedicated themselves to preparing large-scale urban renovation plans.

The vision of Le Corbusier, Swiss architect and influential urbanist, strongly influenced the urban renewal movement. He suggested replacing existing cities with rational urban centres, planned with an eye to efficiency and intended to raise living standards for all. To resolve problems posed by the complexity of urban phenomena, Canadian city planners began to separate functions such as residence, workplace, and recreation in an attempt to control growth. In this model, residences and industries occupied increasingly discrete spaces, intensifying a trend set by earlier land-use zoning practices. Ownership of private automobiles expanded greatly in the postwar period, both a reflection and cause of the need to travel between the home and the workplace.

Along with urban planning came increasing state interventionism, notably by the federal government, which created the Canadian Mortgage and Housing Corporation to stimulate residential construction and to provide financial assistance to municipalities for urban renewal projects. First in Montreal and Toronto and then in Winnipeg, Quebec, Vancouver, and other cities, local authorities began to demolish old dwellings and working-class neighbourhoods in an effort to eradicate the health and social deviance problems associated with those who lived in them. "Slums" were replaced with tall towers of public housing, clustered in residential blocks and often separated from the rest of the city by green spaces. The Regent Park project in Toronto is the emblematic case. This type of development, initially conceived of as a way to open up spaces in the city, led instead to the formation of new ghettos for the poor.

In the postwar period, the urban renewal movement continued to be strongly influenced by an organic metaphor that compared the city to the human body. Updated to explain the necessity of modernizing downtown neighbourhoods, this imagery also influenced the way that planners posed the crucial problem of circulation. As early as 1941, the main plan of Montreal's new Urbanism unit sought to establish "a rational system of principal arteries, which will direct traffic and liberate the vital parts of the urban organism. This system of arteries should therefore reduce congestion in the business district, link urban roads to pathways into the city, relieve crowded streets ... and connect the surrounding towns to the centre." To

Postwar urban development on a large scale.
Regent Park, Toronto, 1968. Photo by Graham Bezant, *Toronto Star*

reduce the construction expenses of this network and ensure the cost-effectiveness of this investment in infrastructure, the plan foresaw the extension of new arteries through the decaying sectors of the city, which presented the double advantage of reducing outlays for expropriation and promoting the demolition of dilapidated and ageing houses. As the director of the unit explained in 1948, this process aimed to provide the city's inhabitants with "the freedom of movement required to make Montreal a good city to live and work in."

Modernizing projects promoted freedom of movement so much so that it became the central indicator of quality of life. The suburb best epitomized this ideal, and a suburbanization wave transformed Canada beginning in the 1950s. Thanks to the construction of highways and the large-scale production of houses, the residential suburb attracted a large proportion

Suburban growth. Aerial view of Lower Sackville, Halifax, Nova Scotia, 2006.
Photo by DJSasso, Wikimedia Creative Commons Licence

of the expanding middle classes, eager to flee the large cities that they perceived as outmoded and crowded, despite the urban renewal projects then underway. They were attracted more by the opportunity to move into new houses, located in well-ventilated environments that included plenty of green spaces, thanks to the lawns and gardens surrounding the homes as well as parks and public playgrounds. Suburbs throughout the Canadian landscape permitted a certain democratization of the ideal of the garden city, but it was based on the bedrock of the nuclear family.

These unprecedented urban and suburban postwar developments profoundly influenced the form and dynamics of Canadian city life. Within a few decades, the demographic weight of downtown cores and suburbs was reversed. From the 1950s to the 1970s, central city areas in major cities lost population to their peripheries, to the extent that, today, more than half of all urbanites are suburban. As cities spread farther and farther afield, this tendency encouraged urban sprawl and a discontinuous urbanization. In Montreal, for instance, urbanized territory beyond the city limits increased by 13 square kilometres from 1932 to 1944, 62 square kilometres from 1944 to 1952, and 337 square kilometres from 1961 to 1971. In Edmonton, the shift of retail businesses to the suburbs surpassed North American norms with the construction of an immense shopping centre in the early 1980s. With subsequent expansion, the West Edmonton Mall now includes some eight hundred retail outlets.

Since the early 1960s, these urbanization patterns have attracted a raft of critiques. From the perspective of the city core, reformers began to defend the old urban heritage, attempting to save it from the wrecking ball. But the most heated and lively criticisms concentrated on the suburbs, creating a negative perception of this form of urbanization and blaming it for the simultaneous destruction of urban cores and rural areas. As early as 1961, a federal-provincial conference on the theme "resources for tomorrow" tackled the pressure that urban sprawl placed on agricultural lands. At the same time, early environmentalists focused on suburbanization as a principal cause of the destruction of nature. Because agriculture and urbanization both occupy a relatively narrow band of territory in the south, the battle against urban sprawl was particularly vociferous in Canada.

Condemnations of the suburb echoed criticisms of earlier urban forms. The low density of the built environment, spatial segregation, and reliance on the automobile supposedly promoted individualism, competitiveness, and conservatism among suburbanites. The reversal of perspectives was striking. No longer was the deviant an inhabitant of the poor neighbourhoods of old downtown cores; it was now the suburban dweller, who was held responsible for automobile pollution, the destruction of nature, and even the obesity epidemic. The common practice of referring dismissively to suburban zones by their telephone codes – the 905 in Toronto or 450 in Montreal – perfectly expresses the attitude of new urban elites towards these groups.

Because critics posed this problem in terms of spatial distribution, their solutions reflected their starting assumptions. In the 1980s, they began to embrace the idea of the sustainable city as an answer to the suburban plague. This new model reflected a new respect for density and mixed use, two features of urban landscapes that had long been criticized in Canada. The promotion of sustainable urbanism resulted fairly quickly in the re-vitalization and reassessment of old central neighbourhoods. The century-long tendency among elites to move into new and better-quality houses on the city's fringe, leaving ageing houses to the least favoured social classes, was reversed as young professionals and members of the so-called creative class invested sweat equity in the gentrification of inner-city neighbour-hoods and pushed the less-well-off to the peripheries. These "urban pioneers" and other members of the socioeconomic elite who followed them were the primary beneficiaries of the sustainable city. The gentrification of Vancouver was particularly spectacular in this regard, to the extent that planners started to worry about population decline.

More and more prized, urban density was now promoted through the ideal of the walkable or bikeable city, where all the services of everyday life were located close to home. Those urbanites able to afford gentrified neigh-bourhoods generally favoured mass transit and urban sociability, in the belief that they were promoting tolerance, community spirit, and civic pride. Although their perspective was the exact opposite of elites in earlier periods, the underlying logic remained the same. Some attributed new merits to urban life, different from the characteristics that they associated with suburbanites, whom they viewed as an undifferentiated lot. Typically, this rhetoric downplayed the class and ethnic differences that existed within

A highly gentrified neighbourhood in Montreal's Mile End district, 2010.
The photograph emphasizes urban sociability, which is now considered
a desirable quality of city life by urban elites. Photo by Alain Rouiller,
Wikimedia Creative Commons Licence

suburban populations, as well as the broader socioeconomic factors that had contributed to sprawl in the first place.

In most large Canadian cities, planners devised new reform proposals for urban design based on the concept of sustainable development. These models also promoted the creation of several poles or centres of urban development, organized to increase the density and diversity of land use and improve access to public transit. Each of these plans attempted to curtail the expansion of urban territory to protect agricultural lands and natural spaces such as wooded areas, waterways, and wetlands. In the city as on the periphery, the sustainable city model promoted a set of best practices in transit, lifestyle, recycling, and even the consumption of resources. The objective of responsible growth contributed to a normative vision of good urban development, made in the name of environmental protection.

Sustainable city models depend on a concept of urban development that normalizes density and condemns sprawl. But is this perception not utopian and out of sync with the dispersed urban world it confronts, a world in which urbanization is largely suburbanization? Even if the vision of the sustainable addresses the very real problems created by the loss of fertile agricultural land to urban sprawl and the costs associated with commuting, it still fails to address the problem of social inequality and rejects the preferred habitat of most Canadians. Would it not be wise to conceive of a type of sustainable development that suits current urban forms?

The imagined cities of the present and the past are strategic representations that have served at different times to promote certain planning schemes and specific values. Each has favoured particular social groups over others. And each has privileged the relationship between humans and nature in different ways, depending on the key issues of the day. At the turn of the twentieth century, people were preoccupied with the problems of density and public health, which were linked to water supply and waste disposal. At mid-century, planners could not envisage any limits to urban development, in technical, financial, and territorial terms. The heavy consumption of natural resources inherent in suburban sprawl presented no concerns for public authorities. Towards the end of the century, however, people became more aware that urban sprawl placed strong pressures on natural resources and relied on the incessant consumption of energy. Taken together, these urban models remind us just how closely linked our cities are to the natural elements upon which they depend. By recognizing that sociopolitical perceptions and processes shape the nature of "nature" in urban Canada, we come closer to understanding how transformations of the lived environment also serve to constitute society and the power relations that penetrate it.

REFERENCES AND FURTHER READING

There are no book-length overviews of the history of Canadian cities, but a number of important collections of articles can help construct a narrative. See Pierre Filion and Trudi Bunting, eds., *Canadian Cities in Transition: Local through Global Perspectives*, 3rd ed. (Don Mills, ON: Oxford University Press, 2006) and Alan F.J. Artibise and Gilbert A. Stelter, eds., *The Usable Urban Past: Planning and Politics in the Modern Canadian City* (Toronto: Macmillan, 1979).

Figures on rates of urbanization come from Jim Simmons and Larry McCann, "The Canadian Urban System: Growth and Transition," in Filion and Bunting, *Canadian Cities*, 40–64. The idea of the city as an imagined environment is inspired by Caroline Rosenthal's *New York and Toronto Novels after Postmodernism: Explorations of the Urban* (Rochester, NY: Camden House, 2011). She develops this concept initially presented by James Donald in "Metropolis: The City as Text," in *Social and Cultural Forms of Modernity*, edited by Robert Bocock and Kenneth Thompson, 417–61 (Cambridge: Polity Press, 1992).

A classic study of anxiety in nineteenth-century cities is Judith Fingard's *The Dark Side of Life in Victorian Halifax* (Halifax: Pottersfield Press, 1989). In *Peopling the North American City: Montreal, 1840–1900* (Montreal and Kingston: McGill-Queen's University Press, 2011), Sherry Olson and Patricia A. Thornton explore similar themes for Montreal, as does the contemporary analysis by Herbert B. Ames, *"The City Below the Hill": A Sociological Study of a Portion of the City of Montreal, Canada* (Montreal: Bishop Engraving and Printing, 1897) and Terry Copp's *The Anatomy of Poverty: The Condition of the Working Class in Montreal, 1897–1929* (Toronto: McClelland and Stewart, 1974). On Winnipeg, see J.S. Woodsworth, *Strangers within Our Gates, or Coming Canadians* (Toronto: F.C. Stephenson, 1909); on Toronto, see John Lorinc, Michael McClelland, Ellen Scheinberg, and Tatum Taylor, *The Ward: The Life and Loss of Toronto's First Immigrant Neighbourhood* (Toronto: Coach House Press, 2015); and on Vancouver, Kay Anderson, *Vancouver's Chinatown: Racial Discourse in Canada, 1875–1980* (Montreal and Kingston: McGill-Queen's University Press, 1991). An excellent source for material on the urban reform movement is Paul Rutherford, ed.,

Saving the Canadian City, the First Phase, 1880–1920: An Anthology of Early Articles on Urban Reform (Toronto: University of Toronto Press, 1974). Hasting's "if any part of the body is cut" is quoted on page 132.

The rapid urban growth of the early twentieth century is covered in Artibise and Stelter, "Planning," in their collection, *Usable Urban Past,* 167–75. For more information on Adams's career and ideas, see Michael Simpson, "Thomas Adams in Canada, 1914–1930," *Urban History Review/Revue d'histoire urbaine* 11, 2 (1982): 1–15. Thomas Adams pronounced on urban-rural disequilibrium in *Rural Planning: A Study of Rural Conditions and Problems in Canada* (Ottawa: Commission of Conservation, 1917), 17. The influence of the city beautiful movement is traced in Walter H. van Nus, "The Fate of City Beautiful Thought in Canada, 1893–1930," in *The Canadian City: Essays in Urban History,* edited by Gilbert A. Stelter and Alan F.J. Artibise, 162–85 (Toronto: McClelland and Stewart, 1977), and for a detailed study of one garden suburb, see Jill Delaney, "The Garden Suburb of Lindenlea, Ottawa: A Model Project for the First Federal Housing Policy, 1918–24," *Urban History Review/Revue d'histoire urbaine* 19, 2 (1991): 151–65. The Hydrostone development in Halifax is treated in J.C. Weaver, "Reconstruction of the Richmond District in Halifax: A Canadian Episode in Public Housing and Town Planning, 1918–1921," *Plan Canada* 16, 1 (1976): 36–47.

Richard Harris looks at the development of middle-class suburbs in the early twentieth century in *Creeping Conformity: How Canada Became Suburban, 1900–1960* (Toronto: University of Toronto Press, 2004), as does Larry D. McCann in "Suburbs of Desire: The Suburban Landscapes of Canadian Cities, ca. 1900–1950," in *Changing Suburbs: Foundation, Form and Function,* edited by Richard Harris and Peter Larkham, 111–45 (New York: Routledge, 1999). McCann provides a photo essay on an elite neighbourhood in Victoria, BC, in "John Olmsted's Uplands: 'Victoria's Celebrated Residential Park' – A Photo Essay," *BC Studies* 181 (Spring 2014): 11–37. On the desire to live close to nature, see Michèle Dagenais, "Se rapprocher de la nature: Le rôle de la villégiature dans la colonisation de Montréal," in *Faire et fuir la ville: Espaces publics de culture et de loisirs à Montréal et Toronto aux XIXe et XXe siècles,* 187–209 (Quebec: Presses de l'Université

Laval, 2006). Len J. Evenden and G.E. Walker examine the changing geography of the suburbs in "From Periphery to Centre: The Changing Geography of the Suburbs," in *The Changing Social Geography of Canadian Cities*, edited by Larry Bourne and David Ley, 234–51 (Montreal and Kingston: McGill-Queen's University Press, 1993). For one early critique of suburban development (from the 1950s), see N. Pearson, "Hell Is a Suburb: What Kind of Neighbourhoods Do We Want?" *Community Planning Review* 7, 3 (1956): 124–28.

André Corboz looks at the impact of Le Corbusier in "L'urbanisme du XXe siècle: Equisse d'un profil," in *De la ville au patrimoine urbain: Histoires de formes et de sens*, edited by André Corboz and Lucie K. Morisset, 245–55 (Quebec: Presses de l'Université du Québec, 2009). Jill Grant, "Shaped by Planning: The Canadian City through Time," in Filion and Bunting, *Canadian Cities*, 320–37, examines the process of replacing slums with high-rise towers. Sean Purdy explores the special case of Regent Park in "'Ripped Off' by the System: Housing Policy, Poverty, and Territorial Stigmatization in Regent Park Housing Project, 1951–1981," *Labour/Le Travail* 52 (Fall 2003): 45–108. For Vancouver, see Mike Harcourt and Ken Cameron, with Sean Rossiter, *City Making in Paradise: Nine Decisions That Saved Vancouver* (Vancouver: Douglas and McIntyre, 1997), Chap. 2.

The translated quotation from Montreal's Urbanism office can be found in *Urbanisation de Montréal, plan directeur, rapport préliminaire* (Montreal: Service d'urbanisme, 1944), 17–18. The quotation about "freedom of movement" is from Claire Poitras, "A City on the Move: The Surprising Consequences of Highways," in *Metropolitan Natures: Environmental Histories of Montreal*, edited by Stéphane Castonguay and Michèle Dagenais (Pittsburgh: University of Pittsburgh Press, 2011), 175. On the development of suburbs in relation to the growth of roads and highways, also see Graeme Wynn, *Canada and Arctic North America: An Environmental History* (Santa Barbara, CA: ABC Clio, 2007). The figures on suburban sprawl in Montreal come from David B. Hanna, "Les réseaux de transport et leur rôle dans l'étalement urbain de Montréal," in *Barcelona – Montréal: Desarrollo urbano comparado/Développement urbain comparé*, edited by Horacio Capel and Paul-André Linteau (Barcelona: Publicacions de la Universitat de

Barcelona, 1998), 129. On global suburbanization trends in the postwar period, see Jon C. Teaford, "Suburbia and Post-Suburbia: A Brief History," in *International Perspectives on Suburbanization: A Post-Suburban World?*, edited by Nicolas A. Phelps and Fulong Wu, 15–34 (London: Palgrave Macmillan, 2011).

On the process of gentrification, see David Ley, *The New Middle Class and the Remaking of the Central City* (New York: Oxford University Press, 1996), and Pierre Filion and Trudi Bunting, "The Structuring Parameters of Twenty-First-Century Urbanization," in Filion and Bunting, *Canadian Cities*, 237–42. Proposals for reforming urbanization patterns in Vancouver and Montreal reveal the importance of sustainable development as a key concept. Both cities' regional growth strategies for 2011 can be found on their websites. On the normative elements involved in the sustainable city, see Michèle Dagenais, "The Sustainable City: A New Label for the Progressive Cities of the 21st Century? Some Remarks on the Case of Montreal," *Informationen zur Modernen Stadtgeschichte* 2 (2010): 22–33.

My thanks to Colin Coates, who generously translated this chapter into English and whose comments helped to sharpen the argument.

The X15 pit filled to the top with water at the
abandoned Pine Point Mine, Northwest Territories, 2008.
Photo by Arn Keeling

NEVER JUST A HOLE IN THE GROUND

―――

Arn Keeling and John Sandlos

M
INING HAS A LONG history in Canada. Sixteenth-century explorers
Jacques Cartier and Martin Frobisher carried ore eastward across
the Atlantic on the return legs of their early voyages in the belief that they
had discovered mineral riches. Coal was extracted from the cliffs of Cape
Breton to warm the houses of Fortress Louisbourg in the eighteenth century.
And in 1945, when the Dominion Bureau of Statistics published a
"Chronological Record of Canadian Mining Events, 1604–1943," the simple
list of one- and two-line entries ran to fifteen pages of small type, single-
spaced. Miners and the towns in which they worked have even entered the
pantheon of Canadian lore in poems and folk songs. In Nova Scotia, Stan
Rogers reminds us that "the Rawdon Hills once were touched by gold."
The "Ballad of Springhill" leaves no doubt that "bone and blood is the price
of coal." The cremation of Sam McGee was only one of the "strange things
done in the midnight sun / By the men who moil for gold." And who can
forget Stompin' Tom Connors's ode to the nickel-mining capital of Ontario:
"Well, the girls are out to bingo and the boys are gettin' stinko / We think
no more of Inco on a Sudbury Saturday Night"? Popular images of Canadian
mining celebrate its role in the settlement of town, region, and nation. Today,
these images are often accompanied by the insistent claim or refrain – most

often put forward by the industry itself – that mining is a sustainable enterprise. But what does the land itself, the hard rock upon which this country has been built, tell us?

Hard rock mining, spurred by railroads, technological developments, and industrial growth, was a major driver of regional expansion and environmental change in the second half of the nineteenth century, when the tentacles of an expanding world economy reached out to the newly valuable resources of remote mining sites in Canada. The process was typified in the Slocan Valley of southeastern British Columbia, where extraction began in 1894 on a minuscule scale with pick and shovel high on the mountainside. Within five years the narrow valley was served by spur lines of two transcontinental railways and Sandon, a town of around two thousand people, had emerged amid trails and aerial tramways that brought silver and lead ore to concentrating mills. Most of the country's greatest mining centres, places such as Sudbury, Cobalt, Timmins, Rouyn-Noranda, and Flin Flon, were opened up in similarly tumultuous fashion after 1885. As demand soared, driven by rising global markets for raw materials and energy resources, Canada became a major producer of lead, zinc, nickel, iron, uranium, and other industrial minerals. The value of Canadian mineral production increased more than six-fold in the thirty years after 1899.

Between 1940 and the late 1970s, the output from Canada's mines soared in value at a comparable rate, from $5 billion to nearly $30 billion. Early in the new millennium, production exceeded $40 billion, and in 2015, mining's contribution to the national GDP was pegged at $56 billion. Today, Canada is one of the world's most important mining nations. It produces more than sixty minerals and metals and ranks among the top five producers of thirteen major commodities, including potash (1st), uranium and nickel (2nd), cobalt and aluminum (3rd), and diamonds, graphite, and gold (5th). Large mineral-processing facilities such as refineries and smelters grew in tandem with the mines, and the Canadian firms Inco,

In 1897 Sandon, British Columbia, was the site
of two railroads and a burgeoning town.
Courtesy of the Royal BC Museum and Archives, Image C–05028

Noranda, Alcan, Cominco, Falconbridge, and Barrick became global industry leaders.

Reflecting on the industry between the wars, Canada's pre-eminent economic historian, Harold Innis, saw mining as a "frontier" activity in two senses: the spatial (it opened new territory for settlement) and the economic (it created the conditions for the emergence of "a highly-integrated advanced type of industrial community"). A mine was never just a hole in the ground. It included many different types of development activities: exploration (which led to forest fires and the bulldozing or hand-cutting of seismic lines that criss-crossed regions); the construction of roads, railroads, and airstrips; the often voracious consumption of local forests for fuel and timber; and the expansion of oil, gas, or hydroelectric projects to meet the typically high energy demands of mineral production. These ancillary developments, Innis suggested, would build a platform for modern industrialism and the creation of an integrated national economy by generating infrastructure, stimulating internal markets, encouraging settlement, promoting technological innovations, pooling capital, and supplying the minerals that are vital to industrial production.

Innis's enthusiasm for mineral-led development caused him to overlook the vulnerability of remote mines and communities to downturns in the commodity cycle. Price shocks and other perturbations can lead to the abandonment of mines, communities, and infrastructure. Indeed, large-scale mineral extraction generally poses significant problems of investment and financing. Considerable expenditures (in exploration, equipment, and infrastructure) must precede production, often by years, and returns on that investment are characterized by a falling rate of profit because of declining ore grades and increased costs of production. These cycles of investment and return are also affected by business cycles that do not necessarily correspond to development and production schedules and rates. The result is an often precarious preproduction period as companies seek capital, work promising deposits, and nervously watch markets for signs of price shifts. Thereafter, any mine is vulnerable to sudden shocks from major market shifts, which can be prompted by the discovery of substantial ore deposits elsewhere, declines in demand for mineral products, the removal of special price and marketing arrangements, and so on.

Few mining centres suffered quite as marked or as swift a decline as Sandon in the Slocan Valley. In 1897, the town had electric streetlights, seventeen hotels, fifty or so commercial enterprises, a sawmill, a brewery, two newspapers, and law, medical, assay, insurance, and brokerage offices. It was linked by speculative capital to thriving centres of investment and seemed set for prosperity. In 1900, it burned to the ground. Though it was rebuilt, it never recaptured its original grandeur, and the Slocan boom was well and truly over by 1910. Half a century on, in the 1960s, mining's often acute sensitivity to market conditions was driven home again when the end of the US military's stockpiling program, with its price guarantees, brought about the near collapse of Canada's uranium industry.

In the 1970s, these problems led critics to question the mining industry's impact on regions and economies in Canada. The geographer John Bradbury pointed out that mining created instability, dependency, and uneven development in Canada's resource hinterland. Mining towns, he argued, failed to overcome the problems of "isolation, community impermanence, instability, labor migrations, demographic distortions, and economic dependency." Fuelled by the rhetoric of colonial expansion, hinterland mineral developments had, indeed, promoted the construction of large-scale infrastructure and hydroelectric power developments, but in the Quebec-Labrador borderlands, for instance, these investments failed to generate the industrial spinoff developments envisaged by their promoters. Mining in the region continued to be unstable because of declining ore grades and price fluctuations, which culminated in the closure of the Iron Ore Company mine at Schefferville in 1982 and the near-complete collapse of the community. In Bradbury's view, rather than building an economic foundation for further industrialization, mining regions remained trapped in a system that produced economic booms and "whiplash declines." The post–2000 commodities super cycle, which was followed by a rapid downturn in mineral prices and the industry's fortunes, only reinforces Bradbury's critique. Although the life of a mine may range from a few years to almost a century, mining is always an ephemeral activity because the resource itself is finite. As "the grandsons of the mining men" well understood, as they attempted to scratch a living from the poor farms of the Rawdon Hills, "the glory left the hole."

In this sense, mining seems to be the quintessence of unsustainable resource exploitation. Minerals such as iron, gold, copper, or diamonds are the material products of geological processes turned into "resources" through specific economic, sociological, and technological conditions. Shifts in the costs of production or the value of the commodity might slow or quicken extraction, but any single ore body will eventually be exhausted or become uneconomic. Cyclical patterns of boom and bust are so typical of mining operations that mining is taken to exemplify "extractive" development. Poor farmers are scorned as "soil miners"; depleted fisheries and forests are said to have been "mined."

Yet mining's defenders will argue that there have been no global mineral supply shortages, even after centuries of increasingly intense extraction. New technologies have allowed humans to exploit previously unrecoverable, low-grade deposits. And improved recycling programs keep minerals in use for longer periods of time. Industry advocates in Canada and elsewhere insist that mining is not a narrow hit-and-run development activity but a generator of wealth that will provide long-term value for future genera- tions once that wealth is reinvested in private ventures or public infrastruc- ture. Even if mineral reserves must, inevitably, decline over time, the industry maintains that they will create value for no one – in present or future generations – if they are left in the ground. In their view, which echoes that of Innis, the wealth generated by mining offsets the environmental and economic challenges that accompany extraction. Recent attempts to improve the industry's environmental performance and earn a "social licence to operate," such as the Mining Association of Canada's Towards Sustainable Mining initiative, are by no means trivial.

Historical experience and trends in Canada suggest, however, that the mining industry remains fundamentally unsustainable for two reasons. First, it has generally been a profoundly unstable base for economic de- velopment in peripheral regions of Canada, often leaving abandoned communities and severe environmental damage in its wake. Second, the long-term downward trend in the quality of ore bodies in Canada (and globally) has meant that industry must apply more energy and produce more waste rock and tailings in pursuit of ever-shrinking percentages of valuable minerals. Attempts to rebrand the industry as a sustainable enterprise largely ignore the historical, environmental, and socioeconomic consequences of mining, as well as the fundamental ecological contradictions of our mineral and energy-intensive society.

A fundamental problem is the finitude of the resource. Mineral deposits are formed and transformed over geological time scales. Notions of a resource cycle, derived from ecosystem models and predicated on phases of depletion and regeneration, simply do not apply. Nor do traditional concepts of conservation. Indeed, early twentieth-century miners referred to minerals as a "wasting asset" that could not be conserved in the traditional sense of ensuring perpetual harvests or long-term and sustained yields. Mines are inescapably temporary, time-limited ventures. Although technological innovations or new discoveries may extend the life of a mine (or attract miners to exploit abandoned mines and tailings), the material resource itself cannot be regenerated. Even for long-lived operations, closure or abandonment is a key feature of the mine's natural history.

For all that, the global supply of minerals has actually increased over time. The discovery of new deposits has played a role, but technological improvements that enable exploitation of low-grade deposits (or stockpiled mine waste), dismissed as uneconomical a century ago, have extended the economic life of particular mines and districts. However, such a cornucopian argument – that the supply of minerals is unlimited so long as we continue to apply human ingenuity to increasingly low-quality resource stocks – ignores the industry's environmental impacts. Technological developments in early twentieth-century copper mining led to open-pit mining, which relies on heavy machinery and fossil-fuel energy to extract very low-grade ore and on chemical processing techniques to separate the mineral. In environmental terms, the impact of this new "disassembly line" was devastating. Open-pit mines produced enormous volumes of waste rock and tailings, and chemical byproducts such as cyanide (used to separate minerals from ore) and toxic heavy metals (arsenic, lead, cadmium, and so on) present in the ore body were spewed into the environment. Because of dramatic increases in the amount of material involved, ever-greater energy inputs were required. These processes left indelible imprints on the Canadian landscape in the form of gigantic open pits at places such as the Jeffrey Mine in Asbestos, Quebec, the Island Copper Mine in British Columbia, and the Ekati and Diavik diamond mines in Northwest Territories.

This story has been repeated time after time. Ore grades have declined for almost all minerals of significance. As the ratio of minerals to ore goes down, indicators of unsustainability, including the production of green-house gases, increase. Here lies the basic conundrum facing advocates of sustainable mining: as we mine out the world's remaining mineral deposits, we must apply more energy, move more earth, and create more pollution to sustain or increase rates of production.

In Canada, in keeping with global trends, lead and copper grades have declined markedly. Nickel and zinc grades have held steady, however, because of large finds such as at Voisey's Bay, Newfoundland. Uranium ore grades have actually improved because of discoveries in northern Saskatchewan and Nunavut. In terms of absolute supply, however, known reserves for almost all base metals have declined markedly, as have silver reserves among the precious metals. Reserves of other metals such as iron are considered plentiful.

Yet sustainability remains a problem. Since the 1950s, iron production in Canada has been dominated by the exploitation of low-grade taconite in deposits along the Quebec-Labrador border. This activity became possible only in the mid-twentieth century with the discovery of a cost-effective way to convert taconite into iron pellets for shipping. As with copper production a half-century earlier, this technological "solution" required high-energy and waste-intensive open-pit mining. First used in the United States, this development led to protracted legal battles over the dumping

Mines #19, Westar Open Pit Coal Mine, Sparwood, BC, 1985.
Edward Burtynsky's photographs brilliantly capture the scale and
impact of open-pit mining and other industrial developments.
Photo © Edward Burtynsky. Courtesy Metivier Gallery, Toronto

of huge volumes of tailings in Lake Superior. On the Labrador-Quebec border, the pelletizing and upgrading of taconite also produced vast quantities of waste rock and a massive transformation of the landscape. Technology may allow humans to exploit ever-lower grade deposits to meet increasing global demand, and a big discovery might delay the decline of ore quality within an individual Canadian mineral sector; however, at some point, the costs of moving so much earth will outweigh the benefits. Bringing tiny fractions of useful materials and energy into the production stream will create a "peak minerals" scenario in which the exploitation of certain minerals will become uneconomic.

A broken and abandoned tailings pipeline at the Gunnar Mine,
Lake Athabasca, Saskatchewan. This Cold War–era uranium mine operated
from 1955 to 1963, leaving behind millions of tonnes of radioactive tailings that
flowed into the lake. The site is now being remediated at public expense.
Photo by Arn Keeling

Moreover, mining's modification of surface and subsurface environments
often persists for decades, even centuries after the supposed end of a mine.
On the surface, mining entails the removal of more or less extensive areas
of soil and vegetation. Open-pit and strip mining completely remove topsoil
as "overburden," leaving behind a landscape hostile to recolonizing vegetation. Similarly, the disposal of waste rock and tailings provides dramatic,
visible, and long-lasting evidence of mining's environmental impact.
Globally, mining produces the largest proportion of total industrial waste.
These are not simply rock piles or tailing ponds. They can be chemical and
physical environmental hazards: tailings impoundments erode and fade,
heavy metals and process chemicals leach slowly into local waterways, and
acid mine drainage can lead to acute environmental toxicity.

The toxic legacies of abandoned mines remain one of the industry's foremost environmental challenges. There are an estimated ten thousand abandoned mines in Canada. They range from small "dog hole" mines and trenches to extensive polluting sites. The Britannia Beach mine near Squamish, BC, spewed acid effluent into Howe Sound during its operation and for decades after its closure in 1974. The cleanup cost tens of millions of dollars. At the Faro Mine in Yukon, which closed in 1998, there are ongoing concerns about the geotechnical stability of dams, acid mine drainage at the tailings pond, and heavy-metal contamination of surface water in the area. Annual maintenance costs for the site are $7.2 million, with the final remediation bill estimated at nearly a billion dollars. The unstable tailings pond also represents a serious threat to the Pelly River. The challenge of managing these vast waste streams was starkly illustrated by the massive Mount Polley tailings dam failure in central BC in 2014, which released over 25 million cubic metres of contaminated tailings into local waters.

Even in cases where toxicity is not a significant issue, damage to the landscape can take decades to heal. At the Pine Point mine in Northwest Territories, which closed in 1989, the landscape is still pockmarked with barren waste-rock piles and with dead lakes formed from mined-out open pits.

Environmental disasters and long-term problems with toxicity defy the argument that mining is merely a short-term transformation of the landscape. The toxic legacies associated with waste rock and tailings ponds are often impossible to repair completely and require permanent monitoring and containment programs at significant, often public expense. These long-term care costs are not typically factored into the "weak sustainability" argument mobilized by mining advocates, the argument that the wealth generated for future generations will outweigh the costs of depleting the resource and rehabilitating the land. In theoretical terms, this wealth-generation argument requires that we measure only the value of a mining operation's manufactured capital and fail to account for its impact on natural capital such as ecosystem services, food, water, and other renewable resources. Although it can be difficult to quantify these costs, there is no denying that the environmental liabilities of mining throw doubt on the selective cost-benefit analyses of mining advocates.

The absurdity of measuring only the benefits and not the liabilities of mining is exemplified by gold mining in Yellowknife. In 2002, two senior bureaucrats in Northwest Territories portrayed gold mining in the Yellowknife mining district as a sustainable endeavour because "the city of Yellowknife will long outlive the gold mines that it was founded on." By their count, the district has yielded 13.5 million ounces of gold and cumulative revenues of about $5.5 billion since 1938. The mines "converted the gold contained in the rocks underlying Yellowknife into a stream of highly significant cash flows" and "are responsible for much of the early 'built capital' in the city including ... hydro power developments ... and a significant amount of the downtown Yellowknife housing stock." They also note the (lesser) roles of government and civil society in wealth and infrastructure creation. Nowhere, however, do these authors mention that the Giant Mine had been depositing arsenic trioxide (collected from air-pollution control equipment) in underground chambers since 1951. In 1999, the mine's owners declared bankruptcy, and by the time the mine finally closed in 2004, 237,000 tonnes of arsenic dust had been stored in the mine, posing an extreme toxic threat as the water table started to rise. Following a contentious environmental assessment, the federal government planned to freeze the arsenic underground permanently using passive air-exchange technology at an initial estimated public cost of nearly $1 billion, an amount far exceeding the estimated $454 million (in 2002 dollars) in government revenues received during the entire life of the mine. Indeed, given that the site may have to be monitored and water pumped

Aerial view of Giant Mine, including tanks,
company-owned housing, and other buildings, Yellowknife, 1948.
From 1949 to 1951, the mine's roaster stack emitted over 7,400 kilograms
per day of arsenic trioxide into the local environment. Pollution controls
gradually reduced stack emissions until roasting ceased in 1999. Photo by
Henry Busse. Courtesy of Northwest Territories Archives, N–1979–052: 1947

indefinitely (barring a permanent solution involving the removal of the
arsenic), costs for perpetual care will mount over unimaginable periods of
time and might well exceed the total value of gold produced at the mine.
Although this is an extreme example and most mining companies today
are required to post some form of financial security to offset the cost of
remediation and monitoring, critics suggest that such levies may not fully
cover long-term liabilities or the ongoing health and environmental impacts
associated with mining.

Postclosure environmental issues at sites such as Giant Mine represent
only one of the many ways that mines maintain an "afterlife" after abandonment. Mines live on in human memories of work underground and in the

history and heritage of Canada's many unique mining towns. Mines may also awaken from the dead when waste ore, suddenly made valuable, lures the return of investment and human activity or when long-delayed efforts to repair the damage of former developments introduce new risks through the mobilization or long-term containment of toxic material. These resurrected or "zombie" mines are not simply legacies of the "bad old days" of poor environmental practices and lax regulation – they pose real threats to communities and landscapes, in the present and future, as people are forced to grapple with cleaning up and paying for degraded environments.

The so-called externalities associated with mineral development are not, of course, confined to mine sites and local environments. Just as people, capital, things, and energy converge at mine sites, so minerals and the byproducts of mining travel outward. Minerals and other materials are transported from sites through the chains of commodity production, marketing, and distribution. Where the ore goes matters. It matters because additional value (in Canada, or elsewhere) can potentially be captured when the mineral is processed into its elemental form or incorporated into finished products. But it also matters because of where and how the products of mining are ultimately used. These "downstream" impacts became clear when Canadian uranium production became entangled in the advent of nuclear warfare during the Second World War and Cold War. Canada's major uranium mines were located in remote areas of Northwest Territories, northern Saskatchewan, and Northern Ontario, but uranium mining had far-reaching environmental and geopolitical consequences. It led, for instance, to the widespread contamination of the landscape of Port Hope, Ontario, where the state-owned Eldorado company refined uranium oxide concentrates for the US military. In addition to supplying the Manhattan Project during the Second World War, Canadian uranium was sold to India in the 1970s (ostensibly for power development) and assisted that country's acquisition of nuclear weapons. Although debates in Canada have often focused on our failure to realize "added value" by processing primary resources before exporting them, the environmental impacts of mineral smelting have often been devastating – as residents who lived near major smelters at Rouyn-Noranda, Sudbury, or Trail can attest.

The Canadian mining industry has long relied on unfettered (indeed, subsidized) access to mineral frontiers to sustain its expansion and growth. It has fostered the expansion of capital and labour in a seemingly endless search for new minerals. But the industry has also carried with it often severe environmental, social, and economic consequences for people who lived near mines or mineral-processing facilities. As an industry that is sometimes promoted as a boon to remote regions, mining, because of its volatility and dependence on global markets, is a shaky foundation for building long-term sustainable communities. Although the industry has expanded its geographic reach and production rates, its claim that it is moving towards environmental sustainability can't stand up against local evidence and global trends pointing to declining ore grades, increasing waste production, and the long-term environmental costs of abandoned mines.

Sustainability indicators and programs such as Towards Sustainable Mining are now widely touted in Canadian (and international) mining circles. But questions remain about the utility and enforceability of these indicators and programs, the lack of hard targets for environmental performance, and the ability of these initiatives to account for the long-term consequences of past mining practices. A focus on intensity-based indicators (improvements in energy use and waste production per tonne of ore mined) rather than absolute reductions can result in improved environmental performance, but historical trends towards lower-grade ore have resulted in more and more ore being excavated. As a consequence, total energy use and waste production have increased.

One critic has suggested that sustainability reporting in the global mineral industry is a strategy companies use "to inoculate themselves against critique by converting these [sustainability] discourses into the premises of an audit culture, in which reform is simulated rather than enacted." To achieve sustainability, companies must acknowledge and address the environmental impact of mining practices and develop specific and demanding regulatory standards for the remediation of the landscapes surrounding abandoned mines. They will have to make concerted and sustained efforts to limit or eliminate heavy metal contamination, radiation, and acid mine drainage. It is one thing to say you are moving towards sustainable mining practices; it is quite another to establish the thresholds that must be crossed to achieve this goal.

Mining is central to the economies and ways of life of the developed world. Although minerals and metals account for a relatively small fraction of the Canadian economy (about 3.4 percent of GDP in 2012), mining remains a regionally significant industry, especially in the provincial norths and territories. Most Canadians are surrounded by mineral products: we have copper in our electric wires, our electricity is generated from coal or uranium, we use diamonds to show our commitment to a loved one, and our computers contain rare earth minerals. By contrast, for most of us, the environmental impacts of mining are hidden from our everyday lives, even though they are paradoxically massive in scope. If the mining industry is to achieve any meaningful degree of sustainability, both the producers and consumers of mineral products – that is, all Canadians – will have to face up to the environmental costs and legacies associated with this industry.

REFERENCES AND FURTHER READING

Much of the mining history of Canada has been written at the regional scale or focuses on a case study of a local mining centre, such as R. Cole Harris's account of Sandon in "Industry and the Good Life around Idaho Peak," in his *The*

Resettlement of British Columbia (Vancouver: UBC Press, 1998). For broader national trends in mining history, a wide range of current and historical statistics on mineral exploration, production, trade, and so on are available through the Natural Resources Canada website. Jeremy Mouat's *Metal Mining in Canada, 1840–1950* (Ottawa: National Museum of Science and Technology, 2000) contains an excellent overview (and bibliography) of mining technology in this period. D.A. Cranstone's *A History of Mining and Mineral Exploration in Canada and Outlook for the Future* (Ottawa: Natural Resources Canada, 2002) also contains some useful data on ore production rates and reserves. One of the earliest academic studies of mining in Canada is Harold A. Innis's *Settlement and the Mining Frontier* (Toronto: MacMillan, 1936), which traces the development of the Klondike and Kootenay regions and extols the potential of mining development along the Hudson Bay Railroad. The "highly-integrated advanced type" quote was drawn from its pages. Ironically, the geographer John Bradbury invoked Innis's insights to argue, in a series of papers, that iron mining along the Quebec-Labrador border had failed to produce a balanced and diversified industrial economy. The "isolation, community impermanence" (164) and "international corporate empire" (163) quotes are from his "Towards an Alternative Theory of Resource-Based Town Development in Canada," *Economic Geography* 55, 2 (1979): 147–66; "whiplash declines" is from "The Impact of Industrial Cycles in the Mining Sector: The Case of the Quebec-Labrador Region in Canada," *International Journal of Urban and Regional Research* 8, 3 (1984): 311–31. For works that add an analysis of the broad-scale environmental impacts of mining on northern environments, see Arn Keeling, "'Born in an Atomic Test Tube': Landscapes of Cyclonic Development at Uranium City, Saskatchewan," *Canadian Geographer* 54, 2 (2010): 228–52, and Liza Piper, *The Industrial Transformation of Subarctic Canada* (Vancouver: UBC Press, 2009).

Mining fits uncomfortably in the model of what R.A. Clapp called the resource cycle, with its implied potential for sustainability. Economic geographer Homer Aschmann's article, "The Natural History of a Mine," *Economic Geography* 46, 2 (1970): 172–89, suggests mines have natural cycles of development, renewal, and decline. Industry-driven versions of this mining-cycle model represent mining as, if not renewable, broadly sustainable. Examples include the Canadian-based Towards Sustainable Mining program and industry-supported publications such as Georgina Peachman's *101 Things to Do with a Hole in the Ground* (Cornwall, ON: Post-Mining Alliance, 2009). These initiatives derive in part from the industry's efforts to enhance its public image and acceptability, also known as its "social licence to operate," a phrase whose adoption by the industry is described in John R. Owen and Deanna Kemp's "Social Licence and Mining: A Critical Perspective," *Resources Policy* 38 (2013): 29–35. For critiques of the sustainable mining argument, see Ariana Waye, Denise Young, Jeremy P. Richards, and Joseph Doucet, "Sustainable Development and Mining: An Exploratory Examination of the Roles of Government and Industry," in *Mining, Society and a Sustainable World*, edited by J.P. Richards, 151–82 (Berlin: Springer, 2009), and Stuart Kirsch, "Sustainable Mining," *Dialectical Anthropology* 34 (2010): 87–93.

We drew on material about the fundamental historical relationship between declining ore grades and increasing environmental impacts from Timothy LeCain's masterful study *Mass Destruction: The Men and Giant Mines That Wired America and Scarred the Planet* (New Jersey: Rutgers University Press, 2009), and from a series of data-driven studies by Gavin Mudd's research team at Monash University, Australia. His analysis of Canadian mining trends is in "Historical Trends in Base Metal Mining: Backcasting to Understand the Sustainability of Mining" (paper presented at 48th Annual Conference of Metallurgists, Canadian Metallurgical Society, Sudbury, Ontario, August 2009), http://users.monash.edu.au/~gmudd/files/2009-CMS-03-Base-Metals.pdf. For the problem of abandoned mines in Canada, see W.O. Mackasey's report, "Abandoned Mines in Canada" (unpublished report prepared for MiningWatch Canada by WOM Geological Associates, 2000), and the Cal Data report, "Capacity Building for a National Inventory of Orphaned/Abandoned Mines in Canada" (prepared for National Orphaned and Abandoned Mines Initiative, 2005). We introduced the notion of zombie mines in "Zombie Mines and the (Over)burden of History," *Solutions Journal* 4, 3 (2013): 80–83.

For the application of the sustainable mining argument to the specific case of Giant Mine, see Warwick Bullen and Malcolm Robb, "Socio-economic Contribution of Gold Mining in the Yellowknife Mining District," 2004, available online. The comment on "built capital" is on page 5. For analysis of long-term environmental problems at Giant Mine, see Alternatives North, *From Despair to Wisdom: Perpetual Care and the Future of Giant Mine* (report on a community workshop, September 26–27, 2011), available online. The "inoculate themselves against critique" quote is from Kirsch, "Sustainable Mining," 87.

Wolves hunting elk
on the railway overpass at Banff, February 21, 2016.
Photo by Christopher Martin

EVERY CREEPING THING ...

Ken Cruikshank

READING HIS BIBLE ONE night during the London Conference that
framed the British North America Act, Leonard Tilley, one of the Fathers
of Confederation, was struck by the declaration of Psalm 72:8: "He shall
have dominion ... from sea to sea, and from the river unto the ends of the
earth." So, the story goes, Canada came to be characterized as a "Dominion"
rather than a "kingdom," and the new country found its motto – "A Mari
usque ad Mare." This account may be apocryphal, but it captures the nation-
building project envisaged in 1867: to acquire and maintain a continental
territory extending from the Atlantic to the Pacific and eventually to the
Arctic. Viewing the nation-building challenge from his New Brunswick
perspective, Tilley made sure that the BNA Act mandated construction
of a railway between Halifax and the St. Lawrence Valley. In the years
since, successive Canadian governments have supported efforts to facilitate
the flow of people, goods, and information from sea to sea, first through
the construction of transcontinental railways, then through the building
of an all-Canadian highway and pipeline, the creation of a national airline,
and the development of a sea-to-sea-to-sea microwave telecommunications
network. Tilley's "Dominion" has been realized by Canadians using technology to overcome geographical challenges.

It is no surprise, then, that Canadian scholars have become well known for taking transportation and communication seriously – and for thinking that everyone else should do so too. One Canadian, Harold Innis, gained international renown for developing the staples approach to economic history, which includes the idea that changes in transportation and communication technology shape and disrupt networks of trade in natural products. Later, Innis and another Canadian, Marshall McLuhan, acquired a global following as they sought to understand the broader social and cultural impacts of shifting forms of communication. Contrary to scholars who focused narrowly on the messages conveyed by various media, they contended that the materiality of any particular medium affects its social and cultural impact: "the medium is the message."

Neither Innis nor McLuhan thought much about a quite different materiality: the impact of communications on the natural world. Environmental scholars in other countries have explored the ecological footprints of various transportation technologies. Some, for example, have considered the role of the automobile in producing a new energy regime, in transforming the demand for and production of critical materials such as rubber, and in contributing to a new landscape of waste. American environmental historian William Cronon has extended the notion of an ecological footprint to consider the transformation of land and life wrought by the annihilation of space. His argument surely applies to Canada as well – that railway and telegraph technology made the abstraction and commodification of products possible and, in doing so, helped alienate the urban consumer from the ecological consequences of production.

There is another, equally important, way of thinking about communication and the material world. The St. Lawrence Seaway inadvertently transformed the aquatic environment of the Great Lakes by allowing ships from around the world to introduce entirely new and disruptive species, such as zebra mussels and round gobies. Focusing on such changes shifts our attention back to those transportation and communication networks that fascinated Innis but demands that we examine them from a different perspective. Ships pass through corridors, in the form of rivers, seaways, and canals. Trains and motor vehicles need corridors for their rails, roads, and bridges. Airplanes need runways. Telegraphs, telephones, and even cellphones also require a material network, including wires, cables, and towers. The transcontinental ambitions of our nation's leaders – and their collective efforts to ensure the mobility of people, goods, and information across the nation – have interacted and interfered with the mobility of the nonhuman natural world. In ways we are only now struggling to understand, our rights-of-way, our runways, and our telecommunication towers have affected – to paraphrase the book of Genesis in Tilley's Bible – the fish, fowl, and "every creeping thing that creepeth upon the earth."

To communicate over long distances and to create national networks, Canadians carved rail and roadways through the wilderness, far beyond the limits of their settlements. Political leaders supported the expansion of the railway network for almost a century, encouraging construction of some ninety-two thousand kilometres of track by 1935. The railway companies spent the rest of the twentieth century abandoning almost half of what had been built, retreating, in part, because of competition from motor vehicles. To support the use of those vehicles, governments expanded the road network throughout the twentieth century. Early in the twenty-first century, it was 1.4 million kilometres long – and this excludes great stretches of lesser, private roads. There are between six thousand and eight thousand kilometres of logging roads in Ontario's Algonquin Park alone.

Animals need corridors too. They move daily and seasonally to survive, responding to climate, to the changing availability and exhaustion of food sources, and to the movement of predators and prey. They disperse more permanently from one area to another as their habitat changes. One effect of this dispersal is to spread the gene pool and avoid inbreeding. Conservation biologists have become increasingly concerned to ensure that species can move as freely as possible between different natural areas. They emphasize the troubling consequences of isolation and the importance of travel and dispersal through corridors. Human rights-of-way have the potential to disrupt the corridors that animals need.

Building any right-of-way entails clearing plants and trees and compacting the soil – and often much more in the way of environmental change. To make rights-of-way more level, straighter, free of flooding, and generally more efficient for railways and motor vehicles, engineers raised them with ballast, lowered them by cutting through hills, and filled in wetlands, creeks, and ponds. Loggers cut down forests to make railway ties, utility poles, bridges, and guardrail posts. Then, to make these objects last longer, lumber companies treated the wood with creosote, a coal tar substance laced with polycyclic aromatic hydrocarbons (PAHs). Other manufacturers had used this same substance as an insecticide, herbicide, fungicide, and animal repellent in rope and canvas materials. Governments paved roads with another petroleum-based substance, bitumen, to reduce the friction and dust of driving. In the 1940s, they began applying salt to those impervious, paved roads in winter, to make driving safer. By the 1960s, local and provincial governments in Ontario had spread nearly twenty thousand tonnes of salt on Ontario roads each winter, and three to four times that amount by the end of the twentieth century. In short, human corridors of communication transformed environments by introducing novel and sometimes toxic materials – Environment Canada considered labelling road salt as a toxin in 2001 – and by altering the topography, hydrology, and the very nature of surface materials, soils, and water.

The novel ecologies produced by these interventions favoured some species over others. Roads allowed plants more resistant to salt, common reeds for example, to thrive and crowd out others. Rights-of-way created lengthy edge effects, exposing the forest floor to light and heat and changing the vegetation along these corridors. Earlier melting of winter snow made these spaces very attractive to animals, as they offered the earliest sources of food in spring. Rights-of-way also generated new pathways facilitating the travel and migration of certain species: in Nova Scotia, lynx made use of lightly used roads to migrate. Roads also created dangerous zones for others.

Open spaces offer little or no protection from predators. Some species – rabbits, hares, and rodents – are especially endangered by the lack of cover provided by sparse vegetation along rights-of-way. Many early railways ran through narrow corridors. By the end of the nineteenth century, however, the Canadian Pacific Railway required contractors to clear trees and stumps for at least fifty feet (fifteen metres) on both sides of the centre line of the railway as a practical measure to prevent trees from falling on the track. In the early twentieth century, government regulators responded to concerns about railway-induced forest fires by extending the zone to three hundred feet (ninety metres) on each side of the centre line. This fireguard had to be kept entirely free of trees, weeds, and other vegetation as well as "other inflammable materials." In practice, this frequently meant clearing more than a six-hundred-foot-wide (180 metre) area so that combustible materials cleared from the corridor could be accumulated beyond its specified limits. The wider the corridor became, the more it became a barrier to some species and an opportunity for others.

Railways and roads also introduced novel, bewildering, and increasingly large and fast predators – locomotives, trucks, and automobiles – that took their toll on mammals large and small and on other creatures. In the second half of the twentieth century, from 1951 to 1998, trains travelling in a region near Jasper collided with large animals twenty-seven times annually, and motor vehicles struck fifty large animals each year. Elk, deer, and moose – in that order – were the most frequent victims. In 1972, scientists studying roadkill along some 137 miles (220 kilometres) of gravel lanes, paved roads, and divided highways in southeastern Ontario identified other less noticed victims of fatal accidents. On average each day, motor vehicles took the lives of two birds, three herptiles such as frogs, snakes, salamanders, or turtles, and three small- or medium-sized mammals

Canadian Pacific Railway work crew laying track
in the Lower Fraser Valley, 1881. Rights-of-way opened spaces
that created obstacles to the mobility of some species and altered
vegetation within the neighbouring forest. These rights-of-way grew ever
wider as efforts were made to control the dangers of fire and wildlife.
Courtesy of the Royal BC Museum and Archives, Image A–07021

such as groundhogs, skunks, or chipmunks. On its own, this death toll had little impact on populations, but the new mechanical predators that stalked rights-of-way also reshaped behaviour. The 1972 study reported that reptiles and medium-sized mammals were most likely to be killed by fast-moving

A sign warning motorists of the danger of moose in Newfoundland.
Photo by Stefan Reicheneder

traffic on multilane highways, but that birds, amphibians, and smaller
mammals met their fate in greater numbers on two-laned paved highways
and roads. One reason for the difference was that smaller mammals and
amphibians (and birds such as the pinnated grouse, or greater prairie
chicken, perhaps) did not venture to cross the larger highways. They were
not the only ones: biologists tracking fifty-one male and female bears
in Banff National Park found that only five males ever crossed the Trans-
Canada Highway, and only one crossed it regularly. Only six males and
eight females crossed a much less busy secondary highway. As human-built
rights-of-way criss-crossed the land, as they became busier and wider, and
as encounters with old and new predators became more likely, animals
learned to stay away from them.

No wonder, then, that an early twentieth-century Indian agent in Alberta complained that a new railway running through the Stoney Reserve

was forcing Nakoda hunters to leave the reserve in search of game. Similarly, an Ontario game inspector reported that the coming of a railway to his area meant that local and visiting hunters were finding that deer and squirrels were now "extinct" and that muskrat and mink were "scarce." Roads were no better. Conservation biologists working in the 1990s discovered that fewer kinds of plants, birds, mammals, reptiles, and amphibians could be found within two kilometres of a local road than in the rest of the wetland. They wondered when this had started happening and began looking at old natural inventories and maps. The key event? The paving of the road in the middle of the twentieth century. Within ten years of paving, there were fewer species of birds, reptiles, and amphibians near the asphalt road; several decades later, plant diversity began to decline.

In the past few decades, road planners have paid more attention to the consequences, for the natural world, of the routes they develop, creating interest in questions of road ecology. This heightened sensitivity is most evident in efforts to facilitate animal mobility. When work began on widening the TransCanada highway through Banff National Park, local conservationists and road engineers built overpasses and underpasses – not for motor vehicles but for animals. Undoubtedly, concerns about the potential for more human collisions with large animals helped to justify the investment, but fencing along the highway and the creation of crossings also improved nonhuman corridors. Road construction crews built the first crossings in 1996, and by 2014 they had created six overpasses and thirty-nine underpasses designed to facilitate the movement of wildlife. Individual species gradually adapted to the new crossings, learning where they were and which form of crossing worked best. Grizzly bear crossings increased from seven in 1996 to over one hundred a decade later. The Ontario government built its first animal overpass when it expanded a stretch of highway through cottage country and, in other parts of the province, it built special fencing, underpasses, and culverts to counteract increasing road density. One of the more unusual crossings may be the one underneath a raised portion of a controversial expressway in the east end of Hamilton. The city hired engineers and biologists to design a series of seventeen posts that would facilitate the continuing movement of southern flying squirrels across their newly bisected valley. They have since added platforms as well as hiding places on the posts because the flying squirrels did not appear to be using the new crossing.

While Canadians struggled to reconcile their demand for vehicular rights-of-way with the natural environment, they also relied on a form of travel that created novel challenges. At the end of the Second World War, civilian airplanes carried over eight hundred thousand passengers through Canadian airports; by 2010, almost 78 million passengers flew through Canada's five busiest airports. While airlines did not need rights-of-way (other than flight paths to reduce the risks of midair collisions), they did require increasingly elaborate spaces for takeoff and landing. To some extent, these spaces created many of the same problems as rights-of-way: flattened landscapes, filled-in wetlands, and the introduction of disruptive substances into the landscape, including chemicals such as propylene glycol, which is required to de-ice airplanes in Canada's winter weather. Propylene glycol can be fatal if ingested by animals and, as runoff, it can deplete dissolved oxygen in nearby waters. Airport managers have reintroduced special wetlands at some airports to serve as catch basins and natural treatment plants for the runoff.

Shortly after the widespread adoption of the jet engine, owners and pilots worried about a particular form of interference from nature. When the movements of large birds or flocks of small birds crossed aircraft flight paths, they could damage planes and even cause them to crash. Between 1958 and 1962, Air Canada spent about $240,000 each year on parts repairs owing to bird strikes. Responding to industry and military concerns, the National Research Council struck a special committee on bird strikes in 1962. Safety could be improved and repair costs reduced by making planes more resilient, but researchers discovered that airports offered distinctive ecological spaces that heightened the probability of interactions with some birds. The wide-open spaces typical of airports kept many predators away, favouring the presence of gulls, doves, starlings, swallows, and sparrows who found good places to perch and nest on various airport structures. Starlings, robins, and gulls found excellent insect and earthworm feeding areas on closely cropped vegetation near runways. But allowing plants and grasses to grow was no solution, because they provided cover for smaller mammals such as mice that attracted raptors.

No one was thinking about birds when an airport was located on Sea Island in the Fraser River delta, an important resting and feeding point for birds migrating on the Pacific flyway. Settlers had already begun to alter the delta habitat by building dykes and developing farms over former marshland. Planes started using part of the island as an airfield in 1929, and two years later, the city acquired 475 acres for a municipal airport. By 1960, Vancouver International Airport controlled 3,600 acres on the island, although it only needed 1,000 acres for its operations.

Control was important, however, as the airport's managers tried to deal with the bird problem. Between 1963 and the opening of a modernized airport in 1968, managers removed all hedges, cut tall grass, cleaned out ditches, and smoothed out rough areas on the airport property. They eliminated many farms and restricted activities on others. They removed a local garbage dump and a series of old pilings on the river, and they covered major buildings to prevent nesting. They even considered covering the tidal flats with dredged sand. All of these efforts were intended to destroy bird habitat. Here and at other airports, managers used chemicals to rid the property of insects and worms, and wetlands or grasslands were destroyed. The number of birds struck by jets hardly threatened bird populations, but the efforts to prevent such strikes so dramatically altered the local habitat that birds were forced elsewhere to feed and nest.

In a wider context, some birds adapted well to urban development while others did not, just as some were assisted by conservation measures while

Air Canada Boeing 777–333(ER) C-FIVQ swarmed by birds, 2009.
Although this photo was taken near Heathrow Airport, the potential for birds
of varying species to interfere with the operation of jets is present at major
international airports everywhere, including Vancouver, whose airport
is located on the Pacific flyway. Courtesy of AirTeamImages

others were not. Bird populations changed dramatically in the last quarter of the twentieth century. Aerial insectivores and grassland birds declined dramatically. The number of ducks, geese, gulls, and various raptors increased. Some of the very birds that caused problems for aviation thrived and, for all of the environmental manipulation that took place near airports, the frequency of strikes continued to range between two and five for every ten thousand takeoffs or landings. This ratio is higher in Canada than in the United States (where there were 142,000 strikes between 1990 and 2013, including the encounter with Canada geese that forced a US Airways plane down in the Hudson River), and it is worse at some airports, such as Vancouver International, than others. Some airport managers, including at Toronto's Pearson airport, began using specially trained falcons to try to direct other birds away from flight paths. Late in 2017, Edmonton

International Airport conducted a three-month long experiment with "Robird," a drone built (at considerable cost) to emulate the hunting behaviour and mimic the appearance of a female falcon, in an effort to direct birds away from flight paths. "Sharing the skies" – as Transport Canada's guide to wildlife management at airports is called – has proved challenging for people and birds alike.

Increased use of rights-of-way and airports during the past 150 years went hand in hand with increasing use of telecommunications technology. For much of this period, the telegraph and telephone network contributed to and shared other rights-of-way. Following the Second World War, however, Canada's telephone companies faced new challenges. The volume of long-distance telephone calls outstripped both population and economic growth and threatened to overwhelm the thinly constructed system of copper wires and creosote-soaked poles. In the 1950s, the presidents of Bell Telephone of Canada and the Canadian Broadcasting Corporation championed the use of microwave frequencies to beam telephone messages and broadcast radio and television across the nation: just one microwave channel handled the equivalent of 1,200 individual telephone conversations, all at once. Canada's railways were also interested in the new technology. In 1958, Canada's various telephone companies and the CBC invested $50 million to construct a transcontinental microwave system. By 1967, the Canadian National and Canadian Pacific railways had collaborated to complete a second national system.

The microwave system appeared to free communication technology from its grounding in the material world. But not quite. To make the system work, companies had to construct microwave towers within "sight" of one another, about fifty kilometres apart: the first transcontinental spine depended on the construction of 139 microwave towers, and that number soon grew. These towers created their own new spaces and interference with the natural world. Towers took up a lot of space on the ground, required access to some power, and needed roads large enough to carry sizeable structures both for construction and ongoing maintenance. All of these spaces also required firebreaks, which required the clearing of large areas. Companies sought to economize and acquired spaces close to existing rights-of-way, but this was not always possible, particularly when beaming signals through the Canadian Rockies.

An assessment of the site of a microwave tower decommissioned in the 1990s reveals the new materiality of microwave communications. The railway companies constructed the Pyramid Mountain tower ten kilometres northwest of Jasper in 1963 as part of their microwave system. They leased enough land from Parks Canada to build a twelve-kilometre road through the wilderness, a garage site for snowplowing equipment within 250 metres of Pyramid Lake, and a diesel-fuelled tramline running from the base of the mountain to the summit, where they constructed the tower. They located the base of the tram within one hundred metres of a creek running into the lake and stored some fuel there. At the summit, they constructed the tower, a tram station, four above-ground diesel fuel storage tanks and a fifth underground tank. In maintaining the operations of the tower, they frequently dumped used crankcase oil at both the base and the summit. Ten years after the companies stopped using the tower, environmental consultants hired to help clean up the site still found elevated levels of xylene and hydrocarbons at both ends of the tram. Human communication had disrupted the habitats of marmots, pikas, and mountain goats.

Microwave technology does not require a lot of power, but companies used fuel to drive generators to light towers and ensure that they were visible to airplanes. The lights might have kept some birds from flying into microwave towers, but they confused others. Collisions increased when low-lying clouds, fog, smoke, or haze interacted with the lights to produce an illuminated area around the tower that disrupted normal navigational cues. Some birds responded by flying around the tower like moths to a flame until they either struck it, collided with other equally confused birds, or simply collapsed from exhaustion. Warblers, ovenbirds, and at least

Microwave radio tower and cable car, Pyramid Mountain,
Jasper, Alberta, 1964. A tower is not just a tower, as became evident from
environmental studies when the tower was decommissioned. Photographer unknown.
Courtesy of the Canada Science and Technology Museum, CN000320

eighteen other species are particularly prone to accidents at communication towers. More than half of those species are already endangered by other human changes to their habitat. The towers added one more threat.

In the early twenty-first century, some microwave towers and telephone systems are being replaced by optical fibres, cellphones, and other portable devices. These developments are transforming peoples' lives and cultural experiences in interesting and exciting ways. Many consumers embrace the freedoms offered by "mobile communications" but forget how much the technology remains grounded in the material world. Cellphones need a lot of antennae and a lot of places to put those antennae. In cities, they may be less than five hundred metres apart, and even in the best, flattest, most open countryside, they cannot be separated by much more than fifty kilometres. Initially, antennae could be sited about forty metres above the ground in urban areas, and communications companies often made use of existing structures, such as stadium light poles, water towers, and especially rooftops, rather than new towers. But the extension of ever-longer cellular communications corridors depends on the construction of more and more towers, some of them up to 125 metres high.

That's what the people of a small community thirty kilometres up the Ottawa River from the nation's capital discovered in the early 2010s. Communications company Videotron Quebec planned to erect an eighty-two-metre tall telecommunications tower near homes and right beside a nature preserve in Pontiac. Members of the community became concerned that the tower would endanger migratory birds using the preserve and undermine efforts to reintroduce the endangered eastern loggerhead shrike to the area. Although Videotron dodged a formal environmental assessment, it could not ignore community concerns: the company was soon looking for a different location. It found another on a farm a few kilometres away, equally unpopular with the local community, but farther from the nature preserve. For both the people of Pontiac and Videotron, the conflict illustrated just how much mobile communications depended on immobile and potentially troublesome structures.

The current communications revolution, like all those before it, has the potential to disrupt wildlife and fisheries habitat and interfere with the mobility of "every creeping thing that creepeth upon the earth." Nor is this revolution replacing all of the earlier rights-of-way and runways created to move people and goods from sea to sea to sea. As Canadians come to value biodiversity and ecological resilience and seek to restrain their dominion over nature, they will need to recognize and mitigate the inevitable environmental costs of their transportation and communication networks.

REFERENCES AND FURTHER READING

When Graeme Wynn and Colin Coates asked me to write an essay on communications and the nature of Canada, I immediately thought of key works that might send this essay in many different directions. The early books and essays of Harold Innis explored changing human interactions with and exploitation of the natural world in northern North America and attended to the role of transportation technology. His later works offered a meditation on the significance of changes in communication to the development of human civilizations and influenced the communications theorist, Marshall McLuhan. William Cronon's *Nature's Metropolis: Chicago and the Great West* (New York: W.W. Norton, 1991) brilliantly connects railways and telegraphs to commodification and, hence, to fundamental changes in human interactions with nature in the American west and northeast. Wolfgang Schivelbusch's *The Railway Journey: The Industrialization of Time and Space in the Nineteenth Century* (Berkeley: University of California Press, 1986) encouraged subsequent scholars to think about the cultural experience of new transportation technology, while more specific studies such as David Louter's *Windshield Wilderness: Cars, Roads, and Nature in Washington's National Parks* (Seattle: University of Washington Press, 2006) have connected transportation to ideas about nature.

Although I clearly have lifted a phrase from McLuhan, four works more directly influenced the eventual direction I took. Graeme Wynn's chapter on "corridors of modernization" in his *Canada and Arctic North America: An Environmental History* (Santa Barbara, CA: ABC Clio, 2007) was suggestive, and I was further inspired to think along these lines by journalist Jeff Alexander's fine *Pandora's Locks: The Opening of the Great Lakes–St. Lawrence Seaway* (East Lansing: Michigan State University Press, 2009), which extends and expands upon Wynn's ideas about the St. Lawrence Seaway as a corridor for invasive species. As a result of reading Wynn and Alexander, I found myself particularly interested in those essays that discussed the impact of transportation on wildlife and vegetation in the important edited collection *The Ecology of Transportation: Managing Mobility for the Environment*, edited by John and Julia N. Davenport (Dordrecht: Springer, 2006). I found two essays particularly helpful and stimulating: Marcel P. Huuser and Anthony P. Clevenger's "Habitat and Corridor Function of Rights-of-Way," 233–54, and Tom Kelly and John Allan's "Ecological Effects of Aviation," 5–24.

I then began to think along these lines in relation to different modes of transportation and communication over time. For a quick visual overview, and knowing how much transportation and communication systems lend themselves to mapping, I reviewed the *Atlas of Canada*, beginning with the first edition (1906) and ending with the sixth edition (1999–2009). The atlases are all conveniently located online at Natural Resources Canada's Map Archives.

And then I started to do a lot more reading. On railways and their rights of way, J. Gordon Nelson and A.R. Byrne's "Man as an Instrument of Landscape Change: Fires, Floods, and National Parks in the Bow Valley," *Geographical Review* 56, 2 (1966): 226–38; Stephen Pyne's *Awful Splendour: A Fire History of Canada* (Vancouver: UBC Press, 2008); and Heather Anne Longworth's "Tracks, Tunnels and Trestles: An Environmental History of the Construction of the Canadian Pacific Railway" (master's thesis, University of Victoria, 2009) all point towards floods and fires and efforts to prevent them. On roads, the seminal *Road Ecology: Science and Solutions*, edited by Richard T.T. Forman and colleagues (Washington, DC: Island Press, 2003) led me to many Canadian studies. Most notably, see D.J. Oxley, M.B. Fenton, and G.R. Carmody, "The Effects of Roads on Populations of Small Mammals," *Journal of Applied Ecology* 11, 1 (1974): 51–59; C. Scott Findlay and Jeff Houlihan, "Anthropogenic Correlates of Species Richness in Southeastern Ontario Wetlands," *Conservation Biology* 11, 4 (1997): 1000–9; and C. Scott Findlay and Josée Bourdages, "Response Time of Wetland Biodiversity to Road Construction on Adjacent Lands," *Conservation Biology* 14, 1 (2000): 86–94. On bears, see M.L. Gibeau and S. Herrero, "Roads, Rails, and Grizzly Bears in the Bow River Valley, Alberta," in *Proceedings of the International Conference on Ecology and Transportation*, edited by G.L. Evink, 104–8 (Tallahassee: Florida Department of Transportation, 1998). William Lowry briefly discusses the impact of roads on national parks in Canada in *The Capacity for Wonder: Preserving National Parks* (Washington, DC: Brookings Institute, 1994). There are several government- or industry-sponsored studies that gather national information on collisions with large animals, including L.P. Tardif and Associates Inc., *Final Report: Collisions Involving Motor Vehicles and Large Animals in Canada* (Ottawa: Transport Canada, Road Safety Directorate, 2003), and Ward G.M. Vanlaar, Kari E. Gunson, Stephen W. Brown, and Robyn D. Robertson, *Wildlife Collisions in Canada: A Review of the Literature and Compendium of Existing Data Sources* (Ottawa: Traffic Injury Research Foundation, 2012). The mapping and related work in Adam Fenech, Brent Taylor, Roger Hansell, and Graham Whitelaw, *Major Road Changes in Southern Ontario, 1935–1995: Implications for Protected Areas* (Toronto: Integrated Mapping Assessment Project, University of Toronto, 2000) proved invaluable. *Safe Passages: Highways, Wildlife, and Habitat Connectivity*, edited by Jon P. Beckmann, Anthony P. Clevenger, Marcel P. Huijser, and Jodi A. Hilty (Washington, DC: Island Press, 2010) contains an essay on the Banff wildlife crossings and an extensive bibliography of related work, including numerous works whose lead author is Anthony P. Clevenger.

On aviation, H. Blokpoel's *Bird Hazards to Aircraft: Problems and Prevention of Bird/Aircraft Collisions* (Ottawa: Canadian Wildlife Service, 1976) is essential, and the significance of airports in his analysis is updated and extended in B. Mackinnon, ed., *Sharing the Skies: An Aviation Industry Guide to the Management of Wildlife Hazards* (Ottawa: Transport Canada, 2001). Two master's theses separated by almost thirty years, D.R. Halladay's "Avian Ecology as It Relates to the Bird Hazard Problem at Vancouver Airport" (University of British Columbia, 1968) and Sharla M. Daviduik's "Management of Birds at Vancouver International Airport" (Simon Fraser University, 1999), convinced me to focus more on Vancouver Airport, although I also looked at ecological studies related to the "new Toronto airport" and Mirabel in the 1970s. See Transport Canada, *Ecology and the New Toronto Airport* (Ottawa: Transport Canada, 1972) and Pierre

Dansereau, Peter Brooke Clibbon, and Gilles Paré, *Atlas EZAIM: Écologie de la zone de l'aéroport international de Montréal* (Montreal: Presses de l'Université de Montréal, 1975).

On communication towers, Masten Brolsma and Court Sandau's *Decommissioning of Pyramid Mountain Microwave Facility* (Calgary: Jacques Whitford, 2005) helped me think through a number of issues of materiality. Travis Longcore and colleagues summarize a wide number of studies on communication towers and birds in "Avian Mortality at Communication Towers in the United States and Canada: Which Species, How Many, and Where?," *Biological Conservation* 158 (2013): 410–19. There have been numerous small controversies about cellphone towers; the one at Pontiac happened to be well documented owing to James Riordan's activism and letters to the government, including Petitions 301 and 301B in the environmental petitions catalogue on the Auditor General's website, and his submission to Industry Canada's consultation on its tower siting procedures.

"WHAT WILL HE GROW TO?"

Coal and Steam
consider the potential of electricity, from *Punch*, June 25, 1881.
Courtesy of Toronto Public Library

THE POWER OF CANADA

Steve Penfold

I N 1989, THE FEDERAL department of Energy, Mines and Resources published *Energy: The Power of Canada*, a short but impressive volume. It tells the story of Canadian energy. Wood, coal, petroleum, and hydro receive their due, in succession, carrying the story from the colonial era to its late twentieth-century culmination in an emerging "multiple fuels era." In a hundred pages, the book offers optimistic accounts of technological progress, industrial research, commercial innovation, and national growth. It is glossy and colourful, filled with photographs that draw on almost every imaginable cliché of the machine and the garden: an offshore oil rig is set against the red sky at dusk, and flip the page to a maple leaf covered in glistening raindrops. This is not a critical account. As a publication of the federal government, it wears its nationalism prominently and honestly, celebrating the increasing efficiency of Canadian industry and detailing energy-saving improvements to homes. Its very title hints at this boosterish approach and Marcel Masse, the incumbent minister, reinforced his department's self-serving message when he remarked, in the volume's preface, that it was "impossible to understand Canada or imagine its future without knowing something about energy." Indeed, Masse continued, the country's "chronological, constitutional and to some extent emotional

Energy and the human conquest of nature,
a British Columbia Electric Railway logo. The designer of this
logo, Vancouverite J.D. Beatson, experimented with different forms,
seeking a "virile, symbolical design, emblematical of 'ELECTRIC ENERGY,'
the motive force giving Transportation, Light, Heat, Power."
Courtesy of British Columbia Hydro and Power Authority
(BC Hydro), H0096/2

history ... [had] its parallel in the exploitation and discovery of different kinds of fuel."

Such claims demand attention, and there are many good reasons to pay close attention to this book. Its title alone encourages further reflection. The play on *energy* and *power* assumes a relationship between the social and the material; the possessive *of Canada* suggests a particular view of national ownership and sovereignty; the word *Canada* itself presupposes a single geographic space. Taken together, the three key words that form the title of this book speak to the inseparability of energy and social development, and I use them here to clarify and extend the uncomplicated story it offers, first, by examining the modern processes that transform nature into energy for human consumption; second, by exploring the inherently political and social qualities of energy; and, finally, by suggesting that the history of energy in Canada can be framed by national boundaries but is not determined by them. Overall, this is to emphasize that energy (like other resources) is a socionatural creation: it is embedded in the environment but requires human actions to mobilize invention, development, and institutions to realize its potential. At its most basic, energy is nature dominated and transformed.

In Canada, as elsewhere, modern energy began when humans asserted dominion over nature. "For industrial man," the Royal Commission on Energy claimed almost six decades ago, energy supplies "are the orb and sceptre that more than anything else represent the degree of his sovereignty over nature." This view was widely shared across space and time. The specific metaphors could change – with oil boosters speaking the language of extraction and hydro developers using words such as *harness* – but everyone agreed that nature was just waiting for human use and ingenuity. "Because of its particular climate and topography," Quebec premier Robert Bourassa famously wrote in his account of the James Bay Project, "Quebec is a vast hydroelectric plant in-the-bud and every day millions of potential kilowatt-hours flow downhill and out to sea. What a waste!"

Overcoming distance was another powerful dynamic in Canadian energy history. Before about 1850, key sources of energy – wind, water, flame, muscle – were employed close to where they were produced. This imposed important limits on human potential, shaping settlement patterns, economic development, and even social formations. Industries clustered near sources of flowing water; communities came together around wind- or water-driven gristmills; humans traversed distance by knowing nature and their own bodies. By contrast, modern power reached out. Eugene Holman, the president of Standard Oil of New Jersey, made this point clearly to the Empire Club of Canada in April 1951: "There is no relation between the places where oil is found and where it is used," he noted. "Oil is found where nature put it. It is consumed where populations have concentrated and industry flourishes." In Canada, transportation systems had to transcend particularly vast spaces.

Holman was speaking four years after the iconic discovery of oil at Leduc in 1947 – really, the beginning of Alberta's history as a petrostate – but that discovery would have been meaningless without reliable connections to markets. Pipelines soon moved oil east and west out of the province. These were massive projects. The Trans Mountain linked Alberta to Vancouver and Seattle across seven hundred miles of mountains and rivers, cleared a fifty-foot strip through forests and valleys, and required over one hundred thousand welds to make the pipe. If a vast territory caused great difficulties, it also attracted overheated rhetoric. "All the latest weapons employed by engineers in modern pipeline construction converge on the theatres of war," one Canadian Broadcasting Corporation story declared. "A squad of brush commandos armed with saws and axes start a daily skirmish ... The enemy, one by one, toppling to cries of Timber! The stumps lie like tombstones in a forest graveyard."

Giant projects produced big transformations. Hydro engineers blew up tons of rock, moved massive piles of earth, and transformed rivers into lakes. The High Arrow Dam in British Columbia, commissioned in 1968, raised water levels around the town of Castlegar by thirty-six feet, flooded over twenty-five thousand acres of land, and displaced two thousand human and countless nonhuman residents of the area. In 1974, Quebec's massive James Bay Project included the diversion of three rivers into La Grande, more than doubling its normal flow. The village of Fort George was relocated, and the largest dam on that project was almost five hundred metres long.

Oil companies deployed different technologies to similarly striking effect. The closest equivalent to the monumental presence of the big dam was the offshore rig (the largest towered more than one hundred metres above the sea) and the Alberta oil sands (where development disturbed over eight hundred square kilometres of land by 2013). Long before these big projects, in the years after Leduc, Alberta farmers had complained that oil companies cut fences, stripped crops, and carelessly allowed wells to leak oil and salt water. Pipelines also leaked and burst: between 1961 and 2013, the Trans Mountain experienced eighty-one spills totalling almost 6 million litres of oil. The causes were multiple – technological failure, acts of nature, and human error – and in many ways followed inevitably from the complexity and scale of the pipeline system.

For all the epic language, energy moved forward through a series of banal – even boring – processes. Energy sources needed to be developed: technology installed, scientific knowledge formed, labour deployed, raw nature processed into useable forms. Engineers, scientists, planners, and entrepreneurs engaged nature in multiple ways, but dominion was implicit in deeds, both in the meaning of acts (as technical problems to be solved, projects to be built, and so on) and ownership (rights and powers to be leased, bought, and sold). Similarly, while energy capitalists built vast networks across space, they also transcended the more banal distance between the gasoline pump and your car or between the electricity grid and your computer. Most Canadians experience energy as electric sockets, not as eloquent speeches. Utility companies often sold appliances as forms of domestic liberation, and car manufacturers promoted the freedom of speed and individual mobility, but technologies that started as exciting and transformative soon became normal, part of a common-sense landscape of power that set the terms of Canadian life.

SUMMER FREEDOM ⚱ ⚱ ⚱ ⚱ ⚱

AWAY FROM THE KITCHEN

PLAN to spend more time in leisure and out-of-door sports during these lovely days. An electric range offers the solution to the many exhausting hours spent in a sweltering kitchen.

Electric cookery means finger-tip control, speedy and unvarying heat at the turn of a switch is yours at any time of the day or night. No wood or coal to lug or pile —no stoking—no filth and ashes—no red hot stove top to lean over. Low cost—less than 1c per meal per person.

Above is shown the all-enamel cabinet model Hotpoint with automatic oven heat control, offered at $143.85. Only $8.75 down delivers it to your kitchen—the balance will be spread over a term of 18 months in the form of additions to your monthly light bills. This and dozens of other lovely ranges are on display at all B. C. Electric stores—call and see them!

COOK ELECTRICALLY

British Columbia Electric Railway Co. Ltd.

"Summer Freedom," *Utility Topics,* August 1931.
Electricity supposedly offered cleaner and more efficient energy to homemakers. In fact, women were often reluctant to embrace this new technology in the kitchen. Courtesy of BC Hydro

In this sense, technological success was often no better in environmental terms than failure. Probably the most ubiquitous "spill" in the petroleum commodity chain occurs at the end of the tailpipes on millions of Canadian cars. By 1972, Toronto cars alone spewed over four hundred thousand tonnes of carbon monoxide every year; between 1990 and 2007, greenhouse gas emissions from private vehicles in Canada increased at twice the rate of the population. Methylmercury, which enters the food chain through reservoirs, is an analogous result of energy "success" in hydro.

Those taken-for-granted technological events nonetheless occurred at the end of an energy system that remained profoundly, if only partially, natural. The beginning point of almost all this useable energy is the sun. Plants use photosynthesis to grow, producing calories for direct consumption (think grain) or indirect use (think grain fed to a dairy cow that gives milk). Other plants produce fuel for burning. An energy historian looks at a forest and sees solar energy being stored in combustible trees, edible plants, and equally edible animals eating those plants. Modern fossil fuels are simply thousands of years of this process put underground for many more thousands of years: coal is "the subterranean forest" and oil the remains of ancient marine life, both fossilized by years of oxygen deprivation, bacterial work, and decay. The big transition from biomass to fossil fuels hardly reversed these basic material facts. It simply allowed Canadians to exploit millennia of the same energetic process buried underground. The sun fuels wind and hydro power as well: it produces differential heat and pressure so that air flows from place to place. That airflow can spin windmills or cause evaporation, which ultimately provides the falling water that hydro engineers capture in their dams and turbines; both processes produce electricity. And since nuclear and geothermal still represent a small fraction of both world and Canadian energy production, we remain "children of the sun."

Even as vast systems transformed solar capital into useable energy flows, many material and natural dynamics remained. In the most obvious sense, energy development is structured by the natural endowments of a place. Many Canadian regions, including coal-rich Nova Scotia, embraced the secular religion of progress through electricity – but few, including Nova Scotia, had good and consistent sources of falling water. Even today, when the grid connects Nova Scotia to hydro sites in other places, most of the province's electricity (about 60 percent) comes from coal-fired thermal plants. Similarly, the process of transcending distance relied on a series of foundational natural facts. On the one hand, fossil fuels move long distances because of their energy density. On the other, oil, gas, and electricity move easily because they flow. Density and flow remain the natural foundation of modern energy. Technology and science might adjust those basic facts – as with, say, the chemical thinning of the tar sands before transport – but they can never fully transcend them.

Moreover, development spaces are themselves subject to natural processes. Water seeps into a coal mine and slowly floods the pit. For companies, water was a nuisance not a commodity, yet removing it was a necessary result of engaging nature to make energy. Managers deployed pumps, pipes, labour, and energy to "mine" water and haul it to the surface. In Nova Scotia, technological systems often hauled much more water than coal. Nor could "natural" processes always be controlled. "Man and machine" might win the "war" against nature (in the words of the CBC's report on Trans Mountain), but the environment waged ongoing guerilla warfare against occupying forces. The oft-quoted lament "blood on the coal" spoke clearly to the inability of technological systems to control the geologic or energetic processes of the mine – rocks bumped and fell, while gas and coal powder explosively transcended the dominion of capital and labour, often with deadly results. Similarly, frost could break a pipeline, while seeping water caused erosion and cracking. The consequences could be extreme. In 1957, frost ruptured a gas line near a house in Oakville, Ontario. The owner, Ralph Clark, lit a cigarette in the kitchen, "and an explosion hurled him 20 feet into the next room." Clark's predicament revealed at once the transcendence of distance (systems brought distant gas to the Ontario town, where it could heat houses or blow them up) and the limits of technology (pipes remained vulnerable to various natural processes). Cracking, like energy development, stood at the literal and figurative intersection of nature and technology. Making nature into energy, then, was never just a matter of asserting dominion.

Nature is transformed through a series of social, political, and economic relationships. Modern forms of energy allow humans to engage with the world in new ways. Light pushes back darkness; artificial heat overcomes winter cold; industrial processes are sped up. Some of the most poetic rhetoric about the power of energy has celebrated the transcendence of distance. "We have seen the power of steam suddenly dry up the Atlantic to less than half its breadth," wrote one British commentator in 1839, an idea that would be echoed in reference to future transportation technologies such as railways, cars, and airplanes, all of which substituted mechanical for organic work and converted natural obstacles from sweat and effort to smoke and vibration. Yet it was not just the natural energy content of coal that compressed distance; that trans-Atlantic ship moved because its owners organized energy and labour into a system that had a single goal and direction. "Coal meant power in the physical, economic and political sense," G.W. Taylor wrote in his history of British Columbia mining: "Countries or individuals who owned or developed coal deposits became the world's industrial leaders."

Systems and networks define modern energy. Drilling and mining go deep, enormous dams cut across vast rivers, and grids of wires and pipes connect production to consumption. Development at this scale requires massive investments and ongoing coordination, and in a capitalist system these are generally left to big business.

Nova Scotia coal eventually fell under the influence of Montreal and American financiers, while in the twentieth century, oil and electricity were dominated by enormous companies such as Montreal Light and Power and Imperial Oil (itself a subsidiary of the more massive Standard Oil of New Jersey, one of the "Seven Sisters" that controlled 85 percent of global petroleum reserves and 88 percent of Canada's refining capacity in 1940). Energy systems always left space for small players, like self-employed electricians who installed sockets or the petty entrepreneurs who opened gas stations. But the actions of such minor operators found meaning only within the "networks of power" they inhabited.

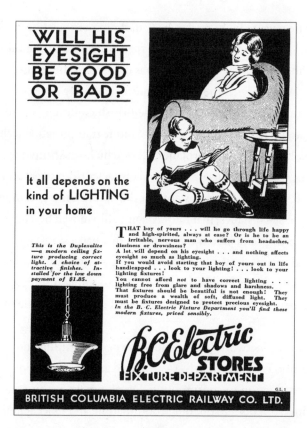

"Will his eyesight be good or bad?," *Utility Topics,* April 1931.
Improving on nature and reshaping humankind with electricity.
Courtesy of BC Hydro

Governments often got involved at a large scale as well. Starting in 1906 with Ontario Hydro, public companies in many provinces became developers and distributors of power, while various governments became involved at different points in oil, coal, and nuclear power. Governments also supported distance-spanning technologies, coordinating pipeline development, spurring rural electrification, and managing social and political conflict. At times, state action tried to impose order on frenzied and inefficient development. In the 1920s, governments began experimenting with petroleum conservation laws to curtail overdrilling and other wasteful practices, rationing production to save capitalists from themselves.

In a more fundamental sense, the whole energy system began with political choices. The early development of oil in the West operated in a context where law and custom facilitated both European settlement and resource development. Property was divided: homesteaders received surface title, but governments (first federal, then provincial after 1930) retained most subsurface rights, which were leased to individuals and companies under shifting terms. Of course, it was hardly possible to separate surface and subsurface in practice since oil companies needed to alter the agricultural landscape to actually drill. Conflict between farmers and drillers was endemic.

Indeed, the politics of development often meant managing conflict. "People in the way" often objected, though resistance more often altered or delayed plans than blocked them entirely. Alberta farmers framed their grievances in terms of financial loss and within moral economies of land and community, but when the Alberta government set up an Arbitration Board in 1947, it aimed to facilitate development.

In the 1960s, rural British Columbians objected to hydro developments on the Arrow Lakes – not the fact of power development so much as the form it took, which sought to remake rather than reinforce community geographies and did not compensate for losses of land that were social and emotional. From a rather different direction, the Cree launched a similar critique of Hydro-Québec's projects at James Bay in the 1960s and 1970s, eventually blunting the hardest edge of energy colonialism by forcing compromise on key terms of timing, compensation, and control. In energy history, it is never easy to distinguish environmental and social consequences.

Nature played a part in energy conflicts. The underground landscape of coal mining endowed miners with considerable power at key moments. Seams ran deep underground, and (until at least the 1920s) coal was mined in small rooms with primitive technologies. Companies depended on workers whom they could not supervise effectively. These environmental conditions sustained (though did not necessarily create) the miner's sense of independence. Even water became a political resource. During the great Nova Scotia coal strikes of the 1920s, trade unionists debated the disposition of water pumps. Radicals such as J.B. McLachlan endorsed a "100 percent strike," shutting down the pumps and letting the mines flood.

More moderate miners were prepared to shut down the mines but thought flooding them too extreme. In coal mines, nature was transformed and exploited but remained present in multiple ways: tunnels became artificial rivers, and water (as much as coal) became a tool of social conflict. While other energy conflicts expressed different forms of natural politics, the fate of the pits became a function of all the main strands of energy history: geology, hydrology, technology, and ideology.

What, in the end, does all this have to do with Canada? At various points in its history, Canada has looked somewhat distinctive in energy terms: at the end of the Second World War, it was a "hydro-electric superpower"; today, it is an aspiring titan in unconventional sources of petroleum (the oil sands). In a broader sense, we took much longer to navigate the transition from biomass to fossil fuel than many other countries. Still, on all the most fundamental questions, Canadian energy history seems in line with the story of most industrialized or industrializing countries over the twentieth century. Canadians have more territory, more rivers, and more bitumen-encrusted sand than many other nations, but we have shared much with other developed parts of the world: the sense that nature should be used and developed, the gradual embrace of fossil fuels and big hydro, the need to build connections across space, and the underexamined fact that massive energy flows are the foundation of the modern good life. Indeed, if the sun is the ultimate source of almost all useable power, then the globe would be the most logical starting point for energy history, but because technological, economic, and political systems can capture energy so differently, we would still need to account for the particularities of place.

By what act of historical imagination should that place be Canada? National dreams have been common in Canadian energy history, but they have never gone very well. As early as the 1860s, Canadians struggled with the problem of what historian John McDougall calls a "national policy" for fuel. Nova Scotia politicians hoped Confederation would increase coal shipments to lucrative central Canadian markets. During the First World War, when Ontario faced wintertime "coal famines" as a consequence of large coal strikes in Pennsylvania, it petitioned the federal government to mandate economical transport between the Maritimes and central Canada. In the 1950s, when technological progress made ultra-long-distance electricity lines possible, many planners and politicians articulated dreams of a national power grid, which would ensure stable supplies and bind the country together. At the same time, pipeline building consumed Parliament, and the federal government eventually became committed to an all-Canadian distribution route for natural gas. Long before the infamous National Energy Program of 1980 – a series of federal policies that aimed to Canadianize the oil industry in the name of security of supply and sharing of benefits – pan-Canadian dreams of power animated politicians and public alike.

A truly pan-national energy system was never built. For all its vast nature, Canada has always imported energy (not to mention capital, technology, and know-how), largely because American and overseas sources remained geographically convenient and economically viable. It was, after all, striking miners in Pennsylvania who threatened Ontario's coal supplies in the 1910s and 1920s, just as it was politicized Middle East producers who deployed the oil weapon in 1973 (and 2015–16), and an American circuit breaker that plunged central Canada into a blackout in 2003. Although energy and transmission systems connect disparate places to one another, the nation still lacks a direct sea-to-sea electricity connection, partly because the provinces prefer regional and continental links to nationalist projects.

Canada's pipeline system also remains a hybrid of national dreams and geographic realities. The federal government ensured that gas lines would follow an all-Canadian route north of the Great Lakes (with lines to the United States as well), but pipelines never succeeded in delivering Alberta's gas farther than Montreal, and the National Oil Policy that governed marketing after 1960 explicitly divided the country at the Ottawa Valley, assigning points west to Alberta oil and points east to cheaper overseas supplies. Finally, the political and economic failure of the National Energy Program – dismantled even before it was completely implemented – remains a touchstone of bad energy policy today, a paradigm of oppressive Ottawa policies imposed on unwilling energy-rich provinces.

The failure of these national dreams, like energy development itself, was both natural and social. In the first instance, nature endowed different parts of the country with different kinds and quantities of resources. Canadian supplies of coal lay in the west and east, far from the large markets in the centre, which were easily served by large fields in nearby Pennsylvania. Oil was also unevenly distributed, ensuring some Canadian places would be producers and some consumers. Even electricity, which seems like a single form of energy when distributed through the grid, can be traced back to different natures across the country. Today, British Columbia relies mostly on hydro, Saskatchewan on coal, and Ontario on nuclear power.

Yet such natural differences also take their meaning from politics. Alberta's oil only became a Canadian problem because nineteenth-century dreams of a continental empire – a Dominion stretching from sea to sea to sea – were successful, often over the objections of various Indigenous people and expansionist Americans.

Moreover, the political creation that made this transcendent Dominion – Confederation – possible after 1867 set up an institutional structure that made natural differences into political conflicts. The British North America Act assigned natural resources to the provinces and interprovincial commerce to Ottawa (though Alberta, Saskatchewan, and Manitoba did not get control of their resources until 1930). Yet modern energy had to be both made and moved – it required both asserting dominion and transcending distance – so provincial and federal powers could hardly be kept separate in practice. National dreams have often failed, but energy development remains profoundly federal in character, with Ottawa present at almost every turn and intergovernmental conflict almost inevitable. Canada was never a homogeneous energy space, but neither was it an empty lot where global forces simply played out; federal institutions shaped energy conflict in important ways.

Although John A. Macdonald imagined a dominant federal government, the BNA Act did not grant anyone jurisdiction over the sun. Canadian energy history has never been much more than a particular version of a much larger international story. Region and province seemed more powerful on the ground than any national frame, partly because Canada's borders remain an arbitrary political imposition over a number of distinct geophysical zones while provinces retain crucial powers over natural resources. Perhaps it is best to see Canadian energy history as socionatural but only partly national. Energy remains a hybrid of material, environmental, political, and social dynamics. Big concepts such as dominion produce evocative images and quotations, but even acts of domination remain embedded in natural systems, just as projects of transcendence require multiple engagements with the environment. But neither the social nor natural dynamics of power lead us very clearly to the nation. In one sense, Marcel Masse was right: it is impossible to understand Canada without knowing something about energy. What we should know, however, is not that energy is the power of Canada but that energy is a hybrid of domination and limits, human action and natural facts, with few transcendent truths to make life easy for nationalists or historians.

REFERENCES AND FURTHER READING

Key surveys of international energy history include Rolf Peter Sieferle, *Subterranean Forest: Energy Systems and the Industrial Revolution* (London: White Horse Press, 2001); Alfred W. Crosby Jr., *Children of the Sun: A History of Humanity's Unappeasable Appetite for Energy* (New York: Norton, 2006); and Vaclav Smil, *Energy in World History* (Boulder: Westview Press, 1994). For Canada, see Richard Unger and John Thistle, *Energy Consumption in Canada in the 19th and 20th Centuries* (Naples: Consiglio Nazionale delle Ricerche, Istituto di Studi sulle Società del Mediterraneo, 2013) and R.W. Sandwell, ed., *Powering Up Canada: Essays on the History of Heat, Light and Work from 1600* (Montreal and Kingston: McGill-Queen's University Press, 2016).

The Marcel Masse quotation is from the preface to *Energy: The Power of Canada* (Markham, ON: Fitzhenry and Whiteside, 1989). The Royal Commission on Energy quotation, from 1959, is cited in Earle Gray, *Forty Years in the Public Interest: A History of the National Energy Board* (Vancouver: Douglas and McIntyre, 2000), 106, and the Robert Bourassa quotation is from his book, *Power from the North* (Scarborough, ON: Prentice Hall Canada, 1985), 4. The Eugene Holman quotation is from his 1951 address to the Empire Club of Canada: "Freedom and Energy Go Together," *The Empire Club of Canada Addresses,* April 19, 1951. The quotations about the Trans Mountain come from Neill Wilson and Frank J. Taylor, *Building of the Trans Mountain, Canada's First Oil Pipeline across the Rockies* (Vancouver: Trans Mountain Oil Pipe Line, 1954) and from "Trans Mountain Pipeline to Carry Alberta Oil to Vancouver," *CBC Digital Archives,* 1954, http://www.cbc.ca/player/play/2139946078.

On energy use by ordinary people, see Bruce Stadfeld, "Electric Space: Social and Natural Transformations in British Columbia's Hydroelectric Industry to World War Two" (PhD diss., University of Manitoba, 2002); Dorotea Gucciardo, "Wired: How Canada Became Electrified" (PhD diss., University of Western Ontario, 2011); and Dimitry Anastakis, *Car Nation: An Illustrated History of Canada's Transformation behind the Wheel* (Toronto: Lorimer, 2008). Automobile pollution statistics come from Dimitry Anastakis, "A 'War on Pollution'? Canadian Responses to the Automotive Emissions Problem, 1970–1980," *Canadian Historical Review* 90, 1 (2009): 99–136, and Statistics Canada, "Greenhouse Gas Emissions from Private Vehicles in Canada, 1900 to 2007," www.statcan.gc.ca/pub/16-001-m/2010012/part-partie1-eng.htm.

On natural processes in energy development, see Edmund Russell and colleagues' "The Nature of Power: Synthesizing the History of Technology and Environmental History," *Technology and Culture* 52 (April 2011): 246–59; Richard White, *The Organic Machine: The Remaking of the Columbia River* (New York: Hill and Wang, 1995); and Thomas Mitchell, *Carbon Democracy: Political Power in the Age of Oil* (London: Verso Books, 2011). I calculated the coal-water ratios from statistics in W.J. Dick, *Conservation of Coal in Canada* (Toronto: Bryant Press, 1914), 51–71. The CBC quotation is from "Trans Mountain Pipeline to Carry Alberta Oil to Vancouver," while Gray, *Forty Years in the Public Interest*, discusses various problems of frost and corrosion in pipeline maintenance. The Clark example was reported in "Gas Explosion Injures Five," *Globe and Mail*, January 26, 1957, 17.

The material on hydro developments in BC and Quebec is drawn from Tina Loo, "Disturbing the Peace: Environmental Change and the Scales of Justice on a Northern River," *Environmental History* 12, 4 (2007): 895–919, and Caroline Desbiens, *Power from the North: Territory, Identity, and the Culture of Hydroelectricity in Quebec* (Vancouver: UBC Press, 2013). On the oil sands, see Paul Chastko, *Developing Alberta's Oil Sands: From Karl Clark to Kyoto* (Calgary: University of Calgary Press, 2004). On Alberta farmers, see Erik Lizée's "Betrayed: Leduc, Manning and Surface Rights in Alberta, 1947–55," *Prairie Forum* 35, 1 (2010): 77–100. The information on the Trans Mountain Pipeline comes from Sean Kheraj, "Historical Background Report: Trans Mountain Pipeline, 1947–2013" (report for the City of Vancouver, 2015).

The British commentator is cited in Wolfgang Schivelbusch, *The Railway Journey: The Industrialization of Time and Space in the Nineteenth Century* (Berkeley:

University of California Press, 1986), 10, while the Geoffrey W. Taylor quotation comes from *Mining: The History of Mining in British Columbia* (Saanichton: Hancock House, 1978), 71.

On "hydro as myth," see H.V. Nelles, *The Politics of Development: Forests, Mines, and Hydro-electric Power in Ontario, 1849–1941*, 2nd ed. (Montreal and Kingston: McGill-Queen's University Press, 2005); for Nova Scotia, see Lionel King "The Electrification of Nova Scotia, 1884–1973: Technological Modernization as a Response to Regional Disparity" (PhD diss., University of Toronto, 1999). The figures on coal and electricity generation were provided by Nova Scotia Power for 2014.

On big business in fossil fuels, see David Frank, "The Cape Breton Coal Industry and the Rise and Fall of the British Empire Steel Corporation," *Acadiensis* 7, 1 (1977): 3–34, and Hugh Grant, "The Petroleum Industry and Canadian Economic Development: An Economic History, 1900–1961" (PhD diss., University of Toronto, 1986). On bigness in electricity, see H.V. Nelles and Christopher Armstrong, *Monopoly's Moment: The Organization and Regulation of Canadian Utilities, 1830–1930* (Philadelphia: Temple University Press, 1986); Karl Froschauer, *White Gold: Hydroelectric Power in Canada* (Vancouver: UBC Press, 1999); and Thomas P. Hughes, *Networks of Power: Electrification in Western Society, 1880–1930* (Baltimore: Johns Hopkins University Press, 1983). Nelles covers the origins of Ontario Hydro in *The Politics of Development*. On government regulation in oil, see David Breen, *Alberta's Petroleum Industry and the Conservation Board* (Edmonton: University of Alberta Press, 1993), and Lizée, "Betrayed."

The points about "people in the way" are from Lizée, "Betrayed," and Tina Loo, "People in the Way: Modernity, Environment, and Society on the Arrow Lakes," *BC Studies* 142–43 (Summer-Autumn 2004): 161–96. The classic studies of labour in Maritime coal areas are David Frank, "Contested Terrain: Workers' Control in the Cape Breton Coal Mines," in *On the Job: Confronting the Labour Process in Canada*, edited by Craig Heron and Robert Storey, 102–23 (Montreal and Kingston: McGill-Queen's University Press, 1984), and Ian McKay, "The

Realm of Uncertainty: The Experience of Work in the Cumberland Coal Mines, 1873–1927," *Acadiensis* 16, 1 (1986): 3–57.

Unger and Thistle's *Energy Consumption in Canada* can be used to chart the international resonance of Canadian energy history but also its particularities. On national dreams in fuel and electricity, see John McDougall, *Fuels and the National Policy* (Toronto: Butterworths, 1982) and Froschauer's *White Gold*.

The phrase *empty lot* is borrowed from Ian McKay's influential study "The Liberal Order Framework: A Prospectus for a Reconnaissance of Canadian History," *Canadian Historical Review* 81, 4 (2000): 617–45.

The scientific modelling of nature –
the National Research Council's model of the St. Lawrence Seaway.
Many other models were built by Ontario Hydro and by the Waterways
Experiment Station in Vicksburg, Mississippi. Noting that none of the
Canadian models has been seen for decades, Daniel Macfarlane, author of
*Negotiating a River: Canada, the US, and the Creation of the St. Lawrence
Seaway*, remarked: "Until they turn up, we will have to be satisfied with
viewing the real deal – even if the Niagara and St. Lawrence waterscapes
are, in certain respects, as much technological artifacts as the models."
Hydraulics Lab St. Lawrence Seaway Model 1967 002,
courtesy of the National Research Council Archives

QUESTIONS OF SCALE

Tina Loo

I N   A   W I D E L Y   I N F L U E N T I A L   book, *Seeing Like a State: How Certain Schemes to Improve the Human Condition Have Failed,* anthropologist James C. Scott coined the term *high modernism.* It described an ideology of development that had animated the large, centrally planned projects undertaken by nation-states around the world in the twentieth century, and especially after the Second World War in Canada. High modernism is distinguished by the conviction that people armed with the tools of science and technology can master nature – including their own – and design a better world for everyone. Canadian historians have long recognized the importance of large-scale nation-building projects such as railways. These expensive infrastructures had significant environmental effects, but after the Second World War, the scale of projects and their subsequent environmental impacts were of a different order altogether.

Globally, high modernist developments took many forms, from the movement of rural Tanzanians into towns to the clearing of slums and the building of ideal cities in the forests of Brazil and on the tundra of Arctic Canada. High modernism also underpinned the consolidation and rationalization of land use. In the Soviet Union and China, peasant farmers were collectivized and their operations governed by an industrial logic. In North America, forests were subjected to new types of scientific management under the assumption that trees could be managed in ways similar to those used for grain crops. Almost everywhere, it seemed, rivers were tamed and controlled under the high modernist impulse. The hydroelectric power produced by massive dams would transform – modernize and industrialize – economies and societies. Generally, high modernist developments were intended to improve the human condition. They were justified by appeals to nationalist ends, but they were also entangled in Cold War geopolitics. Opening the Moses-Saunders Dam on the St. Lawrence River in 1958, the chairman of Ontario Hydro compared it to the Kuibyshev hydro project on the Volga River. The Soviet dam might have had a slightly greater generating capacity than "Big Mo," but "the free and independent workers of the U.S.A. and Canada" had built their great structure more quickly than their communist counterparts.

The idea of progress was absolutely central to high modernist development, and it depended upon seeing nature in utilitarian terms, as a bundle of "resources" that existed for the benefit of people. Forests were valued in terms of board feet; the prairie was measured by its carrying capacity; rivers became conduits of kilowatt hours. When high modernist politicians saw waterfalls, they were not moved, as nineteenth-century Romantics were, by that combination of terror and beauty that told them they were in the presence of God. Rather than regarding them as sublime or picturesque, Quebec premier Robert Bourassa considered waterfalls inefficient. They were examples of nature's improvidence, allowing "millions of potential kilowatt-hours [to] flow downhill and out to sea. What a waste!" In all, the James Bay Project initiated in northern Quebec during Bourassa's premiership diverted and dammed nine rivers and flooded an area the size of Belgium. The extent of the inundation changed caribou migration patterns and altered the local climate. In addition, mercury released by the decomposing vegetation in the years immediately after the flooding contaminated whitefish and northern pike at levels well above World Health Organization standards, threatening the well-being of the Cree who consumed them.

An obvious example of high modernism, the massive hydroelectric
facility at La Grande, Quebec. Quebec began the extensive
development of northern waterways in the 1970s.
Photo by Jean Gagnon, Wikimedia Creative Commons Licence

Possessed of the same "developmentalist nationalism" as his Quebec
counterpart, British Columbia's recently elected premier W.A.C. Bennett
gazed down at the Peace River in the 1950s and saw a modern province.
Wild nature meant little to such disciples of high modernism; their eyes
saw nature transformed. Contemplating the muddy flow of the Peace,
Bennett rhapsodized: "I see dams. And I see power. And I see development.
I see roads, highways, bridges, and growing communities. I see cities –
prosperous cities with schools, hospitals and universities. I see beautiful
homes with housewives baking bread." For Bennett, "living better electric-
ally" meant liberation from a past dominated by single men leading rough
lives in the woods and mining camps. Dams would generate industry,
breadwinner wages, and domesticity.

265

In New Brunswick, regional development initiatives also saw environmental and social transformation proceeding hand in hand. Generating electricity was a way to modernize this "backward" province by creating a working class from a society of rural smallholders. Inspired by the Tennessee Valley Authority, the Mactaquac Regional Development Program aimed to produce a labour force for industry and the service sector, which involved remaking families as much as it depended on damming the St. John River. Vocational training was offered to men, home economics advice to women. The latter included demonstrations of fondue making, instruction on casseroles, and a short course on sewing. Rural New Brunswickers were reoriented to the time-work discipline of the new economy and the middle-class expectations of modern family life.

In the hands of the state, science and technology would fashion a better future. Even landscape aesthetics could be improved by the transformation of nature. For high modernists, beauty was to be found in the monumental built form. Canada's massive dams became tourist sites, places where millions of people could see nature harnessed – miraculously "cured" of its wastefulness – thanks to the awesome power of human ingenuity. There is no better example of the hubris of such conviction than the North American Water and Power Alliance (NAWAPA), a transcontinental water transfer plan. Designed by the Los Angeles engineering firm Ralph M. Parsons Corporation in 1964, it aimed to divert "unused" water from the north and west of North America, including rivers in Canada, to serve the arid regions of the United States and Mexico. An "invasive technonatural apparatus," it involved hundreds of separate construction projects – 240 reservoirs, 112 irrigation systems, and 17 navigation channels. As one US hydrological engineer commented, "NAWAPA is the kind of thing you think about when you're smoking pot."

High Modernism's potency rests upon such reductive and schematic ways of seeing – upon perspectives that radically simplify time and space even as they render nature in utilitarian terms. The power and the pitfalls

The North American Water and Power Alliance (NAWAPA)
was a continent-wide water management and diversion scheme
developed in 1964 by engineers at California's Parson Corporation. It speaks
to the grandiose ambition that was characteristic of high modernism.
Cartography by Eric Leinberger

of such reasoning are beautifully illustrated by the conceptualization
of bird migration paths as flyways. This way of thinking about the seasonal movements of millions of migratory birds was developed as a biological concept in the 1930s and encompasses continents and hemispheres.
It abstracts the myriad movements of uncountable numbers of birds –

movements shaped by shifting winds, storms, the ever-changing productivity and availability of feeding grounds, and hunters – into a few clean,
simple lines traced across maps that encompass enormous areas of the
earth's surface. Eschewing detail – most flyway maps pay no attention
to the species involved and simply show "bird" migration routes – this
conceptual innovation recast the administrative organization of bird
conservation. At a time when multiple bureaucracies hobbled the implementation of conservation measures, there was much to recommend the
idea that protecting "fugitive resources" required the adoption of a bird's
eye view. Plenty of challenges remained in the development of sufficiently
strong and broad-ranging authority to coordinate conservation efforts, but
few people argued that there was a problem with the expansive concept
of the flyway itself and the way of seeing that it exemplifies.

Although the concept is associated with ornithologist Frederick Lincoln
of the US Biological Survey, it was not the outcome of his own labours but
of a huge continent-wide bird-banding program that enrolled a variety of
people, from professional ornithologists and farmers to rod and gun club
members. As recent efforts to create wildlife corridors for mammals across
eastern and western North America attest, conservationists believe a high
modernist approach can be used to protect other species.

Wherever they were deployed, the "brute force technologies" of the high
modernist era transformed landscapes and lives, leaving behind a legacy
of dislocation, disorientation, dependence, depression, and death. People
and other animals lost their homes and habitats, as well as their bearings
in environments re-engineered by high modernism. From Kwadacha
(formerly Fort Ware) on the Finlay River in northern British Columbia to
Nitassinan, the lands of the Innu in northern Quebec and Labrador, the
disorientation people experienced was deepened by the loss of independence that came with the destruction of the lands on which their livelihoods
depended.

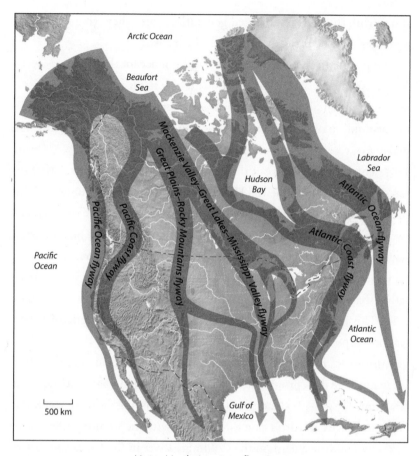

Major North American flyways –
the end-of-summer migrations of millions of birds reduced to a few informative
ribbons across the continent. Cartography by Eric Leinberger

Some, like the men who lost their small fruit farms or who found their traplines sitting on desiccated wetlands, never found their way again, falling victim to depression and, occasionally, to suicide, or to a landscape made newly hazardous. For the Cheslatta t'en, victims of the flooding caused by the Kenney Dam on BC's Nechako River in 1956, the trauma of past events lives on: bones scoured from a graveyard inundated in the course of spilling water from the dam re-emerged generations after they were interred, a reminder that the past can never really be buried.

The people in the way of progress did not accept their fate passively. They pushed back and in the process laid bare the limits of development, revealing much about people's relations with the state and that state's understanding of nature. Outside the courtroom where BC Hydro was making its case for a water licence to build a dam on the Arrow Lakes in 1961, which would flood out thousands of Kootenay residents, a *Vancouver Sun* journalist interviewed Hazel Stark about what she thought of the proceedings. "This is just a hearing," she said, "when is there to be an answering?" Upset at the prospect of losing his orchard to the St. Lawrence power project, one man in Iroquois, Ontario, tried to make the state answer for its actions by forcing Ontario Hydro to "tabulate a history of each tree" rather than determine what his land was worth by averages and comparables. This required a kind of parsing to which the high modernist state was not disposed.

Authorities preferred other ways of dealing with change. Blueprints for many large dam projects in Canada used text and image to juxtapose a "traditional" past with a "modern" future while ignoring the present entirely. For instance, BC Hydro's case for flooding settlements along the Arrow Lakes by building a dam on the Columbia River in the 1960s contrasted an early twentieth-century past of sternwheelers and scattered, rural small holdings with a future centred on the car and a road system that would connect Kootenay communities to one another, the province, and the continent. Then-current conditions in the valley were completely disregarded.

The pastness of places lost to the waters of the rising reservoirs of high modernist development projects was enshrined in the historical sites built to commemorate them. At both Upper Canada Village, which was created as part of the St. Lawrence Seaway and Power Project, and Kings Landing in New Brunswick, which was part of the Mactaquac Regional Development Plan, historically and architecturally significant buildings were moved out of the flood plain and re-established elsewhere to represent "pioneer" life in the nineteenth century. Many of those whose lives were turned upside down by the great projects were then hired to engage in their own folklorization as the animators of "living history" museums.

The changes effected by high modernism were more than devastating. I mean that figuratively: a single word cannot capture the meaning of change as it was experienced by those displaced. But I also mean it literally, in the sense that there is more to change than devastation. Taking a cue from recent work in nonequilibrium ecology, which argues that changes reverberate and find expression in many forms, we should attend to what change creates as well as what it degrades or destroys. The disturbances associated with the construction of high modernist projects such as dams brought new communities into being, including places such as Mackenzie (where the pulp and paper industry depends on the reservoir created by the Bennett Dam and the transportation it affords) and Arvida, the company town created around the aluminum smelter that was powered by dams near Lac St. Jean and on the Saguenay River in Quebec. To acknowledge as much is to recognize that even as they destroyed some lives and altered many landscapes, high modernist projects also reshaped the terrain on which we must now search for solutions.

In a similar vein, these projects forged new political landscapes even as they changed the economic geography of the country. The eight powerhouses and five reservoirs of the James Bay hydroelectric project that reconfigured political identities along with the land offer a fine illustration of this point. Hydroelectricity made Quebec modern; nationalizing power and building the James Bay Project transformed Quebecers from colonial subjects to masters of their own house, "hydro-québécois." At the same time, hydroelectricity gave rise to Cree nationalism. Confronted with the James Bay development and the destruction of their homeland, the Cree reorganized themselves politically, creating a new organization in 1974 to represent their collective interests. As a political body that represents all of the Cree and advocates for their rights, the Grand Council of the Crees not only changed the landscape of provincial politics, it also shifted environmental politics beyond the boundaries of Quebec and Canada.

In the 1990s, the Grand Council took its battle against Hydro-Québec to American consumers, whose demand for electricity was driving the company's expansion. By forging alliances with Robert Kennedy Jr. and the Natural Resources Defense Council, the Cree played the politics of scale skilfully, succeeding in making their problems the world's problems. But this had costs. Grand Chief Matthew Coon Come lamented that fighting for his people meant that he spent "too much time walking on cement," which frayed his connections to his home community and the land. Imposed on them, high modernist development contributed to the formation of a new leadership class among the Cree as well as to a pan-Cree political identity.

Hydroelectric development also shaped politics and political identity in Newfoundland. If James Bay embodied Quebec's nationalist ambitions, the Churchill Falls hydroelectric project came to exemplify Newfoundland's colonial status in Confederation – at least to Newfoundlanders. Hopeful that a dam at Churchill Falls would bring prosperity to Newfoundland, in the 1960s Premier Joey Smallwood negotiated an agreement with the government of Quebec, through whose territory the power would have to travel, providing for the sale of electricity at a guaranteed, and as it turned out, very low price. When electricity prices soared in the 1980s, Hydro-Québec re-sold the electricity from Churchill Falls at huge profits, much to the chagrin and annoyance of the government of Newfoundland, which found itself unable to renegotiate the Smallwood deal or get around it.

It would take another dam, at Muskrat Falls, and another deal, with Nova Scotia, to bring an end to Newfoundland's history of hydro colonialism and to create a new identity. The language the provincial government chose in announcing the deal was significant, linking development and self-determination. "Our people are proud nationalists who believe it is only by affirming our identity as Newfoundlanders and Labradorians that we will realize our goal of economic equality within the federation," stated the province's lieutenant-governor in the 2007 Speech from the Throne. The speech echoed the classic phrase of Quebec's Quiet Revolution in the 1960s: "Our people are ready to take charge of our future and, under My First Minister's leadership, our province will achieve self-reliance by becoming masters of our own house."

Simplifying space and time can make enormous changes seem both possible and necessary. But such simplifications have also prevented high modernist projects from delivering entirely on what they promised: there are costs, as well as benefits, to managing nature and improving the human condition. To see like a state is to deny the complexity and diversity of nature and the many and complex relationships that link people and the biophysical world. Devaluing what they did not understand and destroying what they could not see, the agents of the high modernist state had vision but lacked wisdom – or so the usual critique asserts. Resource towns and industrial farms could be planned or engineered, but the embodied, improvisational, tacit and, above all, historical knowledge that creates a particular way of being in the world and allows people to feel settled in place could not be created by decree.

Yet this critique is also a simplification – a distillation of certain elements from a more complex reality. Building a dam involved an intense engagement with nature; it required and resulted in an understanding that was far from simple. The maps made in planning each large dam speak to that engagement and the knowledge that resulted. Colourful charts of bedrock geology and soils that exposed the invisible underground showed where a large and heavy structure like a dam might be located. The Canadian Federal Department of Mines and Surveys circulated eighty-nine detailed maps of the entire length of the Canadian portion of the Columbia River, the product of twenty-seven survey parties working over a seven-year period. The men who produced this knowledge spent weeks bushwacking and battling bears and bugs. Their maps, drawn at a scale of one inch to the half mile, show bogs, scrub, rapids, and trees (coniferous, deciduous, and fruit, each with its own symbol). The human landscape is rendered with a similar attention to detail: there are separate symbols for churches with spires and those without.

The writings of engineer Ralph Peck, who worked on many of Canada's and North America's large dam projects, speak similarly to the knowledge about nature produced by high modernist development. For Peck, the material structure of a dam was the result of a conversation between an engineer's expertise and the irreducible materiality of the geology and soils present in a particular locale. In his 1959 report on soil mechanics for the Peace River project, he argued, "The design of an earth or rockfill dam must necessarily be suited to the materials available in the locality. As such knowledge becomes available, various possibilities for the design of the dam suggest themselves."

Despite his discipline's move into the laboratory and towards modelling, Peck remained committed to the idea that knowing nature came from working in it, from the particular experience gained on specific large projects located in specific places. Writing in the inaugural issue of a new geo-engineering journal, he emphasized that the particularity of place had to be taken seriously, as a limit on generalization: "The inherent heterogeneity of soils and rocks ... will always refocus our profession's attention back to the importance of case histories."

More broadly, Peck believed fieldwork taught respect. Good engineering was about improvising and acknowledging the limits of one's own knowledge and living within the limits of what nature offered. For engineers, one of the joys of the job was problem solving, figuring out how to make something work in circumstances that could only be altered or controlled to a point. As Peck put it, "We, as human beings, can observe Nature and we can learn from her. We can't dictate to her. Nature, on the other hand, can dictate to us and she will ... We have to try to accept

Nature on her terms, not to try to have Nature accept us on our terms, because she won't and she doesn't have to."

Peck's way of knowing nature was a kind of local knowledge drawn from intense engagement with a place but not necessarily dependent on prolonged familiarity with it. This knowledge could be detached from the setting in which it was formulated and used to effect change elsewhere, sometimes far from where it had been generated. In that respect, it re-sembled a case study reported in print, or a set of maps. But it was also embodied. Construction workers and engineers who moved from job to job around the world took their experience with particular places with them.

Much recent scholarship is critical of high modernist development. Fault-finders lament the collateral damage that abstraction and generaliza-tion inflict on those whom development projects are supposed to help. Life is not lived at thirty-five thousand feet, yet the state and its agents used such a broad, general view to shape future lives and landscapes. In rejecting a world of "the few and the big" and in embracing one composed of the "small and the many," these critics of high modernism appear to have much in common with some of today's most prominent environmentalists who insist that small is beautiful and local is better. Indeed, the social and en-vironmental damage inflicted by high modernism in the second half of the twentieth century paved the way for the embrace of the local in the twenty-first.

Yet it is worth remembering that it was a synoptic (broadscale) view of our own home that spurred interest in the modern environmental move-ment. Taken in December 1968 by the Apollo 8 astronauts, the photo *Earthrise* conveyed the planet's beauty and fragility. Above all, it captured the earth's wholeness. Seen from space, the differences that divided people were invisible. As astronaut Frank Borman reflected, "Raging nationalistic interests, famines, wars, pestilences don't show up from that distance. We are one hunk of ground, water, air, clouds, floating around in space. From out there it really is 'one world.'" Encapsulating the "planetary thinking"

The classic synoptic perspective. *Earthrise* was taken
by the astronauts of Apollo 8 on Christmas Eve, 1968. NASA

that was being articulated from many different quarters, *Earthrise* was part
of a new way of seeing that gave expression to a powerful new environmental
sensibility.

So we are reminded that important though it is, an emphasis on the
local can become a problem if it occurs to the exclusion of other scales.
We know that everything is connected to everything else. Any standard
ecology textbook makes the point that life is not lived on one scale and
that disturbances reverberate because of the connections that exist among
populations, ecosystems, and the biosphere. Attending to the connections
among scales is crucial to ecological and social health. Mitigating development's excesses and doing development better will come only if we think

and work across scales, both spatial and temporal. High modernist developments fundamentally changed environments and peoples, but the synoptic
perspective that underpinned them remains valuable. Meeting the challenge
of living in the Anthropocene requires us to engage with change at all
scales, from the local to the global.

REFERENCES AND FURTHER READING

Daniel Macfarlane's quote on Canadian models is from "Model Environments:
Engineering the Niagara and St. Lawrence Megaprojects," NiCHE blogpost,
August 24, 2016.

The key book here is, of course, James C. Scott's *Seeing Like a State: How
Certain Schemes to Improve the Human Condition Have Failed* (New Haven, CT:
Yale University Press, 1998). The 1958 comment regarding the Moses-Saunders
Dam is from Daniel Macfarlane, *Negotiating a River: Canada, the US, and the
Creation of the St. Lawrence Seaway* (Vancouver: UBC Press, 2014), 282n26.

Bourassa's description of Quebec as a "vast hydroelectric plant" is from
Caroline Desbiens, *Power from the North: Territory, Identity, and the Culture of
Hydroelectricity in Quebec* (Vancouver: UBC Press, 2013), 18. The large literature
on the environmental and social impacts of the James Bay Project includes
many technical reports. *Social and Environmental Impacts of the James Bay
Hydroelectric Project*, edited by James F. Hornig (Montreal and Kingston: McGill-
Queen's University Press, 1999), is a good place to start.

W.A.C. Bennett's "dams into domesticity" statement is much quoted. See
Tina Loo, "People in the Way: Modernity, Environment, and Society on the
Arrow Lakes," *BC Studies* 142–43 (Summer-Autumn 2004): 161–96. On the
Mactaquac Project, see Joshua John Dickison, "Making New Brunswickers
Modern: Natural and Human Resource Development in Mactaquac Regional
Development Plan, 1965–1975" (master's thesis, University of New Brunswick,
2006); and James L. Kenny and Andrew G. Secord, "Engineering Modernity:

Hydroelectric Development in New Brunswick, 1945–1970," *Acadiensis* 39, 1 (2010): 3–26.

For the North American Water and Power Alliance, see Benjamin Forest and Patrick Forest, "Engineering the North American Waterscape: The High Modernist Mapping of Continental Water Projects," *Political Geography* 31, 3 (2012): 167–83, and Marc Reisner, *Cadillac Desert: The American West and Its Disappearing Water,* rev. ed. (New York: Penguin Books, 1993), which includes the quote about smoking pot on page 493.

On the flyway, see Robert M. Wilson, *Seeking Refuge: Birds and Landscapes of the Pacific Flyway* (Seattle: University of Washington Press, 2010), Chap. 3.

On the impacts of the Kenney Dam on the Cheslatta t'en, see Matthew D. Evenden, *Fish versus Power: An Environmental History of the Fraser River* (Cambridge: Cambridge University Press, 2004), Chap. 5, and J.E. Windsor and J.A. McVey, "Annihilation of Both Place and Sense of Place: The Experience of the Cheslatta t'en Canadian First Nation within the Context of Large-Scale Environmental Projects," *Geographical Journal* 171, 2 (2005): 146–65. Hazel Stark's opinion on the water licence hearings is from Loo, "People in the Way." The story of the man who sought compensation for each and every tree is from Lionel Chevrier, *The St. Lawrence Seaway* (Toronto: Macmillan, 1959), 102 and 107.

On Upper Canada Village, see Macfarlane, *Negotiating a River,* 164–65, and Joy Parr, *Sensing Changes: Technologies, Environments, and the Everyday* (Vancouver: UBC Press, 2010), Chap. 4.

On Arvida and the James Bay Project, see José E. Igartua, *Arvida au Saguenay: Naissance d'une ville industrielle* (Montreal and Kingston: McGill-Queen's University Press, 1996), and Desbiens, *Power from the North.* Coon Come's observation about "walking on cement" is from *Power: One River, Two Nations,* directed by Magnus Isaacson (Montreal: National Film Board of Canada, 1996). On Churchill Falls and the quote from the 2007 Speech from the Throne, see Jerry Bannister, "A River Runs through It: Churchill Falls and the End of Newfoundland History" *Acadiensis* 41, 1 (2012): 211–25.

On engineer Ralph Peck, dam building, and engagement with nature, see Tina Loo and Meg Stanley, "An Environmental History of Progress: Damming the Peace and Columbia Rivers," *Canadian Historical Review* 92, 3 (2011): 399–427. The Ralph Peck quote is from his "Nature Ignores Specialties," *Geotechnical News*, March 1983, 12–15. The term *brute force technology* is from Paul Josephson, *Industrialized Nature, Brute Force Technology and the Transformation of the Natural World* (Washington, DC: Island Press, 2002).

On the world of the "few and the big" versus that of the "small and the many," see Bill McKibben, "The Era of Small and Many: Reversing the Trend of Generations," *Orion Magazine* November-December 2011, 10–11. For the effects of the *Earthrise* photograph, see Robert Poole, *Earthrise: How Man First Saw Earth* (New Haven: Yale University Press, 2008); the Borman quote is on page 2. Also see Ursula Heise, *Sense of Place and Sense of Planet: The Environmental Imagination of the Global* (New York: Oxford University Press, 2008).

Members of Voice of Women protest
on the steps of Parliament, September 25, 1961.
The pacifist group deployed images of suburban responsibility to navigate
tense Cold War politics. Their baby tooth survey engaged many thousands
of Canadian women who would have been reluctant to participate
in protests such as this one. Library and Archives Canada,
Duncan Cameron fonds, a209888

A GENDERED SENSE OF NATURE

Joanna Dean

CONIC PHOTOGRAPHS OF THE first Greenpeace voyage depict a scruffy, bearded crew setting off to bear witness to the nuclear bomb tests at Amchitka Island. Only men were permitted on the voyage, and the stories told are filled with male bravado. Filed away in the archives, however, is a photograph that tells another story. It shows a bemused Dave Birmingham, the marine engineer on the epic voyage, being kissed by his wife, Deeno. According to Greenpeace lore, Dave had joined the vessel at the urging of his activist wife. As he explained, "She said they needed an engineer, so I thought I'd better go." Deeno Birmingham was the president and "the key mover and shaker" of the BC chapter of Voice of Women, or VOW. The photograph of their embrace captures a forgotten link between Greenpeace (familiar to Canadians for its masculine counterculture theatrics) and VOW (known, to the extent it is known at all, for motherhood and pacifism). In contrast with Greenpeace's iconic photographs, VOW's are all suburban respectability. They show middle-class women in pearls, hats, and white gloves. What, then, should we make of this kiss?

The photograph of the marital embrace is a telling entry point into questions of gender and nature: by revealing the connections between suburban mothers and macho men, the photograph brings women's activism out of the shadows and presses us to think more deeply about how

Deeno Birmingham, the president of the BC chapter of Voice of Women, volunteered her husband, Dave, as the engineer on the *Greenpeace I* and *Greenpeace II*. This photograph of their embrace appeared in the newsletter of the BC chapter of the Voice of Women in December 1971 with ringing endorsements of the voyage to Amchitka. Photo by Flett Studios. Courtesy of University of British Columbia Library, Rare Books and Special Collections, BC Voice of Women Collection, Box 1, file 1–11, Scrapbook, Amchitka clippings, and Mary Ruth Amundsen

gender plays out in the material world. Men have loomed large in Canadian environmental history. Wilderness, parks, and the North have generally been defined as masculine arenas. It was, by and large, men such as J.B. Harkin, the "father" of Canada's national parks, who were given the education and authority to lead early conservation movements, and it was men who spoke most loudly on environmental questions. Think of Ernest Thompson Seton, Grey Owl, Jack Miner, and Farley Mowat. Even the historians who write about the environment have been disproportionately male. The women whose voices have emerged have been dismissed as amateurs (think of Catharine Parr Traill), eccentrics (Emily Carr), or, more recently, ecofeminists (the women at Clayoquot Sound). Elizabeth May, the leader of Canada's Green Party, argued in 1990 that women are essentially different from men: "We operate more from an intuitive thought process. We are biologically and spiritually connected to the cosmos, its planetary shifts, the earth's tides and phases of the moon. We are more nurturing, more concerned with the flow and flux of life – people, plants, animals, even seas." The argument that women are naturally more connected to the cosmos does not sit well with feminists, who are rightfully suspicious of any attempt to consign women to the natural world. Queer theorists are even more uncomfortable with the invocation of a tidy binary of male and female; they point us to a natural world that is sexed in endlessly playful and diverse ways.

The story of the Birminghams' embrace takes us in a new direction. It points to the entanglement of both men and women in a physical world made toxic by nuclear fallout. Nature was no longer something "out there" and separate from humanity but something within. Toxins permeate bodies, percolate through breast milk and semen, and work their way down through the generations. The story starts in the early 1960s, a decade before the Amchitka voyage. Like many Canadians of my generation, I have a small personal stake in it. My young mother, Ankaret Dean, met a neighbour, Annie Lind, for coffee in the bedroom community of Oakville, near Toronto. Lind pointed to the clouds drifting across Lake Ontario and explained that they bore radioactive isotopes, the fallout of nuclear weapons testing in Nevada. Clouds filled with fallout were drifting across the continent, and isotopes such as strontium-90 fell with the rain, to be taken up in the grass and in the milk of grazing cows and, eventually, in the bones and teeth of young children. Lind was a member of Voice of Women, and she urged my alarmed young mother to send my baby teeth to be tested for strontium-90. "It was all rather disappointing," my mother recalled recently, "they never got back to me."

The baby tooth survey was one of the most effective publicity campaigns in Canadian history. Between 1961 and 1966, mothers sent thirty thousand baby teeth to the University of Toronto to be tested for strontium-90.

Historians remember this as a protofeminist and antinuclear campaign, but it was also an environmental crusade that politicized a generation of Canadian mothers.

The survey emerged amid heightened Cold War tensions, as the Soviet Union and the United States tested a growing arsenal of nuclear weapons, releasing clouds of fallout into the atmosphere. Canadians, positioned precariously between the nuclear testing grounds of the super-powers, felt particularly vulnerable. The *Toronto Star* raised anxiety in the summer of 1957 with a headline that read "Southern Canada Fallout Is Highest in World; No Safe Dose – Geneticist." In April 1958, when federal scientists refused to release data on fallout radiation, the *Star* protested: "The government says it alone will decide how much poison is good for us, and it alone will know how much poison is descending on us from the skies. This is an outrageous way to treat citizens of a democracy." Later that summer, the *Globe and Mail* noted "widely divergent scientific statements about the fallout hazard" and "major uncertainties" about "how the fallout material enters the food chain" and the damage it might do once in contact with the human body. The federal minister of health, Paul Martin Sr., insisted that testing posed no risk and assured the public that he would seek an end to testing if any impacts were detected. At stake were questions of scientific knowledge and authority. How much fallout was safe? What risks were acceptable? Who could be trusted? These were matters of chance, statistics, and thresholds or, as the German sociologist Ulrich Beck later framed them, they were hazards shrouded by uncontrollability, ignorance, and uncertainty.

Study groups on radiation sprang up in the face of government obfusca-tion, and young mothers often took the lead. In 1958, Marion Kellerman organized the Mother's Committee on Radiation Hazards in West Vancouver. As reported in national newspapers, the simple maternalism of their man-date (Kellerman "just wanted safe milk for her children," wrote one journal-ist) masked the political import of their existence. The following year, Mary

Van Stolk formed a mother's study group in Edmonton, and in 1960, Ethel Kesler formed Citizens for Nuclear Disarmament in Montreal. Kesler's group moved from study to action. Following the example of the Greater St. Louis Citizen's Committee for Nuclear Information, the Montreal group collected baby teeth to measure levels of radioisotopes. Their initiative, like the American one, was a form of citizen science: both combined women volunteers, who did the brunt of the work, with male scientists such as University of Toronto dentist A.M. Hunt, who tested the teeth. Kesler played up her own incompetence: "How a little nobody from Cote St. Luc could get involved in something like this, I don't know." But she was a remarkably effective "little nobody." Kesler's group collected four thousand teeth in the first year and five thousand in the second. "Ordinary people have grabbed leaflets like hotcakes," she said. "Women have held on to our forms for 12 months because they knew their child would be losing a tooth." Two years later, apparently at her urging, the campaign was taken up by VOW and expanded across Canada.

VOW had formed in 1960, when thousands responded to *Toronto Star* columnist Lotta Dempsey's call for women to organize as mothers for disarmament. The group drew on the expertise of newspaper and television women, such as Dempsey, and catapulted into the national arena: within a few days of the first meeting, the leaders met with Prime Minister John Diefenbaker. Within a year, the group had four thousand paid-up members, seven provincial committees, an office, and a paid staff person; by 1962, the group had almost six thousand members across Canada. The organization was founded on the idea that women, as women, needed to be heard in debates about nuclear arms. This perspective was frequently (but not always) expressed as maternalism, which held that women, as mothers, would instinctively want to protect life.

VOW stumbled slightly in its early years as a groundswell of popular support swept it into the public eye before it had determined its goals and its place in volatile Cold War politics. Organizers constantly combatted accusations that they were communist sympathizers, and a thick file of reports from the Royal Canadian Mounted Police indicates that the state took them, and the threat of communist infiltration, seriously.

International tensions over nuclear deployments increased as VOW grew. After a three-year moratorium, the USSR and then the United States resumed nuclear testing in September 1961. In August 1962, milk was withheld from market in Canada because of high levels of iodine-131 (a short-lived radioisotope that lodges in the thyroid); in October, the possibility of nuclear war loomed in the terror of the Cuban Missile Crisis. Then tensions slowly dissipated. On August 5, 1963, the United States, the United Kingdom, and the USSR signed a treaty prohibiting nuclear testing in the atmosphere, in space, and under water. But radioactive isotopes from earlier tests continued to fall from the stratosphere. According to the *Globe and Mail*, "the average level of radioactive Strontium 90 – which can cause bone cancer and leukemia when absorbed in sufficient quantity – measured in a liter of milk in the US" had almost doubled in the year after May 1962. The newspaper reassured readers that "government scientists say there is no cause for alarm."

VOW members lobbied for better monitoring of the dangers. Ursula Franklin, a physicist with the Ontario Research Foundation, joined the group and gave its research a scientific basis. She prepared a study guide on radiation hazards for local groups, and in March 1963, she urged members to lobby members of Parliament, to ask them whether they knew that Canada had higher radiation levels than the United States and the United Kingdom and "a totally inadequate system of monitoring and information." Franklin's research was disseminated in the mainstream media, often without attribution. On May 4, 1963, *Maclean's* magazine announced that "the world is going into the hottest year for fallout since testing began. Canada is the hottest country in the world. Here are the simple steps we should already have taken to protect ourselves." A month later, Franklin presented technical data on increasing levels of radioactive contamination to Judy

LaMarsh, the minister of health and welfare, and called for improvements to radiation monitoring and the publication of data. She also called for the decontamination of milk. In response, LaMarsh set up a new advisory committee on radiation protection. The minutes of the first meeting of the committee reveal a dismissive attitude towards VOW (one scientist refers to their claims as "absurd"), but they also reveal an uneasy respect for the group's public profile and the legitimacy of their demands.

At the same time, VOW took the Montreal baby tooth survey national. Campaigns swept through Toronto, Winnipeg, Regina, Edmonton, and Vancouver as well as smaller centres. The guidelines from Montreal advised women to distribute forms through supermarkets, children's libraries, nursery schools, and home and school associations. They stressed the importance of providing buttons to children who donated their teeth, as a reward, but also to publicize the campaign to other children. VOW leaders were sometimes exasperated by the publicity given the survey, even as they reaped the benefits politically. An RCMP report suggested in 1963 that the survey might have helped the organization regain "lost respectability" and would "combat any future efforts on the part of anyone to discredit them." VOW advised the volunteers to avoid politics and emphasize science: "We try to stress that our collection is for the purpose of collecting facts not at present known, and avoid taking sides on the issue." Of course, the tooth collection was about much more than facts: toothless children and their tiny teeth were powerful symbols that provided a visceral reminder of the vulnerability of infants and the permeability of the body to environmental contaminants.

In the end, VOW sent at least thirty thousand of these highly charged physical markers of invisible toxicity to the University of Toronto. Considering that only some of the women targeted had children of the correct age, and that only some of them would have thought to save the teeth and found time to mail them in, we can assume that hundreds of thousands of people knew about the campaign and understood the impact of nuclear

The tiny baby teeth sent to Voice of Women by thirty thousand Canadian mothers serve as visceral reminders of the vulnerability of infants to the toxicity of nuclear fallout. In British Columbia, the survey had broad public support from health agencies and dentists. Courtesy of University of British Columbia Library, Rare Books and Special Collections, BC Voice of Women Collection, Box 2, file 2–3, Baby Tooth Project, and Nick Eagland

fallout on their children. Their efforts were reinforced by other antinuclear groups, and by 1966, as journalist Barbara Frum noted, Canadians felt as if "we were walking under a perpetually raining cloud of radioactive particles." These fears spread to other invisible toxins and laid the groundwork for modern environmentalism. In 1962, in *Silent Spring*, American scientist Rachel Carson tapped into, and amplified, fears of nuclear fallout to raise similar concerns about pesticides, and in 1967, the CBC tied these same fears to air pollution in a powerful and controversial documentary "Air of Death."

Women who sent in teeth were asked to fill out a card to explain where they had lived while pregnant and whether the infant had been breast- or bottle-fed. The form had scientific purpose: the location of the mother identified where the strontium-90 had been accumulated, but it also served as a reminder of the connections between the mother and infant and the permeability of the female body. Then (as now) the idea that breast milk might contain poisons was deeply repugnant. The baby tooth survey reminded women not only that poison rained down from the clouds but also that poison travelled through their bodies into their infants. It emphasized these connections at a time when the very visible deformities resulting from the administration of thalidomide to pregnant women in Canada between 1959 and 1962 – stunted, flipper-like limbs, hands, and feet – were all too evident. A chilling poem, "To a Thalidomide Baby," in VOW's national newsletter marked the connections.

In March 1966, Hunt completed his study of the teeth and released his findings. He sought to minimize fears: "There was so little Sr 90 in the 30,000 teeth collected from children in five Canadian cities that he had to measure it using 20–70 teeth at a time ... a luminous watch dial could give a count 10,000 times higher." In an interview with Frum for the *Toronto Star,* Hunt conceded that there might be long-term effects, but he noted that "we'll kill ourselves a lot faster with air pollutants." Ursula Franklin was less complacent. She questioned Hunt's numbers and asked: "How many cases of childhood leukemia are permissible?"

As Hunt was concluding his study, the question of nuclear testing returned. Underground nuclear testing was permissible under the 1963 treaty so long as no radioactive debris fell outside the territorial limits of the state responsible. On October 29, 1965, the United States detonated an underground nuclear test on Amchitka Island. Relatively small and unexpected, it went largely unnoticed, but news of a second test (which took place on October 2, 1969) led to massive protests at the American border. Bearing banners that read "Don't Make a Wave" and "It's Your Fault If Our Fault Goes," protesters were driven, in part, by memories of the Alaska earthquake of 1964 and the fear that nuclear testing might trigger another quake or tsunami.

Anxiety about the test peaked in the jurisdiction of one of VOW's strongest provincial chapters. BC-VOW, with 1,085 members, had been second only to Ontario in 1962. Although paid-up memberships dropped to 560 by the end of the decade, the regional newsletter, *BC Voice*, reached one thousand readers, and groups were spread across the province in fifteen centres. The BC chapter organized one of the most effective baby tooth campaigns, legitimized by close links with public health agencies. After 1965, under Deeno Birmingham's leadership, the group expanded its sphere of concern to environmental issues such as resource use, pollution, population control, and recycling. Members were quick to join the protests against the Amchitka explosions, and they joined representatives of the Society for Pollution and Environmental Control, End the Arms Race, and others in the streets outside the American consulate. In his column in the *Vancouver Sun*, environmental activist Bob Hunter reflected: "So there are women who are starting to learn the tricks of organization. That gives me more hope than anything has in years. The power of aroused mothers is famous." To conclude, he urged politicians to take note: "There is a power out there in suburbia, so far harnessed only to charity drives, campaigns and PTAs which if ever properly brought to bear on the great problems of the day, will have an impact so great the result of its being detonated (like the Amchitka A bomb test) cannot be predicted."

In February 1970, VOW members heard about the plans hatched by the newly formed Don't Make a Wave committee to sail a protest ship to Amchitka. They threw their considerable weight behind the idea. Deeno Birmingham and Lille d'Easum were invited to join the committee by d'Easum's friend, Greenpeace founder Dorothy Stowe. Seventy-one-year-old d'Easum wrote the first Greenpeace technical report, *Nuclear Testing in the Aleutians* (March 1970), and Birmingham drew on national VOW networks to raise funds and petition the Canadian government. The Amchitka campaign dominated VOW's national annual meeting in October 1970, and chapters across the country were urged to sell Greenpeace buttons.

The iconic photograph of the scruffy counterculture crew
of the first Greenpeace voyage, which set off to bear witness
to nuclear testing on Amchitka Island. Members of VOW were
on the organizing committee, and when they found out that women were not
permitted on the voyage, they volunteered Deeno Birmingham's husband,
Dave *(upper right)*, one of only two clean-shaven crew members.
Photo by Robert Keziere, "Crew of the Greenpeace – Voyage Documentation
(Vancouver to Amchitka: 1971)," GP019ID. © Greenpeace/Robert Keziere

VOW pressed to have women on the Amchitka voyage, and when that
failed, they provided critical support from shore. A month before the
Greenpeace sailed, VOW leader Beatrice Brigden and a delegation from
Manitoba travelled in a car decorated to symbolize the green "peace ship."
Karen Sanford (leader of the Comox chapter and subsequently an MLA
for the New Democratic Party), phoned every school principal in her area
to ask students to write letters against the blast. When the ship sailed, she
organized a send-off in Comox. VOW's national executive committee,

holding its annual meeting at the time of the ship's departure, sent the following telegram to the *Greenpeace:* "You represent essence of our struggle. We are with you heart and soul." The photograph of Deeno and Dave Birmingham kissing goodbye on the dock symbolized a passing of the torch between a well-established antinuclear women's group and the nascent Greenpeace.

Like the VOW members, the Greenpeace crew had very physical and embodied responses to the toxicity of strontium-90. "I don't care about Strontium 90 in my milk. You get used to anything," Bob Hunter had written sarcastically in his 1968 novel, *Erebus.* "What does it matter that my scrotum is filled with softly-glowing sperms?" They, too, were concerned with future generations. Hunter's fellow journalist, Ben Metcalfe, explained: "We do not consider ourselves radicals. We are conservatives, who insist on conserving the environment for our children and future generations of man." Hunter made the same point more graphically: "What kind of looks are your kids going to give you ten or twenty or thirty years from now when the whole shebang comes crashing down and they die of leukemia or cancer or bone-rot or DDT, or they are driven mad by overcrowding, or wiped out in a nuclear war, and they ask us, Why did you let this happen?"

As their rusty vessel, renamed *Greenpeace,* sailed up the coast of British Columbia towards Amchitka in fall 1971, the crew understood that there was a real likelihood of radiation poisoning from the fallout. According to Hunter, they had worked out an arrangement: "The crewmen who are already fathers – Bohlen, Metcalfe and me – will go on deck after the fallout cloud passes, assuming the test does leak, dressed in slicks, and attempt to wash off the decks and walls. The guys who haven't had any kids yet will stay below in the hope that the dose of radiation they get won't be quite so lethal to their genes." It is a powerful image: fathers out on deck taking the blow to protect future fathers below deck. The crew members of the *Greenpeace* were as explicitly paternal as the women of VOW were maternal.

Many conclusions can be drawn from the parallel stories of VOW and Greenpeace. First, both organizations were shaped by journalists, and both groups were masters of the consciousness-changing "mind bomb." The VOW campaign can be summed up by those milk teeth and their connotations of the deep embeddedness of nuclear fallout in human bodies. Greenpeace, in the early years, can be summed up by the image of small, vulnerable ships on a large ocean, facing down the military might of the superpowers. Both organizations played on Cold War gendering and put it to radical ends. So why do scholars define VOW by its maternalism while no one has paid critical attention to the testosterone that fuelled the rise of Greenpeace? The heightened masculinity wrapped up with Greenpeace's self-image has rarely been seen as a weakness.

Second, these stories suggest a need to reconsider the history of Greenpeace. When the *Greenpeace* sailed, the young activists appeared to have come from nowhere. Historian Frank Zelko attributed their success to the presence of an older generation of pacifist Americans in Vancouver: "The organization may have started life in Canada, but to a large extent, its activist roots lie south of the 49th parallel." Dave Birmingham's presence on board ship points to other roots, in Canadian soil. The news reports of the Amchitka voyage fell on fertile ground because initiatives such as the baby tooth survey had prepared Canadians for the messages delivered by the madcap crew.

The larger conclusion is that we need to pay attention to our bodily responses to the natural world. Strontium-90 threatened the sexual and reproductive powers of men and women equally. The response of Greenpeace's male crew to nuclear fallout was just as bodily as that of the mothers who participated in the survey. The brilliance of the women's campaign lay in its ability to ground an abstract concern – fallout – in the sensuality of bodily experiences and physical relationships. A woman who sent her child's milk teeth in for testing understood strontium-90 to be coursing through her blood and breasts, associated radioisotopes with the intimacy and sensuality of nursing a baby, and "saw" the toxin in her child's baby teeth. A similar imaginary reverberated through the Greenpeace mission. By sailing close to the test, the twelve men were planning to expose their bodies to radioactive fallout; they anticipated radioisotopes raining down upon their bodies, poisoning their semen, and damaging their future generations.

All of this warns against easy claims about the ways in which gender shapes environmental concerns, even as it directs attention to the permeability of both male and female bodies and our shared entanglements in a material world.

REFERENCES AND FURTHER READING

On J.B. Harkin and the invisibility of women in Parks Canada, see Alan MacEachern. "M.B. Williams and the Early Years of Parks Canada," in *A Century of Parks Canada, 1911–2011,* edited by Claire E. Campbell, 21–52 (Calgary: University of Calgary Press, 2011). For Seton, see John Henry Wadland, *Ernest Thompson Seton: Man in Nature and the Progressive Era, 1880–1915* (New York: Arno Press, 1978). For Grey Owl, see Donald B. Smith, *From the Land of the Shadows: The Making of Grey Owl* (Saskatoon: Western Producer Books, 1990). For Miner, see Tina Loo, *States of Nature: Conserving Canada's Wildlife in the Twentieth Century* (Vancouver: UBC Press, 2006), 63–91. For Farley Mowat, see his *Never Cry Wolf* (Toronto: McClelland and Stewart, 1963). For an excellent introduction to the gendering of environmental history, see Melody Hessing, Rebecca Raglon, and Catriona Sandilands, eds., *This Elusive Land: Women and the Canadian Environment* (Vancouver: UBC Press, 2005). For an introduction to Traill, see Rebecca Raglan, "Little Goody Two-Shoes: Reassessing the Work of Catharine Parr Traill," in *The Elusive Land,* 4–18. For Emily Carr, see Maria

Tippett, *Emily Carr: A Biography* (Don Mills, ON: Oxford University Press, 1979). May is quoted in Farley Mowat, *Rescue the Earth! Conversations with the Green Crusaders* (Toronto: McClelland and Stewart, 1990). For Clayoquot Sound and ecofeminism, see Niamh Moore, *The Changing Nature of Eco/Feminism: Telling Stories from Clayoquot Sound* (Vancouver: UBC Press, 2015). On risk, see Ulrich Beck, *Risk Society: Towards a New Modernity* (London: Sage, 1992).

The history of Greenpeace has been much chronicled. Frank Zelko's *Make It a Green Peace! The Rise of Countercultural Environmentalism* (New York: Oxford University Press, 2013) is a good starting point. His reference to American origins is in "Making Greenpeace: The Development of Direct Action Environmentalism in British Columbia," *BC Studies* 142–43 (2004): 197–240. For the drafting of Dave Birmingham, see Steve Erwood, *Greenpeace Chronicles: 40 Years of Protecting the Planet* (Amsterdam: Greenpeace International, 2011). On Greenpeace and mind bombs, see Stephen Dale, *McLuhan's Children: The Greenpeace Message and the Media* (Toronto: Between the Lines, 1996). For a sense of the heightened masculinity of the first voyage, see Robert Hunter, *Greenpeace to Amchitka: An Environmental Odyssey* (Vancouver: Arsenal Pulp Press, 2004).

The fullest history of VOW is a doctoral dissertation by Christine Ball, "The History of the Voice of Women: The Early Years" (University of Toronto, 1994), and the best account of the VOW tooth survey is in Tarah Brookfield, *Cold War Comforts: Canadian Women, Child Safety, and Global Insecurity* (Waterloo, ON: Wilfrid Laurier University Press, 2012). For more on Ann Lind's activism, see the memoir written by her daughter Plum Johnson, *They Left Us Everything: A Memoir* (Toronto: Penguin Canada, 2014).

The 1957 and 1958 newspaper quotes on fallout are from the *Toronto Star*, August 26 and 28, 1957, and April 23, 1958. Hilliard, as quoted in *Chatelaine*, is from Valerie J. Korinek, "It Is a Tough Time to Be in Love: The Darker Side of *Chatelaine* during the Cold War," in *Love, Hate and Fear in Canada's Cold War*, edited by Richard Cavell (Toronto: University of Toronto Press, 2004), 167. The "major uncertainties" quote is from John W. Finney, "Radiation Danger If Tests Go On but Old Fallout Called Small Risk," *Globe and Mail*, August 24, 1959.

Kellerman's interest in safe milk is from *Globe and Mail,* July 25, 1963. For Van Stolk, see *Toronto Star,* June 19, 1959, and Ball, "The History of the Voice of Women," 142. On Ethel Kesler, the "little nobody," and "hotcakes," see "Tooth Report Sought," *Globe and Mail,* July 25, 1963, and "Canadian Woman's Mailbox," *Globe and Mail,* June 1, 1963, 18. On contaminated breast milk, see Kathryn Harrison, "Too Close to Home: Dioxin Contamination of Breast Milk and the Political Agenda" in Hessing, Raglon, and Sandilands, *This Elusive Land,* 213–42. Lotta Dempsey's role is discussed in Ball, "The History of the Voice of Women," 148, and the maternalist cast was expressed in numerous places, such as Helen Tucker, "Letter from the President," insert, *Alberta VOW Newsletter,* undated (after March 7, 1962), Library and Archives Canada (LAC), Voice of Women Fonds, MG 28, I218.

The assessment of 1962–63 fallout levels is from "Fallout Level at New High," *Globe and Mail,* August 13, 1963. The *Maclean's* report was by Barbara Moon; see also Susan Kastner, "Mother of Two, Canada Lacks Fallout Facts," *Toronto Star,* July 26, 1963, 21, and brief to the Minister of National Health and Welfare, "Fallout Monitoring in Canada," LAC, Voice of Women Fonds, MG 28, I218, vol. 5, file 1. For the ways in which the brief was handled, see Judy LaMarsh, memo to cabinet, September 25, 1963, LAC, RG 29, 1982–83/109, vol. 2, Meetings, Advisory Committee on Radiation Protection, 1961, 1963, 1965, 1966, 1969, 1975. In the same volume, see also P.M. Bird, report to the minister of initial meetings of ACRP, held June 8 and 9, 1964, and report to the minister of the second meeting of ACRP, held May 27 and 28, 1965.

The 1963 RCMP report is from LAC, RCMP Division "O," Security Intelligence Background Section, October 23, 1963, Voice of Women, Communist Activities Within, Canada, Part 18, Correspondence 1-8-63 to 23-10-63. See also Part 20, Correspondence 20-12-63 to 15-3-64, RCMP Report Voice of Women (Communist Activities Within) Toronto 18-2-64.

Ellen Shadlock's "To a Thalidomide Baby" appeared in an undated newsletter, LAC, Voice of Women Fonds, MG 28, I218, vol. 4, file 10. Hunt's findings were reported in the *Globe and Mail,* March 19, 1966, and Franklin's leukemia question is from *Toronto Daily Star,* August 13, 1966. Barbara Frum's comments are found in her column "Science," which ran in the weekend supplement, *The Canadian,* which was distributed with the *Ottawa Citizen,* the *Gazette* (Montreal), and other newspapers on August 13, 1966. In it she quotes Franklin. Robert Hunter's "aroused mothers" quote appeared in the *Vancouver Sun,* October 2, 1969. For VOW support of the Greenpeace voyage, see LAC, Voice of Women Fonds, MG 28, I218, vol. 22, and VOW *Voice* (newsletter), September 1971. Hunter's account of the "vague arrangement" is in Hunter, *Vancouver Sun,* September 25, 1970, 33.

Who'll stop the rain?
This question served as the title of a song by John Fogerty,
sung by Creedence Clearwater Revival in 1970, and a 1978 film starring
Michael Moriarty and Nick Nolte. But in 1984 the Canadian Coalition on Acid
Rain gave it pointed and urgent political purpose in this poster and the broader
campaign against the emission of sulphur dioxide and nitrogen oxides into the
atmosphere by the burning of fossil fuels. Courtesy of the University of Waterloo Library,
Special Collections and Archives, Canadian Coalition on Acid Rain fonds, GA 87–2051

ADVOCATES AND ACTIVISTS

Graeme Wynn, with Jennifer Bonnell

THE MOST FAMOUS ENVIRONMENTALIST of recent time is a Canadian. Surprising as this may seem in the company of Al ("Inconvenient Truth") Gore, Gaylord (Earth Day) Nelson, James (Gaia) Lovelock, Kenyan Nobel Peace Prize winner Wangari Maathai, English broadcaster David Attenborough, Indian activist Vandana Shiva, and others, David Suzuki's global pre-eminence was announced in a *Maclean's* cover story in November 2013. Coming just a month after an Angus Reid poll identified him as one of the country's most admired figures, and two years after *Reader's Digest* declared him its "most trusted Canadian," this celebration of Suzuki the environmental crusader no doubt stirred the green patriot hearts of many Canadians. They had, after all, ranked Suzuki fifth (and first among those living) in a 2004 CBC Television contest to identify "The Greatest Canadian" of all time.

But fame is fleeting, subjective, and locally rooted (even when it claims global reach). When the *Guardian* published its list of "Earthshakers: The Top 100 Green Campaigners of All Time" in 2006, Suzuki ranked thirty-fifth, well behind Attenborough, Lovelock, Maathai, Gore, and Shiva and trailing Ken Livingston, the former mayor of London, and Arnold Schwarzenegger, body builder and politician. Even the *Maclean's* story had its contrapuntal note. It pointed out that Suzuki himself had declared environmentalism

David Suzuki on the Hart River, Yukon, 2011.
"Environmentalism," observes Suzuki on his foundation's website,
"isn't a discipline or speciality like law, medicine, plumbing, music or art.
It's a way of seeing our place in the world and recognizing that our
survival, health and happiness are inextricably dependent on nature."
Photo by Juri Peepre, Creative Commons Licence

a failure in spring 2012, and it screamed "David Suzuki Loses Faith in the Cause of His Lifetime" across its front cover. World renown Suzuki may have, the magazine seemed to be saying, but let's not get carried away with too much enthusiasm for his cause. Suzuki, a "force of nature," to borrow the title of a film about his life, was beset by doubts and doubters. The "green movement's chief messenger" had come to wonder "just what he and his compatriots have really accomplished."

Despite this sombre note, David Suzuki offers a singular perspective on the complex story of Canada's modern green movement. In placing Suzuki at the centre of our account of this movement, we make no claim that Suzuki is a hero or a great man who made history. We are fascinated, rather, by the relationships between the individual and his setting in a society created by "the work and lives of countless human beings." In this view, Suzuki was shaped by, and helped to identify, the concerns of his time. He clarified issues and gave voice to many of the anxieties of his contemporaries because he could see more clearly than most "where society was headed and what it needed."

When asked to explain how he became a TV personality, Suzuki often answers, enigmatically, "Pearl Harbor." As the child of Canadian-born parents of Japanese descent, Suzuki was moved in 1942, at the age of five and with his family, from Vancouver to an internment camp in the mountainous interior of British Columbia. Forbidden from returning to the Coast at war's end, the family relocated to southwestern Ontario. A dozen difficult years after the first relocation, the young Suzuki won a scholarship to Amherst College in Massachusetts. Graduation took him to Chicago for a doctorate in genetics, followed by a postdoctoral appointment at Oak Ridges in Tennessee. Disaffected and radicalized by racial segregation in the American South, he returned to Canada. After a year in Edmonton, he took a faculty position at the University of British Columbia in 1963, where he threw himself into genetic research and became a rising star in the field. In the late 1960s, he spent a semester at Berkeley. Student protest was in full swing, and he embraced the counterculture.

Pearl Harbor also led the United States into the Second World War, to the development of nuclear weapons, to Hiroshima and Nagasaki, to the Cold War, the nuclear arms race, and the testing of hydrogen bombs on land and sea. These escalating developments spawned anxiety about the consequences of radioactive fallout, leading to the Voice of Women campaign to measure and prevent the contamination of human bodies and to the Don't Make a Wave rallies that inspired the first Greenpeace voyage to oppose nuclear testing in Amchitka. At much the same time, *Poisons, Pests, and People* (a Canadian film documenting the collateral damage of chemical warfare against destructive pests), Rachel Carson's *Silent Spring,* and a controversial 1967 CBC Television broadcast called *Air of Death* (recounting the grim consequences of toxic emissions from industrial plants and automobile exhausts) brought many Canadians to realize that pollution was poisoning people's lungs and lives.

With ferment as well as pollution in the Canadian air, young people imbibed the former to organize against the latter. Pollution Probe, a major voice against society's polluting ways, began at the University of Toronto and had its counterparts in Edmonton (Save Tomorrow, Oppose Pollution or STOP), in Montreal (Society to Oppose Pollution, also known as STOP), and in Vancouver (Society for Pollution and Environmental Control, or SPEC). Pollution Probe even had a cleverly named Toronto predecessor in GASP (Group Action to Stop Pollution). With the American civil rights movement and its dream of a better world in the background, students across the country also responded to the Paris student uprising against capitalism, consumerism, and entrenched authority in May 1968 and, two years later, to the National Guard shooting of four Kent State University students protesting against escalation of the Vietnam War. Many spoke out against the use of Canadian university facilities to produce weaponry for the US military: "We should not be a cog in a machine which is invading Vietnam," said Professor Chandler Davis at the University of Toronto. Opposition to the war galvanized students; it was "the backdrop against which everything happened."

Influenced by his sojourns in Tennessee and California, Suzuki was in tune with the times in his early years at UBC. Closer in appearance to the stereotypical hippie than a lab-coated scientist, he often seemed to prefer the role of "guide by the side" of undergraduates to the "sage on the stage" persona of more traditional instructors. He joined students in wide-ranging informal discussions and was often engaged in antiwar debates. Extrapolating from his genetic studies, he offered students the view that people are basically fruit flies who hatch out as maggots and defecate all over the environment. He wanted to make the point that it is the few who become really powerful (implying American political and military leaders) who are really dangerous. But for all his activism and his concerns about the links between genetics and racial stereotyping, science and the military, Suzuki found a haven in his laboratory and sanity in science.

When CBC Vancouver came calling, it was to capitalize on Suzuki's growing reputation as someone who could talk about science in lay terms. A series of half-hour television programs, *Suzuki on Science,* went on air in 1971 and 1972. Envisaged as educational programs for a youthful audience, they began with genetics – discussing fertilization and genes, immune systems, and so on – but then encompassed other areas of science. In 1974, Suzuki was appointed host of CBC Television's *Science Magazine,* which ran in prime time. In 1975, he also became the first host of *Quirks and Quarks* on CBC Radio, a show that "made science accessible and interesting to the mainstream listening audience in a unique and offbeat fashion." Recognizing the rapidity with which science and technology had changed the world in two decades, Suzuki wanted to provide a better understanding of what it is to be human and to help listeners choose between the good and the evil that science offered. Frank, passionate, and outspoken, he was increasingly recognized as a media personality, even as many of his fellow scientists grew skeptical of his proselytizing.

In 1979, Suzuki left *Quirks and Quarks,* and *Science Magazine* was amalgamated with a longer-running science program on CBC Television that was renamed, in recognition of Suzuki's celebrity status, *The Nature of Things with David Suzuki.* It was a transformative moment. Hosted by University of Toronto physicists Patterson Hume and Donald Ivey, *The Nature of Things* had been brought to air in 1960. Initially, it dealt with topics such as space technology, the causes of schizophrenia, and the functioning of the brain, and for its first decade it was "inextricably bound up with the scientific project of modernity." Most of its episodes were about knowing and controlling the world through science. Nature, in this view, was "predominantly ... a challenge to human ingenuity" or, as "a garden of the wonderful and the weird," a place worthy of human curiosity. Responding to societal concerns in the late 1960s, the show ran half a dozen episodes on pollution and used "the comparatively new science of ecology" to suggest that humans might need to curb their demands on nature. For all that, *The*

Nature of Things strongly espoused the notion of scientific and technological progress and regarded the future with optimism.

By his own account, Suzuki brought "a human-centered perspective" to
the program that now carried his name, "revelling in our intellect and
culture as special and unique." But the show's producer, Jim Murray (who
had also produced *Science Magazine*), had been deeply influenced by the
ideas of John Livingston, who was in effect the "philosophical guru" of the
new program. Livingston was a self-described naturalist who had worked
with the Audubon Society and with Murray at the CBC in the 1960s before
joining the Faculty of Environmental Studies at York University in 1970.
In 1973, he published *One Cosmic Instant: A Natural History of Human
Arrogance* in which he argued that humans in developed countries had
separated themselves from the natural world that sustained them. Assuming
superiority over nature, they mistakenly believed that humans had absolute
power and authority over the nonhuman. By the end of the decade,
Livingston was elaborating these ideas into a trenchant critique of the
"perceived dichotomies that flow from the 'mind/matter,' 'spirit/flesh' dualism inherent in western cosmologies." These cosmologies, he wrote in his
1981 book *The Fallacy of Wildlife Conservation,* place "man" in the same
relationship to "non-man" as they do intellect to emotion.

To Suzuki, Livingston's ideas on humans and the environment were
"radical, running counter to the thrust of western society." The notion that
"humans as a species" are "out of balance with nature, puffed up with an
unrealistic sense of importance and incorrectly convinced of our right to
exploit nature in any way we choose" was difficult for this highly trained
scientist to accept – accustomed as he was to insisting that the power of
the human brain and the majesty of science set humankind apart from the
rest of nature. Others were making somewhat similar pleas for greater
moral and ethical sensibility towards nature. Among this growing international battery of intellectuals, Canadian academic William Leiss argued,
in a 1972 book titled *The Domination of Nature,* that long-held cultural

attitudes and modern science and technology were profoundly detrimental in their assertion of human mastery over nature. It was only "reluctantly, [and] over time," Suzuki later reflected, that he came "to understand the profundity of the 'deep ecology' and green movements."

By the mid-1980s, Suzuki was collaborating with Livingston and Murray on a groundbreaking, eight-part television series, *A Planet for the Taking*. Examining different belief systems, cultural values, and scientific advances, it traced changing human attitudes towards nature and the impact of technology on the lives of humans, wildlife, and the environment. It called for a major "perceptual shift" in humanity's relationship with nature and the wild. Summing up the message in an interview, Suzuki said that the series was critical of "the Western attitude, which regards humans as special and somehow separate from the rest of nature." This, he continued, rests on the conviction that "we were created in God's image and placed on this planet to have dominion over everything. Our definition of progress is measured by the extent to which we can dominate nature ... We don't consider ourselves part of the Earth's ecosystem or recognize that our actions have enormous impact." The implications were plain to see: "If we continue this way, we will not only extinguish a large number of species, which we've already been doing successfully, but we are going to create a planet that won't ... support us."

Drawing on average an audience of 1.8 million viewers per episode, the series earned Suzuki a United Nations Environment Programme Medal and confirmed his status as Canada's environmental talisman. It also, in some sense, cast his future. As he acknowledged, "After a series like that, we couldn't go back to the programming we had once done. Increasingly, our programs have questioned some of the most cherished notions of progress, the necessity for growth and the overriding concern for jobs and profit." Through the late 1980s and into the 1990s, *The Nature of Things with David Suzuki* presented "a very different conception of nature and its relation to science" than its predecessor programs had during the 1970s. Now, "nature" was fragile and vulnerable; it was the unfortunate and largely helpless victim of an ongoing war waged by men and machines. Technological progress had become a poisoned chalice.

With their wide reach, *A Planet for the Taking* and *The Nature of Things* helped shape Canadian attitudes towards the environment in the final quarter of the twentieth century. But they were not the only influences. Building on their Amchitka intervention, Greenpeace activists cemented their image as campaigners "standing between the natural world and the forces that seek to destroy it" with the use of Zodiacs to disrupt Russian whaling activities off the coast of California in 1975. Two years later, in 1977, Greenpeace attracted global attention to the anti-sealing movement and to its environmental activism by bringing French film star Brigitte Bardot to cuddle a baby seal on the ice off Newfoundland. Philosophically (if not tactically and practically) allied with John Livingston in their commitment to the moral consideration of nonhuman nature, Greenpeace made clever use of the media, of "mind bombs," and of celebrity engagement to capture attention, trace a path of lasting international relevance, and provide a model for many other environmental activists.

Canadians were also given cause to think about environmental issues by some of the country's most prolific, widely read, and much-admired authors. Margaret Atwood's work often invites the reader to consider the vulnerability of human beings, and she sees her writing, in part, as an effort "to warn the world against" the sort of cumulative ecological destruction that "might result in the disappearance of life from the face of the earth." Raconteur, rabble-rouser, and incurable romantic Farley Mowat began his lifelong literary campaign to raise peoples' environmental sensitivity with *Never Cry Wolf* in 1963. *A Whale for the Killing* (1972), set in a Newfoundland outport, was ultimately a lament for modernizing society's loss of traditional attitudes of respect for nature. *Sea of Slaughter* (1984) was a true jeremiad attributing the "massacre" of wildlife in the northeastern Atlantic to the hubris of modern civilization and the failure of resource-management science. Together these works won Mowat a reputation as a fierce champion

This iconic picture of Brigitte Bardot, retired film star
and an increasingly prominent animal rights activist, was taken in 1977.
Bardot's visit to Blanc-Sablon, Quebec, and the seal-hunting "front" was
facilitated by wealthy Swiss conservationist Franz Weber, but it did much
to promote Greenpeace's anti-sealing campaign. The campaign had been
funded by a loan from the International Fund for Animal Welfare, led by
Brian Davis, formerly of the New Brunswick SPCA, who began fostering
public hostility towards the hunt in the mid-1960s.
© Fondation Brigitte Bardot

of Indigenous and ecological causes and "a latter-day prophet who railed
against the rapid destruction of humanity's bonds to animals, plants and
the earth itself."

In January 1982, Suzuki presented an episode of *The Nature of Things*
titled "Windy Bay." It juxtaposed lush temperate rainforest with the devastation of clear-cuts, the biological profusion of the archipelago then known
as the Queen Charlotte Islands (now Haida Gwaii) with the consequences
of logging on Lyell Island, which had begun under government licence in
1975. Opposition orchestrated by the Islands Protection Society, a coalition
of Haida and newcomers dedicated to wilderness preservation, and the
Council of the Haida Nation had gained little traction through the 1970s,

This spectacular image of Nootka Island on the west coast of Vancouver Island, taken by nature and conservation photographer T.J. Watt in 2013, speaks volumes about logging on the BC coast. Although proponents of forestry would argue that these cutblocks are far smaller than many worked in the 1980s, that substantial tracts of forest remain, and that earlier exploited areas have been replanted, opponents stress that the bare ground and sinuous roads of recent operations scar an otherwise beautiful vista, destroy habitat, and expose steep slopes to the ravages of sun, wind, and rain. Photo by T.J. Watt

but Suzuki's television program brought industry's assault on "a priceless inheritance 10,000 years in the making" to national attention and strengthened support for escalating Haida protests against the desecration of the "islands of beauty and wonder" they called "Gwaii Haanas." When the provincial government allowed logging to continue, seventy-two people, including several Haida Elders, were arrested at a blockade on the access road. It soon became clear that there was growing national support for the campaign against logging on South Moresby Island/Gwaii Haanas. In 1988, the BC and Canadian governments designated the area a National Park Reserve with joint management by the Council of the Haida Nation.

Here we see the aftermath of logging in the Klanawa Valley
between Nitinat Lake and Bamfield on southwestern Vancouver Island.
Taken in 2016, this photograph reveals a small, bedraggled patch of forest and
a surface littered with stumps and debris being stripped of soil by a cascading
rivulet fed by the two thousand to six thousand millimetres of precipitation
that fall on the slopes each year. Photo by T.J. Watt

Protests against industrial logging and campaigns for the preservation
of old-growth forest and wilderness in British Columbia proliferated
in the 1970s and 1980s. Their roots might be traced back to the successful
efforts of members of BC Spaces for Nature, who focused the "first ever
citizen-led effort to save wilderness in Canada" on the Nitinat Lake area of
Vancouver Island in 1971, but they all drew oxygen from events in South
Moresby/Gwaii Haanas. High-profile confrontations between government
and industry interests, on the one hand, and Indigenous peoples and environmentalists, on the other, have come to symbolize the struggle. Think
Valhalla Wilderness, Meares Island, the Stein Valley, Clayoquot Sound,
the Carmanah Valley, Strathcona Park, the Purcells, the Spatsizi Plateau
(Stikine), and Tatshenshini. They had their counterparts, large and small

across the country, in Temagami and more recently at Grassy Narrows in Ontario, for example. Many of these campaigns were initiated, organized, and supported by environmental groups or NGOs, such as the Western Canada Wilderness Committee, now simply Wilderness Committee, which in 1991, barely a decade after its foundation, claimed thirty thousand members and revenues of $2.5 million from fees, donations, and the sale of calendars and posters bearing magnificent photographs of "the wilderness." None of these campaigns was as (in)famous as that at Clayoquot Sound in 1993, which saw Australian rock band Midnight Oil perform at the protesters' encampment and led to 932 arrests, making it the largest act of civil disobedience to that point in Canada.

Neither the wilderness nor the environment was far from public consciousness in the 1980s and 1990s. Some counted at least 1,800 environmental groups, large and small, across the country. Enormously varied in size and influence, and pursuing a wide range of agendas, from the defence of home places in Nova Scotia to the promotion of bicycling in Montreal, these groups were by no means unitary in organization or singular in purpose. Still, they contributed to growing environmental awareness. In 1987, nineteen in twenty Canadians were said to favour government spending on wilderness preservation. Of course, people understood *wilderness* in very different ways. For some, it was pristine, roadless territory; for others, simply "forest." What is clear, however, is that both government and public recognition of the importance of "wild places" increased significantly between 1960 and 2000. At the end of the millennium, eight in every ten Canadians (the highest proportion recorded in thirty countries surveyed) claimed that environmental protection was more important than economic growth. Indeed, Environment Canada announced at century's end that 98 percent of Canadians regarded nature as essential to human survival (it is not clear whether the other 2 percent ate or breathed). Yet policy sorely lagged behind public opinion. In 1999, Canada placed twenty-eighth among twenty-nine countries on a composite ranking of twenty-five environmental

Crowds gather in front of the BC legislature on March 18, 1993,
after Paul George, Adrienne Carr, and Joe Foy of the Western Canada Wilderness
Committee camped on the lawn in an effort to speak with Premier Mike Harcourt
about the logging of old-growth forest in Clayoquot Sound. Later that afternoon,
two hundred to three hundred people stormed the legislature during the Speech
from the Throne. Several were arrested, the first of one thousand or so protesters
taken into custody over the next six months. Courtesy of Wilderness Committee

indicators published by the Organisation for Economic Co-operation and
Development.

For three decades and more, environmentalists staked their cause on
confrontation – in Zodiacs on the high seas or by chaining themselves to
industrial equipment, spraying dye on the coats of harp seals, or forming
passive human blockades across the roads upon which loggers and miners
depended. Affronted by such challenges to their legal businesses and,
they insisted, to national economic prosperity, industrialists sought injunc-
tions from a political-legal establishment that generally supported them.
Early in this dance, environmentalists and Indigenous people often stood
side by side, seeming to reinforce the conviction, common since the 1960s,
that Indigenous people had been the continent's first ecologists. Here and

there, landscapes were "saved" from the onslaught of feller bunchers or mechanical shovels, often to be set aside as parks, and business proceeded more or less as usual in other locations.

Reflecting on his first visit to Haida Gwaii fifteen years after the "Windy Bay" shoot, David Suzuki recalled a conversation in which he had asked a Haida artist why he was opposed to logging when the forest industry brought jobs and money into local communities. Guujaaw responded that although he and his people would remain when all the forest was gone, "We won't be Haida anymore. We'll be just like everybody else." Here, Suzuki realized, was a fundamentally different way of looking at the world. "To be Haida is to be intimately connected with the land, the air, the water, the fish, the trees, the birds." What's more, he concluded, it was "absolutely right." This insight formed the core of his 1997 book, *Sacred Balance: Rediscovering Our Place in Nature,* in which he argued (as he has since) that humans "are creatures of the earth, and as such ... utterly dependent on its gifts of air, water, soil, and the energy of the sun."

Once again, Suzuki was more bellwether than clairvoyant in making this claim. *Sacred Balance* had many antecedents, demonstrated by its invocation of a wide range of sources ranging from the Bible and Romantic poets to modern scientists and Indigenous wisdom. The book also echoed Englishman James Lovelock's Gaia principle in its argument that Earth itself is a living organism. And it paralleled arguments being made at about the same time by Canadian forest scientist Stan Rowe, whose late-life writings emphasized human responsibility to Earth and the importance of "seeing humanity in the perspective of the planetary worldview." Human bodies, he wrote, were dependent on Earth for existence. People, other organisms, air, soil, and water are all contained, held together, and supported by "Earth-space." Yet, try as he might, Rowe found it difficult to gain popular support for his ideas; "ecological sense does not come easily to ... moderns and postmoderns," he lamented early in the twenty-first century. Suzuki dressed these claims in new garb and sent them jauntily abroad to challenge prevailing views of Earth as a basket of resources for human consumption.

Easy definitions of environmental conflicts as binary encounters between the interests of frontier development and wilderness protection began to crumble as increasingly assertive Indigenous voices articulated a third understanding of the spaces at issue – they were homelands. This was not a new perspective. Justice Thomas Berger's Mackenzie Valley Pipeline Inquiry enshrined the idea in the title of the 1977 report, *Northern Frontier, Northern Homeland*. But it gained cogency when the UN's Brundtland Commission, in 1987, endorsed the right of Indigenous peoples to a decisive voice in the use of their land and through legal decisions such as that of the Supreme Court of Canada in the *Delgamuukw* case in 1997. Recognizing that poverty-stricken Indigenous communities had legitimate cause to use the resources of their traditional territories, some environmentalists began to back away from their insistence that not one tree should fall. At much the same time, industrialists began to see that escalating opposition in the form of consumer boycott campaigns locked them into a zero-sum game. A growing commitment to collaboration and coexistence – first in Gwaii Haanas, then in Clayoquot Sound, and then with the Great Bear Rainforest Agreement of 2006 – trumped confrontation and suggested the importance of rethinking the human-nature relationship.

These were gains – against a dark backdrop. When Suzuki announced in 2012 that environmentalism had failed, he acknowledged the movement's many achievements, but he regretted its failure to achieve this rethinking: "Recessions, popped financial bubbles, and ... a cacophony of denial" had succeeded in portraying "environmental protection ... as an impediment to economic expansion." Canada, hell-bent on expanding oil production from the Alberta tar sands, was contemplating exports of natural gas, lobbying for pipelines to carry diluted bitumen to market, and stifling the expression of opposition to its policies. It concertedly disregarded mounting evidence and anxiety that such actions were "altering the physical, chemical, and biological properties of the planet on a geological scale."

Five years later, a new government in Ottawa committed Canada to the Paris Climate Accord and offered promise of different things to come. In 2018, it is still not clear what they will be. Juggling the creation of domestic jobs and economic development with global commitments and the planetary future (as many politicians are prone to do), the federal government brokered the implementation of carbon pricing with the provinces (particularly a reluctant Alberta) by promising new pipeline capacity to carry diluted bitumen from the Alberta tar sands to Pacific tidewater and for shipment to Asia. Then opposition to the risks of increased tanker traffic in BC coastal waters and uncertainties about future markets and prices for oil (as alternative sources of energy gain traction) led the Texas-based Kinder Morgan company to divest itself of the Trans Mountain Pipeline. The federal government stepped in to acquire and expand the existing line. But the juggling act continues, and its denouement remains uncertain – especially in light of the August 2018 Federal Court of Appeal judgment (that found flaws in the process by which the pipeline expansion was approved) and stalled development plans. Canada is off the pace needed to meet its carbon emission reduction commitments. Shifting provincial political winds are jeopardizing some earlier cap-and-trade and carbon-pricing agreements. And should the world reduce oil consumption decisively, falling markets may turn an expanded pipeline into a stranded asset. Only time, politics, and our collective commitment will tell.

REFERENCES AND FURTHER READING

The first two paragraphs draw from Jonathon Gatehouse, "The Nature of David Suzuki," *Maclean's*, November 18, 2013; David Adam, "Earthshakers: The Top 100 Green Campaigners of All Time," *The Guardian*, November 28, 2006; and Sturla Gunnarsson, dir., *Force of Nature: The David Suzuki Movie* (Montreal: National

Film Board of Canada, 2010). The third paragraph draws from Margaret MacMillan's discussion of Thomas Carlyle and biography in *History's People: Personalities and the Past* (Toronto: Anansi, 2015), 10–11.

We focus on the recent history of environmentalism: nineteenth-century enthusiasms for natural history; the important Canadian Commission of Conservation, established in 1909; such charismatic twentieth-century figures as Grey Owl and "Wild Goose Jack" Miner; and much else fall beyond our purview. For discussions of earlier manifestations of conservationist sentiment in Canada and of Jack Miner, see Tina Loo, *States of Nature: Conserving Canada's Wildlife in the Twentieth Century* (Vancouver: UBC Press, 2006); George Colpitts, *Game in the Garden: A Human History of Wildlife in Western Canada to 1940* (Vancouver: UBC Press, 2002); and Janet Foster, *Working for Wildlife: The Beginnings of Preservation in Canada* (Toronto: University of Toronto Press, 1978). On Grey Owl, see Donald B. Smith, *From the Land of the Shadows: The Making of Grey Owl* (Saskatoon: Western Producer Prairie Books, 1990), and on the Commission of Conservation, see Michel Girard, *L'écologisme retrouvé: Essor et déclin de la Commission de la conservation du Canada* (Ottawa: Les Presses de l'Université d'Ottawa, 1994).

For more on *The Air of Death*, see Ryan O'Connor, *The First Green Wave: Pollution Probe and the Origins of Environmental Activism in Ontario* (Vancouver: UBC Press, 2014), and for *Poisons, Pests and People*, see Larry Gosnell, dir. (Montreal: National Film Board of Canada, 1960). For the ferment of the 1960s, see O'Connor, *First Green Wave*, and on Greenpeace, see Frank Zelko, *Make It a Green Peace! The Rise of Countercultural Environmentalism* (New York: Oxford University Press, 2013). Also see Roberta Lexier, "'The Backdrop against Which Everything Happened': English-Canadian Student Movements and Off-Campus Movements for Change," *History of Intellectual Culture* 7, 1 (2007): 1–18, which quotes Chandler Davis on page 13 and Martin Loney of SFU and the Canadian Union of Students on the war as "backdrop" on page 1. Suzuki's maggot analogy is available in Clip 3 of Gunnarsson's *Force*, on the NFB website, and in the CBC clip "David Suzuki with His Students: 'We Are All Fruit Flies'," *Telescope*, January 4, 1972 (which is available online and also includes the sanity in science point). For Suzuki's perspective in the 1970s, see the television interview with Roy Bonisteel, "David Suzuki on Making Science Accessible," *Man Alive*, March 8, 1977, available online. The accompanying gloss includes the quotation describing *Quirks and Quarks*. The history of *The Nature of Things* is traced in Glenda Wall, "Science, Nature, and 'The Nature of Things': An Instance of Canadian Environmental Discourse, 1960–1994," *Canadian Journal of Sociology/Cahiers canadiens de sociologie* 24, 1 (1999): 53–85, which includes the "inextricably bound" (55), "human ingenuity" (59), and "wonderful and weird" (68) quotations.

The "science of ecology" quotation is from the incomplete list of *The Nature of Things* episodes at TVArchive.ca. John Livingston's "perceived dichotomies" quotation is from his *The Fallacy of Wildlife Conservation* (Toronto: McClelland and Stewart, 1981), 133. Suzuki's early assessment of Livingston's ideas is from his *Metamorphosis: Stages in a Life* (Toronto: Stoddart Publishing, 1987), 260. His comment about *Planet* is from an interview with Ron Wideman, reported in Mirza Abu Bakr Baig, "English Essays in the Wild Project," available online.

The best place to start for Atwood's environmental perspective is Ron Hatch, "Margaret Atwood, the Land and Ecology," in *Margaret Atwood: Works and Impact*, edited by Reingard M. Nischik, 180–201 (Rochester, NY: Camden House, 2000). The quote about Mowat as a "latter-day prophet" is from *Maclean's*, August 12, 2002, 48–49. The "priceless inheritance" quotation is from Ian Gill, *All That We Say Is Ours: Guujaaw and the Reawakening of the Haida Nation* (Vancouver: Douglas and McIntyre, 2009), 111. For "islands of beauty" and the protest, see David Rossiter, "The Nature of a Blockade: Environmental Politics and the Haida Action on Lyell Island, British Columbia," in *Blockades or Breakthroughs? Aboriginal Peoples Confront the Canadian State*, edited by Yale D. Belanger and P. Whitney Lackenbauer (Montreal and Kingston: McGill-Queen's University Press, 2014), 71. For BC Spaces for Nature and the Nitinat Triangle, see the BC Spaces for Nature website. For the Western Canada Wilderness Committee, see Michael R. Mason, "The Politics of Wilderness Preservation: Environmental Activism and Natural Area Policy in British Columbia" (PhD diss., Cambridge University,

1993), 142–49. Much has been written about the Clayoquot protests and their aftermath. See, among others, Tzeporah Berman, *This Crazy Time: Living Our Environmental Challenge* (Toronto: Knopf Canada, 2011), and Warren Magnusson and Karena Shaw, eds., *A Political Space: Reading the Global through Clayoquot Sound* (Minneapolis: University of Minnesota Press, 2003).

The estimate of 1,800 environmental groups is from Jeremy Wilson, "Green Lobbies: Pressure Groups and Environmental Policy," in *Canadian Environmental Policy: Ecosystems, Politics and Process,* edited by R. Boardman (Toronto: Oxford University Press, 1992), 110–11. For cycling in Montreal, see Daniel Ross, "'Vive la Vélorution!': Le Monde à Bicyclette and the Origins of Cycling Advocacy in Montreal," in *Canadian Countercultures and the Environment,* edited by Colin M. Coates, 127–50 (Calgary: University of Calgary Press, 2016); on Nova Scotia, see Mark Leeming, *In Defence of Home Places: Environmental Activism in Nova Scotia* (Vancouver: UBC Press, 2017). For Environment Canada and OECD and other survey figures, see Larry Pynn, "Environment Tops Poll of Canadians' Concerns: The High Ranking Given Pollution and Conservation Issues is Being Attributed to an Improving Economy," *Vancouver Sun,* September 20, 1999, A4; Environics International, "Public Opinion and the Environment" (opinion poll conducted for Environment Canada, 1999); and David Boyd, *Canada vs the OECD: An Environmental Comparison* (Victoria: Eco-Research Chair of Environmental Law and Policy, 1999) and *Canada vs Sweden: An Environmental Face-Off* (Victoria: Eco-Research Chair of Environmental Law and Policy, 2002). Suzuki's conversation with Guujaaw is recounted in Gill, *All That We Say,* 111, and by Suzuki in Gunnarsson, *Force.* The "creatures of the earth" quotation is from Suzuki's *Sacred Balance: Rediscovering Our Place in Nature* (Vancouver: Greystone Books, 2007). James E. Lovelock's Gaia hypothesis is in his *The Ages of Gaia: A Biography of Our Living Earth* (Oxford: Oxford University Press, 1988). For J. Stan Rowe, see his *Home Place: Essays on Ecology* (Edmonton: NeWest Press, 2002) and *Earth Alive: Essays on Ecology* (Edmonton: NeWest Press, 2006). The last paragraph draws from Suzuki's 2012 blog post "The Fundamental Failure of Environmentalism."

Peter Winkworth, *The Emigrant's Welcome to Canada,*
ca. 1820. In the nineteenth century and before, external
perceptions of Canada often focused on the experiences
of winter. Library and Archives Canada, R9266–3510,
Peter Winkworth Collection of Canadiana, e002511221

CLIMATES OF OUR TIMES

Liza Piper

C LIMATE CHANGE IS UPON us. The world is warming, and the parameters of change can be traced by wild storms, melting ice, and rising waters. Since 2000, English newspapers have carried photo essays depicting life on tiny Pacific atolls threatened by the rising sea. One of Al Gore's *Inconvenient Truths* is that many residents of such places have "already had to evacuate their homes because of rising seas." And the *New York Times* reported that the president of Kiribati feared his country would be flooded and uninhabitable within sixty years. Glaciers in British Columbia and Alberta – which feed rivers essential to agriculture, cities, and hydroelectric power in western Canada – are anticipated to shrink by at least 70 percent by the end of the century. Global warming is now our most pressing environmental issue – and it constitutes one of the most difficult political challenges facing Canadians and others in the early twenty-first century.

Global and local climates have changed through time, and they have often done so dramatically. In broad terms, these changes occurred at three different rates. Some played out over many millennia. About twenty thousand years ago, rising temperatures caused the great ice sheets that covered most of what is now Canada and large areas of northern Europe to melt, and rising sea levels flooded land bridges, including the one between Siberia and Alaska that people had used as a path of migration. Plants, animals,

319

and people eventually flourished in areas once covered by ice or glacial lakes. It took three thousand years for the lens of Laurentide ice that covered the interior parts of Labrador in 5000 BCE to melt away and a similar interval for most of Baffin Island to become ice free during the summer months. As the warming trend continued, trees and grasses grew tall and well beyond the current northern limits of their range. Marine and terrestrial environments in the Arctic Archipelago opened to human occupation. Then the climate cooled, and living things retreated southward. The northern treeline fell back a couple of hundred kilometres or so, to approximately its present limits, but it took a thousand years for this to occur.

Shorter-term fluctuations also affected local and regional climates. The Medieval Warm Period (900 to 1250 CE) was, as the name suggests, a prolonged warm spell. It was followed by the Pacific Episode (1250–1550 CE), which ushered in three hundred years of cooling, and by the Little Ice Age (1550–1850 CE). These shifts affected human communities in profound ways. Warming in medieval times, combined with advanced plant breeding by Indigenous societies, allowed for the northward spread of maize agriculture from Mexico into the northern plains of western Canada. The cooler years that followed encouraged hunting over horticulture along the northernmost reaches of maize cultivation and led some populations, such as the Haudenosaunee (Iroquois), to move into new territories. In the Arctic, communities moved southward in response to heavier sea ice and a scarcity of whales. The Little Ice Age brought advancing glaciers in the North and West and harsh winters during the earliest years of colonial settlement in New France. The warmer, at times wetter, conditions that followed encouraged non-Indigenous agricultural settlement in western Canada and the Subarctic.

Finally, there were times of rapid change, when the climate shifted in the span of a few decades. At this scale, even relatively modest alterations in climatic conditions can pose challenges to human survival. Between 1300 and 1330, for example, falling temperatures made it more difficult for Inuit at southern Baffin Island to harvest marine and terrestrial resources, leading them to migrate to the Labrador and Ungava Peninsulas. Six hundred years later, the drought conditions of the 1920s and 1930s displaced thousands of western Canadian farm families and influenced agricultural practices, settlement patterns, state resource management, and broader welfare-state policies for decades to come.

All of these climate shifts had identifiable physical causes. In the long term, scientists tell us, glaciations alternate with interglacial periods on a 100,000-year cycle (known as the Milankovitch cycle). These fluctuations are caused by long-term variations in the earth's orbit around the sun that affect the incidence of solar radiation in the northern and southern hemispheres and lead to periods of ice and snow accumulation and shorter spells of snow and ice melt, the most recent of which began about twenty thousand years ago. Beginning about 11,000 BCE, catastrophic events, such as the sudden release of vast quantities of pent-up glacial meltwater into the oceans, altered hemispheric and global climates over decades and centuries. Periodic variations in the release of radiation from the sun (on a 2,500-year cycle), smaller-scale changes in the release of solar energy (with a periodicity of about 200 years) and sun-spot cycles (with a 10–12 year interval) have also produced changes in Earth temperature and (as a consequence of the close interconnections of temperatures, ocean currents, winds, and weather) regional and global weather and climates.

Although these forces still have an impact on the planet, the climate of our times is different. About 300 years ago, the beginnings of the Industrial Revolution in Britain initiated a shift in energy systems as society moved from reliance on the kinetic power of wind and water and the muscular effort of animal- and humankind to increasing and accelerating dependence, for motive power, on the energy stored in fossil fuels. This shift produced a cascade of consequences. It quickened production, improved communications, and changed patterns of land use. Meanwhile, the emissions produced in burning these fuels accumulated in the atmosphere. Today, we call them greenhouse gases. Scientists have shown, without doubt, that increasing quantities of these emissions, such as carbon dioxide and nitrous oxide, trap more and more of the energy (heat) radiating from the earth, causing the long-term rise of the average temperature of the atmosphere.

Anthropogenic greenhouse gases have been the main force driving global warming for over sixty years. Indeed, as early as 1961, the Canadian Broadcasting Corporation aired television and radio reports on warming in Northwest Territories, our Arctic and Subarctic environments long being sentinels of climate change. But the effects of these greenhouse gas emissions are not always readily apparent to the casual observer. Since 1945, there have been cooler decades, years, and seasons amid the longer trend of warming. Local experiences can seem to confound the global-warming narrative. In March 1987, my father photographed my then ten-year-old sister in front of a rare sight: loose pack ice in Halifax Harbour. But the long-term consequences of increasing greenhouse gas emissions are clear. Sixteen of the seventeen warmest years *on record* have occurred since 2000. The world is warming at a rate that poses severe threats to life on earth as we know it, and humans have been primarily responsible for creating these circumstances. That is why global climate change is both a pressing environmental issue and a major political challenge.

Historical perspective allows us to understand how changes in the atmosphere have influenced human history, how humans have influenced the atmosphere, and how knowledge of the atmosphere and its dynamics has changed over time. Climate and climate change are both physical things and socially constructed in that they reflect shared understandings of things in nature, but these understandings also change over time and place. Indigenous understandings of climate persist in many parts of northern Canada, for instance, allowing Indigenous people to make connections among things that have long since been severed in Western thought. "The climate," as we understand it, is a product of Victorian science, which sought to separate out an understanding of broader, average atmospheric dynamics from our daily experiences of the weather. These scientists also wanted to divorce these dynamics from magnetism, electricity, and aesthetics, which had been connected to climate in European and Canadian thought. Climates have changed over time, but as these examples suggest, changing understandings of climate can influence how we interpret climate change.

Climate has been integral to colonialism and nation building in what would become Canada. Once Europeans arrived in North America, they tried to make sense of their new world, often by taking weather measurements, mostly for their own, local purposes. Explorers, missionaries, trappers, traders, and farmers recorded temperatures, dates of first and last frosts, wind directions, and the timing of river breakups in diaries, logbooks, post records, and almanacs. What they made of this information remains an open question, but these practices helped acclimatize them to unfamiliar environments. In *Roughing It in the Bush*, published in 1852, Susanna Moodie reflected on her first winter in Canada: "The winter had now fairly set in – the iron winter of 1833. The snow was unusually deep ... and passed in such a miserable dwelling, we felt it very severely." As a new arrival to the country, Moodie would not have been aware that the snow was unusually deep. Two decades later, however, recollections of that particular snowfall had produced a settled understanding of place.

Alongside casual settler meteorologists such as Moodie, formal scientific meteorological endeavours sprang up across the area that became Canada as people attempted to comprehend the nature of large territories. The earliest scientific efforts occurred in the eighteenth century. In 1742, Jean-François Gaultier, the king's physician in New France, established Canada's first meteorological station in Quebec City. He measured the temperature on a daily basis for years and published some of his findings in the *Mémoires de l'Académie royale des sciences* in France.

The Hudson's Bay Company supported a wide range of sciences, including meteorology. In 1769, for instance, it backed British efforts to measure and observe the transit of Venus across the sun from its Fort Prince of Wales post. Instruments shipped to the post included thermometers and barometers, which company employees used to record weather at the fort three times a day for a year. The instruments were then used by the HBC to keep detailed meteorological records well into the early nineteenth century.

In 1771, only a few years after the first instruments arrived in Rupert's Land, the Swiss polymath Johann Heinrich Lambert proposed that the Royal Society fund an ambitious global meteorological network, including a site at Fort Prince of Wales. Nothing came of it, but the Royal Society did, sixty years later, support a network of observatories to "marshal geomagnetic observations on a global scale." The project was suggested by the German geographer Alexander von Humboldt and headed up by Edward Sabine, a soldier and scientist. It included observatories in four locations – Upper Canada, Tasmania, Saint Helena, and the Cape of Good Hope – chosen for their relation to what was then known about the earth's magnetic field.

In Canada, in 1839, Lieutenant Charles Riddell, following Sabine's direction, selected a permanent site for a meteorological and magnetic observatory in Toronto. Regular observations began on January 1, 1840, and have continued ever since. Victorians sought to elevate the observation of the weather to a science and in the process distance it from unscientific lay appraisals. Climate science would be built on formulaic observations of the weather: wind, temperature, precipitation, barometric pressure, and cloud cover. The Toronto Observatory served as the foundation for the Meteorological Service of Canada and the hub for a network of observatories that emerged as the new Dominion asserted its authority over the enormous territory it wished to claim.

Erecting a meteorological network across a vast territory posed logistical problems. John Henry Lefroy, superintendent of the Toronto observatory from 1842 to 1850, initially widened his network by asking Royal Engineers and Royal Artillery officers, who had been keeping their own records since the 1830s, to send their regular weather observations to the Toronto Observatory. Records from stations in Ontario, Quebec, Newfoundland, and Nova Scotia were thus incorporated into the Dominion index. These records served the interests of the promoters of the new Toronto Observatory, who envisaged it as the centre for a navigational and storm-warning network along the St. Lawrence. Then, beginning in the 1850s, Lefroy worked with Egerton Ryerson, chief superintendent of education for Upper Canada, to establish meteorological observatories in country grammar schools. Although it took over a decade to implement the program, continuous observations from schools in Ontario were kept for twenty years between 1866 and 1887.

Over eighteen months in 1843 and 1844, Lefroy also completed an expedition from Lachine, Quebec, to Fort Good Hope on the Mackenzie River. He took magnetic observations at more than three hundred stations and particularly detailed observations (hourly and as frequently as every two minutes) at Fort Chipewyan and Fort Simpson. On his northwest travels, Lefroy passed many existing thermometers, barometers, and ledger books used for weather records in trade and mission posts. If the weather observations were deemed acceptable, the Dominion tried to absorb the data and instrumentation into its index and network building. In cases where data collection was needed, new meteorological stations might be established, marking the extension of the state into some far-flung places.

The deep, sophisticated, and richly contextualized knowledge of local and regional climates held by Indigenous people across Canada, as well as their understanding of the effects of seasonal and other changes on the diversity of northwest life, was often of great help to European scientists, who relied on it to travel, subsist in, and get to know places far from European settlements. But Indigenous knowledge did not come in forms readily intelligible to the new national and global index-making projects of Lefroy, Sabine, Humboldt, and others. Indeed, it would take over a century

Meteorologist Eda Owen
taking readings for the
Dominion Meteorological
Service in Edmonton, 1916.
Courtesy Glenbow Archives,
NA–4844–11

for this knowledge to be widely valued by newcomers and their descendants
and for work to begin to share it across cultures. Indigenous people, for
instance, held memories of climate shifts deep in the past. A story told by
a Deh Gáh Got'îê Dene woman about the beginning of the world recalled
when "it was winter all the time. Always cold. Ashes falling like snow." In
the late nineteenth century, Western scientists identified the White River
Ash that had blanketed much of Dene territory, later connecting this ash
fall to a volcanic eruption circa 720 CE. It took until the 1990s, however,
for Dene oral tradition to figure significantly in non-Indigenous accounts
of this history. The incommensurability of Indigenous knowledge and

Victorian science, and the prevailing lack of interest in bridging the gap, paralleled other exclusions of Indigenous knowledge, cultures, and people from the emerging Canadian body politic.

The North, where Indigenous peoples made up the vast majority of the population, held great sway over meteorological science and the way that newcomers imagined the Canadian climate. Developments in the nineteenth century also ensured that northern environments would be viewed as central to the interconnected study of meteorology and magnetism, rather than as something to be studied on their own terms and from northern perspectives. The North's climate extremes reinforced older perceptions of the Arctic as laboratory, an idea that led to an explosion of northern field studies. The magnetic pole's proximity to the Canadian north offered tantalizing opportunities for new discoveries, and spectacular displays of aurora borealis in Europe in the mid-nineteenth century incited widespread public interest in the North, encouraging further study that became integral to meteorological investigations in Canada. Thus, nineteenth-century Englishmen repeatedly launched scientific and exploratory journeys that sought deeper understanding of weather and climate. Historian of science Trevor Levere notes that "keeping a meteorological record was a favorite occupation of arctic navigators and explorers," including those who came in search of John Franklin. Much of this work was compiled between 1879 and 1885 by the Meteorological Council of Great Britain into the five-volume *Contributions to Our Knowledge of the Meteorology of the Arctic Regions*.

By the mid-nineteenth century, the HBC's efforts to deflect competition from Rupert's Land and chilling images associated with widely publicized British Arctic Expeditions had coloured perceptions of the broader Northwest. In 1849, for instance, Major John Griffiths, sometime commandant of the troops at Fort Garry, wrote to the colonial secretary and dismissed Canada as "a country, where there is eight months winter, and snow on the

Picture of the Polar Regions,
London Illustrated News, October 13, 1849. Northern lights were a
subject of much fascination for nineteenth-century explorers and scientists.
Courtesy of Clara Thomas Archives and Special Collections, York University

ground for the whole period." Central Canadian expansionists revised this perception after 1850. They drew on new understandings of geography and climate (including Humboldt's use of isotherms, rather than latitude, to demarcate seasonal temperature patterns and Lorin Blodgett's work on the climatology of temperate North America) to soften harsh perceptions of the northwestern interior. Their insights were reinforced by new explorations led by John Palliser and Henry Youle Hind in the 1850s and Sandford Fleming in the 1870s. Intended to assess the region's suitability for agriculture and development, Palliser's expedition identified an arid triangle in southern Alberta and Saskatchewan as unsuitable for settlement. Visiting the same area in a wet year little more than a decade later, botanist John Macoun argued that it, like most of the Prairie West, was suited to agriculture and that the badlands were isolated exceptions in a generally fertile region.

Settlement of the Canadian prairies was predicated on distinguishing the "habitable" northwest from the "northerly waste."

Nevertheless, between Confederation and the end of the nineteenth century, nationalists and imperialists rooted a sense of Canadian identity in the nation's northern climate. Ideas linking climate and environment to national character were commonplace in western Europe and North America at the time, and they reached their apogee in Ellsworth Huntington's *Civilization and Climate* (1915). In Canada, according to historian Carl Berger, "The adjective 'northern' came to symbolize energy, strength, self-reliance, health, and purity ... The long winters forced men to cultivate thrift and forethought, and it enabled them to pursue intellectual studies ... The sharp and clear air of northern America was calculated to make perception more accurate and more penetrating." Even as such racialized ideologies lost their appeal in the twentieth century, the importance of the North to Canadian national identity endured and found expression in countless cultural products, from the artwork of the Group of Seven to the comic book hero Nelvana of the Northern Lights.

Although the idea that humans are responsible for climate change has encountered considerable resistance in debates about contemporary global warming, early Canadians were far from skeptical about their capacity to alter local climates. Writers in New France expressed the belief that dense forests caused harsh winters and encouraged readers to clear them. In the 1740s, the perception that summers had grown longer was taken as confirmation of the settlers' beneficial impact on the local environment. Even before the Northwest was remade by exploration and mid-nineteenth-century science as a region suitable to agricultural colonization, promoters had invoked the long-held notion (dating back to at least the sixteenth century) that clearing and cultivation would improve the climate to encourage immigration and settlement.

In the late nineteenth and early twentieth centuries, many Canadians thought of climate as something that humans could manipulate and, therefore, change the course of history. In 1884, J.H. Morgan, forestry commissioner, observed in the annual report for the Department of the Interior that "the inevitable consequences of future neglect [of fire control] will be, among other climatic changes, drought, varied by sudden and destructive floods, and a deterioration of the quality of the soil." Morgan embraced the protection and expansion of wooded areas as one way to "ameliorate" the relatively harsh climate of the West. The idea that farming might improve the climate also endured. In 1910, Kingman Nott Robins, treasurer of Associated Mortgage Investors of Rochester, New York, and a significant land investor in Alberta, wrote: "It is a matter of common observation that the rainfall in a newly settled prairie country increases with settlement, cultivation and tree planting." He cited Louis Agassiz, the Swiss American scientist who theorized that the building of railroads and settlements invariably disturbed the electrical currents in the winds and brought rain. "As the area of cultivable lands is increased," Robins advised, "the danger from early frosts diminishes." In other words: "Rain follows the plow." The catastrophe of western drought in the 1920s and 1930s laid bare the limits of that particular idea.

In the nineteenth century, these beliefs gave way to the idea, prevalent in the twentieth century, that climate change occurred only on very long time scale and without human influence. This shift came about in response to late nineteenth-century efforts to accumulate masses of meteorological data that could then be "mapped onto virtually immutable climatic regions with fixed contours and properties." As climatology became a descriptive endeavour emphasizing averages, climate became the backdrop against which human history played out. To distinguish climate in this fashion required that it be separated out from the other forms of knowledge historically subsumed within the study of meteorology. Those nineteenth-century English scientists at work in the Arctic had connected weather, atmosphere, water, and sky in ways that seem obscure to us today. Robert Fitzroy, describing the newly created Department of Meteorology in the United Kingdom in 1853, stated that, as a science, meteorology required a mastery of "Tides – Currents – Winds – Temperature – Magnetism, Electricity and the Atmosphere." By contrast, to make highly complex phenomena comprehensible, late nineteenth-century scientists detached climate from the relationships that bind the atmosphere to all living and nonliving things.

We do not enjoy the luxury of detachment today. Twenty-first-century climate change is being felt acutely in the North, where permafrost is melting, lakes and rivers are disappearing, and sea ice is receding at an unprecedented rate. Northerners and northern scientists and scholars have become essential voices in discussions about what is happening and what it means. Indigenous northerners held on to expansive understandings of atmospheric and other natural phenomena and their interrelation with human activity. This is apparent in anthropologist Julie Cruikshank's account of glaciers in Yukon surging forward in angry response to the actions of foolish travellers. Anthropologists have also drawn attention to *sila* – a term that refers to ice but also to much more. According to Aqqaluk Lynge, chair of the Inuit Circumpolar Council, "it also means weather, climate, environment, sky, and indeed, the universe." Sila is not "climate." But nineteenth-century attempts to understand the atmosphere, the roots of Western "climate," bore closer resemblance to sila than we might expect.

This expansive scientific understanding of atmosphere did not survive the nineteenth century, however. What remained instead from Victorian science was a climate index that now carries immense authority and persuasive power in Canada and around the globe. Current climate change is consistently framed in reference to the record of instrumental data that NASA draws on, going back to 1880. Most "normals" used in Canada – whether on Environment Canada's website or in describing hot summers, cold winters, and everything in between – depend on the meteorological network first erected in the nineteenth century. This is to say that the instrumental record, with all its persuasive power, encompasses only a narrow – and recent – slice of history. Longer and broader views of this interface, such as those held by Indigenous peoples, remind us that climate and climate change are human-generated concepts.

None of this diminishes the value of the statistical normals upon which contemporary discussions of climate change rest. Without them, and a great deal of other scientific research, we would be as blissfully unaware of our human role in altering the atmosphere as those who first used coal to power factories and send steam engines down "the ringing grooves of change." But it does drive home that, in a world of widely available, poorly connected, and largely separate information flows, insistently focused on the pithy and the immediate, we should beware of simple messages, arresting images, and emotive symbols that purport to explain massively complicated and deeply interconnected phenomena. It's only by ranging back through time that we can readily appreciate the unique challenges posed by the climate of our times.

REFERENCES AND FURTHER READING

Most writing on the reflexive engagements of humans and climate has come from European scholars. Prominent, early contributions to the field include Emmanuel Le Roy Ladurie's *Times of Feast, Times of Famine: A History of Climate since the Year 1000,* translated by B. Bray (Garden City: Doubleday, 1971) and Christian Pfister's "Monthly Temperature and Precipitation in Central Europe 1525–1979: Quantifying Documentary Evidence on Weather and its Effects," in *Climate since A.D. 1500,* edited by R.S. Bradley and P.D. Jones, 118–42 (London: Routledge, 1992). For more recent explorations, see Franz Mauelshagen, "The Anthropocene: A Case for a Climate History of the Nineteenth and Twentieth Centuries," *Zeithistorische Forschungen/Studies in Contemporary History* 9, 1 (2012): online edition, and Wolfgang Behringer, *A Cultural History of Climate,* translated by Patrick Camiller (Cambridge: Polity Press, 2010). Other works that have shaped this essay are Fabien Locher and Jean-Baptiste Fressoz, "Modernity's Frail Climate: A Climate History of Environmental Reflexivity," *Critical Inquiry* 38, 3 (2012): 579–98; Katharine Anderson, *Predicting the Weather: Victorians and the Science of Meteorology* (Chicago: University of Chicago Press, 2005); Theodore Binnema, *"Enlightened Zeal": The Hudson's Bay Company and Scientific Networks, 1670–1870* (Toronto: University of Toronto Press, 2014); and Kirsten Hastrup, "The Icy Breath: Modalities of Climate Knowledge in the Arctic," *Current Anthropology* 53, 2 (2012): 227–30.

Suzanne Zeller explores issues discussed in this essay in several works. Her *Inventing Canada: Early Victorian Science and the Idea of a Transcontinental Nation* (Toronto: University of Toronto Press, 1987) is indispensable for its discussion of Blodgett and conceptions of climate in the mid-nineteenth century. For the "marshal geomagnetic observations" quote, see also her "Humboldt and the Habitability of Canada's Great Northwest," *Geographical Review* 96, 3 (2006): 388. The quotation from Susanna Moodie is from *Roughing It in the Bush* (Montreal: Carleton University Press, 1988), 156.

Dene oral tradition is from D. Wayne Moodie, A.J.W. Catchpole, and Kerry Abel, "Northern Athapaskan Oral Traditions and the White River Volcano," *Ethnohistory* 39, 2 (1992): 162. The "eight months of winter" (10) and "northerly waste" (14) quotations are from Doug Owram, *Promise of Eden: The Canadian Expansionist Movement and the Idea of the West, 1856–1900* (Toronto: University of Toronto Press, 1980). Carl Berger produced lively summaries of the rhetoric of enthusiasts for the harsh northern climate in *The Sense of Power: Studies in the Ideas of Canadian Imperialism* (Toronto: University of Toronto Press, 1970), and the "adjective 'northern'" quotation is on 129. The discussion of Kingman Nott Robins is drawn from David C. Jones, *Empire of Dust: Settling and Abandoning the Prairie Dry Belt* (Edmonton: University of Alberta Press, 1987), 24. "Virtually immutable climatic regions" comes from Locher and Fressoz, "Modernity's Frail Climate," 592. Anderson, *Predicting the Weather,* quotes Fitzroy on page 83. See Hastrup, "Icy Breath," for Lynge's account of sila.

The "ringing grooves of change" is from Tennyson's *Locksley Hall.*

Drip by accumulating drop, Brother John's glacier,
high in the Arctic near Etah, Greenland, recedes to become meltwater –
altering the Arctic ecosystem, contributing to global sea-level rise,
and turning visitors into witnesses of climate change.
Photo by Heather E. McGregor

TIME CHASED ME DOWN,
AND I STOPPED LOOKING AWAY

Heather E. McGregor

AWE

I N AUGUST 2015, I stood on a steep hillside at the end of Foulk Fjord, northern Greenland, at 78°18' North. I was travelling on an Adventure Canada cruise expedition through the Northwest Passage. Earlier that morning, we had left the ice-class cruise ship for a forty-five-minute Zodiac ride up the fjord, past cliffs reaching heights of six hundred metres. We stopped along the way to take pictures of small herds of muskox. They appeared to be clinging precariously to sheer and inhospitable bluffs but, of course, they were happily at home on the ancient rocky pathways they knew well and travelled often.

We disembarked from the Zodiacs, traded the matching rubber boots provided to us for personal hiking shoes, and began walking. We passed several dilapidated hunting shacks that marked the abandoned settlement of Etah. It was, for a long time, a waypoint for generations of migrants – Independence (Paleo-Eskimo), Dorset, Thule, and Inuit – who arrived from the west over the course of four thousand years. Robert Peary, the American who claimed he was first to reach the North Pole, and Knud Rasmussen, renowned Danish explorer and anthropologist, both used it as a departure

335

point for their expeditions. Now, it is seldom visited and more often seen by tourists from far corners of the globe than by anyone local. But, as we walked inland under the surprisingly warm sun on a gloriously clear day, there was a deep feeling of following in the tracks of many who had appreciated this place before.

Travelling with a group of two hundred tourists in the High Arctic, many over the age of sixty, isn't easy. Any injury, emergency, or illness that could not be dealt with by the ship's one doctor would necessitate evacuation by helicopter. During land excursions, passengers could not venture outside the perimeter of staff members carrying rifles and radios, acting as "bear guards" and supervising our every move.

We walked up the valley towards the terminal moraine of Brother John's Glacier. Its orientation allowed us to walk up to the end of the glacier and touch it, even walk inside a shallow ice cave. We spread out along the glacier edge to look at the rocks and water coming out of the oldest ice any of us had ever seen.

Above the moraine, I hiked up to a high promontory. The staff member there was Jason Edmunds, an Inuk from Nain, Nunatsiavut (Labrador). Jason had grown up in the tourism industry; his father worked in the outfitting business. He was head of operations for Adventure Canada and married to the company's CEO, Cedar Swan, whose father founded the family-run company.

> "Good spot up here!" I said.
> "Yes, it is. Beautiful day," he responded.
> "It is so nice. So nice. I can't believe how warm it is. And no
> wind ... no bugs ... This is one of the most gorgeous places
> I've been in the Arctic, on one of the nicest days. It is a bit
> scary how good the weather is," I remarked.
> "Yep." He smiled, agreeing on both points.

We were quiet for a few moments as we watched the movements of our fellow travellers below and listened to commentary on the radio between staff members spying foxes and hares on the hillsides through binoculars.

"I haven't been here for two years," Jason said. "Last time I was here, the glacier went all the way down there," he pointed. "It has receded a lot."

Characteristically, Jason stated this with a smile, but I thought it one of the more serious things he had said to me.

"It used to go all the way down there," he continued, pointing farther downslope. "This is all new land."

My gut sank, as I felt an emotion I could not name. I nodded and made the sound of affirmation that Northerners make when they talk to one another: "Mmmm." We both looked out at the exquisitely bright shine of the ice, the textured grey rocks left bare by the melting, moving glacier, and the oddly lush, multicoloured tundra hillsides where life thrived.

"Will you take a picture of me, Jason?"

It was a silly way to break the pensive silence between us, and as I spoke I recognized the cardboard cut-out of a privileged tourist taking shape in the moment. Jason seemed happy to acquiesce and suggested where I should stand for several shots, commenting that he knew you weren't supposed to take photos directly into the sun, but he thought they always looked cool.

I didn't want to leave Jason's hilltop perch. I wanted to suspend time and place and my experience of them, to stop the glacier from changing

Heather E. McGregor visiting Brother John's Glacier, Etah, Greenland.
Photo by Jason Edmunds

any more; I wanted to preserve what I thought might not be here if I, or my imagined descendants, ever could come back to this precious site. But none of that was possible. All I could do was try to take a memory with me.

Another traveller trudged his way towards us, breathing heavily from the hill climb. It was Roy Scranton, a journalist, author, activist, and Iraq war veteran from Oregon, but living then in New York City. He was on the cruise to write an article on climate change and Arctic tourism for the American magazine *The Nation*. Usually, he was quiet, a solitary observer of the places and events around us, choosing words and conversations carefully and listening closely to others. In conversation with me, on occasion, he expressed passionate critique and concern about participation in a trip that felt fraught with contradiction.

I said to Roy, "Pretty incredible, huh?"

"Yes."

Roy's eyes moved quickly over every detail of the scene below us, trying to take it in, as I had. I mentioned that Jason had said how much the glacier was receding, knowing Roy would want to hear about it for his magazine story. Jason graciously told Roy what he had told me.

Again, my stomach sank, as the intense beauty of what we were seeing crashed into the deep knowledge that this place was being irrevocably altered by human-induced climate change.

I said, "I feel lucky to be here."

"Yes," Roy said, "Yes. And grief."

GRIEF

Clear skies. Warm temperatures. Hardly any wind. Each morning, the cruise ship passengers were given the weather report for the day, and each morning the Arctic seemed just as inviting as the day before ... *all the way through the Northwest Passage.* Ice conditions ultimately blocked our transit along the northern route, which was a relief to anyone who, perhaps naively, wished to insulate the region from dramatic changes associated with increased shipping, tourism, military transit, and other ice-free implications. But we made it through the southern route via Bellot Strait.

As I looked out from the top deck, I was haunted by my growing understanding of climate crisis. Greenland is losing as much as 375 cubic kilometres of ice (or about 75 percent of all the water in Lake Erie) every year. "Drip by drip, drop by drop" as Scranton said, it is going to raise sea levels beyond imagination. Jim Halfpenny, a world leader in seasonal cold research who was travelling as an expert on our expedition, explained that the loss of multiyear ice in the Arctic is approaching a major tipping point. We may see an ice-free North Pole in five, or maybe fifteen, years.

View from the side of the *Ocean Endeavour* cruise ship in the High Arctic.
Photo by Heather E. McGregor

Inuit leaders Jose Kusugak, Sheila Watt-Cloutier, and Mary Simon have tried, over several decades, to draw attention to the impacts of environmental change on Arctic residents, even framing them as a violation of Inuit human rights. But the desire to look away from climate crisis has been hard to overcome. It is a "collective action problem of the highest order," Scranton explains in *Learning to Die in the Anthropocene*. Too hard, too complicated, too emotional. "Global warming is what is called a 'wicked problem': it doesn't offer any clear solutions, only better and worse responses."

It is not only the magnitude of, and fear associated with, climate change that has us looking away; it is the ease with which crises affecting marginalized peoples are perpetually overlooked. Another layer of this "wicked problem" is that Arctic peoples are already saddled with a host of long-term, complex challenges. The crises in northern Indigenous food security, housing, wellness indicators, and education continue. Rob Nixon, a scholar in postcolonial literature, calls events such as these "long emergencies" and "slow violence." How can economic development, so often twinned with natural resource extraction projects, be responsibly pursued alongside efforts to mitigate the impacts of climate change?

I love the Arctic and identify with it, even those parts that are utterly new to me and often quite different from Iqaluit – the place where I grew up and that I think of as home. The expedition took us through High Arctic waters and places I had never been. Just as nostalgia can create a longing for earlier times that we may never have experienced, I clung to the places I visited as if they evoked long-lost memories. I was trying to connect deeply with what I saw, even as I remained aware that I might never have the chance to return. I was trying to make this place into home, even as I knew I did not have the skills or will to survive there, even as I knew I do not belong to the people whose ancestors cared for this land, hunted here, gave birth to children here.

All the while, my experience of place was made possible by the comfortable accommodations of a luxury ship. It was the largest transportation vehicle I had ever been on, remarkably insulated and safe from Arctic risks in comparison to any other mode of travel people use in the region.

Looking out on the ship's wake, I struggled with the accusation that this trip was intensely hypocritical. Everywhere the legacy of colonization; everywhere participation in a fossil-fuel economy; everywhere the disparity between haves and have-nots; everywhere the potential for voyeurism. I wrestled with the contradiction of learning about and witnessing climate change on board a vehicle that represents nothing if not human fossil-fuel hubris – the very hubris that has led to human-generated and irreversible changes to the planet's ecosystems.

According to Scranton's interview with Cedar Swan, Adventure Canada's CEO, the hope was that the experience would make passengers more conscious of the very history of the despoliation it revealed and that the positive increase in social awareness thus achieved would outweigh any negative impacts – not the least of which came from burning ten to twenty tonnes of fuel each day.

But neither Roy nor I were ever sure this was achieved, even through the excellent educational programming offered to this high-paying clientele.

The horizon by which I encountered climate crisis in the summer of 2015 cannot fully be attributed to clear weather. My understanding was conditioned, as always, by place and time. My encounters with melting ice mingled with thoughts of the unprecedented melting in my personal life. It was as if the payment I had to exchange for this incredible journey was a reckoning with the passage of time and a self made from the accumulation of moments and choices strung together in the course of a life.

On board that ship, even while travelling in the company of my dear parents, I felt profoundly lonely. Not long before, I had separated from my husband, then signed divorce papers, and then moved myself from Vancouver to Ottawa to start a new, single life.

For the first time in eleven years, I didn't have a companion in travel and in life. I didn't have someone to see the ice with me, to walk the mushy tundra with me, to watch the birds soar, to marvel at the polar bears, and to be rocked with me at night by gentle swells beneath the ship. Unlike the many travels I had been on with my husband, this once-in-a-lifetime adventure threatened to slip through my fingers without a partner to witness it – to witness me in it.

I had spent one quarter of my life certain in the knowledge of my partnership, certain that it would bring me children, a home, and security in my old age. But as I grew into the self that I could be, and should be, I grew away from the self that could be in that marriage – and if that was possible, what else is possible? What story of the future should I believe in now?

I was at the edge of a significant phase of my life, at the edge of being a graduate student, a young woman, and a wife. Youth doesn't last. Marriages don't last. Jobs and projects don't last. Even communities don't last in our highly mobile way of life. Standing on a ship that is stable, but not still, brought acute attention to the movement of time under my feet.

The melting of glaciers and icebergs signified changes in the world I thought I knew. These, it seemed, were changes unlikely to be reversed, changes that for me and many people I care about are likely to elicit pain. The passing of time and the passing of place, together. I could live another sixty-five years. The Arctic is projected to be free of multiyear ice within twenty-five to fifty years. This will affect everyone on the planet.

Will I be able to live through that loss and the changes that result? Will I want to?

HUMILITY

The sun shone, again, on the warm, quiet September morning when my parents and I disembarked from the *Ocean Endeavour* for the last time in Kugluktuk, Nunavut. We negotiated a special excursion into town on our own, before breakfast and before other passengers would be transferred to the airport for departure.

Kugluktuk, formerly known as Coppermine, had been my parents' first home in the Arctic, before I was born. In 1973, they were hired from Toronto as young teachers for what was then a newly expanded K–9 day school. We walked past the first house they had been assigned by the government, which did not, in those days, have bathroom plumbing. We walked past the school where they had taught, recently expanded and renovated again to meet the needs of a growing population.

We walked out to the crest of a hill from which we could see the wide Coppermine River glistening in the morning light, banked by red and yellow tundra-covered hills. As we walked, we marvelled at what seemed like alien species – large bushes – that had grown taller than us despite being at least two hundred kilometres north of the recognized treeline. We talked about how grizzly bears were coming into this territory. Signs of climate change within our own lifetimes.

Heather E. McGregor photographing bushes in Kugluktuk, Nunavut.
Photo by Catherine McGregor

The past accosted my parents from each familiar site; each memory elicited the young, adventurous, community-driven couple who had found themselves happy here. The present interrupted their descriptions: new buildings here, old ones no longer there; signs of recent commercial enterprise, tourism, community development, and population growth. The future called out in questions about how the enduring signs of poverty might be mitigated and whether children were attending school regularly enough to graduate.

Walking in Kugluktuk, my parents returned to their younger selves as they showed me around town, forty-two years after they had arrived. At the same time, my presence as their adult daughter and their need to explain to the familiar community members we met that they are now retired, were markers of their age. I followed, nodded, listened, witnessed, photographed. I bent down to pick berries just as women had here for generations. My preoccupations with climate science and failed social contracts fell away. I breathed in and out simply as the daughter of two human beings *who had been here before* – who called on me to remember with them – who looked to me to bear their stories. In this, I was no more special than another human in the chain of humans who have lived, suffered, loved, and died. As an only child, I am the one who carries the inheritance of my parents' stories. I might be single, I may not have started my own family yet, but I am no less daughter than I was the day I was born.

The melting I witnessed in my environment and in my personal life led me to ask: Is this crisis or is this just life? Are life and crisis the same thing? Is what I think of as a "new beginning" actually a coming around again?

Grief came from recognizing that the stories I had been told, and that I had told myself, about the future had always been merely hopes, ultimately fictions. It is only ever possible to invest in the conditions we can create in the present; no dose of optimism will guarantee conditions in the future. These insights gave way to a deep melding of openness with determination, a dialogue between humility and resolve. Human experiences arise – and, luckily, we can name them, feel them, and watch them pass. Suffering and grief come from comparing those experiences to what we expected we would experience and from wishing they – and we – were different.

RESOLVE

Three weeks on the Northwest Passage cruise gave me time to think. I left my laptop at home, and there was no internet. It was the longest stretch of digital detox I'd had in five years, maybe more. It was as if time chased me down and called on me to stop looking away. Not only did I think about climate change and personal growth, I thought about how I use my time and energy as a historian and writer. I thought about how much the histories I encounter and write mean to me. I thought about how many more Arctic histories remain undocumented and how few people are involved in such research. But had anything I'd written really made a difference? What purpose is there to continuing research in history when what Northerners face now is the need to make unprecedented adaptations for the future?

Drawing on great thinkers and wisdom traditions, Roy Scranton says the ability to make collective meaning from the worst of human experiences depends on forgoing the pursuit and defence of a singular narrative, or truth, that belongs only to one perspective. He calls for multiple perspectives; not only must we learn to see with eyes that better reflect the diversity of human experience, stretching way beyond a Western viewpoint, but, as Scranton so eloquently put it, "we need to learn to see ... with golden-cheeked warbler eyes, coho salmon eyes, and polar bear eyes, and not even just with eyes at all but with the wild, barely articulate being of clouds and seas and rocks and trees and stars."

In his book, *Learning to Die*, Scranton connects "letting go," and "learning to see," with the metaphorical *and literal* process of learning to die.

Learning to die as an individual means letting go of our predispositions and fear. Learning to die as a civilization means letting go of this particular way of life and its ideas of identity, freedom, success, and progress. These two ways of learning to die come together in the role of the humanist thinker: the one who is willing to stop and ask troublesome questions, the one who is willing to interrupt, the one who resonates on other channels and with slower, deeper rhythms.

In other words, we – as individuals – are all going to die. And our society in its present form will pass too. The sciences of human biology and climate change tell us so. The question then becomes: How will we go down?

Might historians take up the role suggested by Scranton for humanist thinkers? Will we act as undertakers to the death of civilizations predicated on the ideas of identity, freedom, success, and progress that have, among other productions, ruined our Earth? Or will we be midwives to the rebirth of diverse human ideas from the past, about what a meaningful life is? Have we ever interrupted *enough* with troublesome questions and with suggestions that resonate with some other ways of being?

Civil Rights historian Tim Tyson has a pessimistic view of the historian's capacity to contribute to contemporary problem solving: "Historians like to think our scholarship is an act of citizenship, of course, but I would hate to try to make a thumping historical case for its effectiveness. Historians often undermine the hopes that activists live on. We're like bugs in the breakfast cereal, ruining everything with our digging."

What history, and whose history, matters now? Dipesh Chakrabarty is one of the most prominent historians to have considered the conceptual distance between history written before the Anthropocene and since. Arguing that the very idea of historical understanding is challenged by climate catastrophe, he says we must now look beyond our discipline to understand this crisis of "many dimensions."

On the other hand, we cannot leave history behind. Indigenous scholars and intellectuals such as Dwayne Donald, Thomas King, and Murray Sinclair often remind Canadians that re-envisioning relationships among Indigenous and non-Indigenous peoples must be predicated on a recognition of, and accounting for, the history (and ongoing processes) of colonization, dislocation, and dispossession.

Sheila Watt-Cloutier, Inuit activist, spokesperson and former chair of the Inuit Circumpolar Council, says this about the need for socioeconomic change in the Arctic: "I firmly believe that if these systems – whether school systems, judicial systems or health systems – do not contextualize our community's problems, helping individuals, families and communities to understand the historical context from which the problems arise and addressing their roots in a small way, things simply won't get better."

We need explanations for the past, especially when the past created seemingly inexplicable inequities in the present. We need continuity with the past to understand ourselves.

The corollary to the momentarily comforting notion that we can look to the past is that we cannot rely on it to predict the future. In learning, in life, in history, the past only points to possible futures, not to certainty or repetition. Our difficulty making sense of this crisis, and the unknowable future it brings, is rooted in a gap – a gap between what we have told ourselves about what to expect for human life in the twenty-first century and how environmental changes are eroding those expectations.

Perhaps it is possible to acknowledge our grief about the loss of the stories that we invested in most deeply – such as that life would continue to get better as time went on – and then to seek different ways of being that address a changing climate.

To do this, I think people, situated in particular places, will need to see and make sense of themselves in the *stories* of climate change, in the *stories* of humanity living within a crisis, and in the *stories* that guide our actions to mediate it. Changes in the human encounter with climate – that is, how we face it, how we reconcile with it, and how we respond to it – cannot be disconnected from the histories that shape who we understand ourselves to be.

I am concerned that such stories and plans not be imposed from "outside," by outsiders. They should not be disconnected from the histories and memories of human relationships that define particular places. As I have learned from scholars who bring attention to the distinctiveness of Indigenous knowledge systems, as I have written elsewhere, and as Julie Cruikshank suggests in her work and in this volume, Indigenous peoples need space to continue creating and teaching stories about human experience in the past-present-future. This means using their own epistemological and ontological moorings, which are often different from those most historians rely on in the academy.

Evidently, then, we must constantly look to the past as we look to the future. We must do this not to offer a yardstick by which to measure ourselves but to give meaning to the experiences that arise whether or not they are what we expected. The historians we need now are those who teach us how to learn, not what to learn – and why some ways of learning are likely to be more ethical than others.

On my Northwest Passage expedition, paradox surrounded me. The water provided an endless glassy expanse on which to glide, while the hard and threatening edges of innumerable icebergs demanded the captain navigate with care and attention. The sun of long summer days was warm and welcoming, in a place notorious for harsh and deadly conditions. A fossil fuel–intensive cruise across the Arctic made climate crisis feel real for someone raised north of sixty°. With nowhere to escape from the two hundred or so other passengers, I felt a deep longing for companionship. The exquisiteness of such an extremely remote region made me grieve for the globe.

And yet, paradox always surrounds us, in every time, in every place. We have many strategies that help us look away. Sometimes those strategies are for survival, but many times they simply take us deeper into suffering. When we see beneath our distractions and find the courage to sit with whatever may be there, when we come of age, we will need stories to hold us up. We will need a place in time.

REFERENCES AND FURTHER READING

This essay was significantly influenced by conversations with Roy Scranton during and following the Northwest Passage cruise on which we both travelled. His work in journalism and activism (*The Nation*, the *New York Times*) and philosophy and literary theory (*Learning to Die*) offers two strengths: it unapologetically draws public attention to the implications, however visceral, of the impending climate catastrophe, and it outlines some possible shifts in humanist pursuits necessary to make sense of, and live within, the Anthropocene and its productions. Quotations are from "What I Learned on a Luxury Cruise through the Global Warming Apocalypse," *The Nation*, November 9, 2015, 15–16; *Learning to Die in the Anthropocene: Reflections on the End of a Civilization* (San Francisco: City Lights Publishers, 2015), 53 and 24; and *We're Doomed. Now What? Essays on War and Climate Change* (Manhattan: Soho Press, 2018) (no page numbers). Scranton introduced me to Rob Nixon's *Slow Violence and the Environmentalism of the Poor* and to the conceptual tools Nixon elicits from the nexus of postcolonial theory, environmentalist/activist narratives, and socioeconomic contexts detrimentally impacted by globalization.

My use of the language *look away* and *looking away* are derived from Naomi Klein's *This Changes Everything: Capitalism vs the Climate* (New York: Simon and Shuster, 2014). Klein's work explains the possibilities and limitations that have resulted from public- and private-sector responses to climate change science around the world. She advocates for solutions that acknowledge Indigenous rights and keep the asymmetrical legacies of colonization, global capitalism, and development at the forefront.

I quote from Tim Tyson's essay "Can Honest History Allow for Hope? The Obligations of Scholarship Diverge from the Needs of Activists," *The Atlantic*, December 18, 2015.

For more information on the emergence of the concept of the Anthropocene and its relevance to historical understanding in particular, see Dipesh Chakrabarty's "The Climate of History: Four Theses," *Critical Inquiry* 35, 2 (2009): 197–222. With regard to Indigenous ways of knowing and making meaning from the past more generally, an issue I raise in the final section of this essay, I point readers to the work of Jo-ann Archibald, Keith Basso, Julie Cruikshank, Michael Marker, Keith Thor Carlson, and others. All such authors from whom I have learned are cited in my "Exploring Ethnohistory and Indigenous Scholarship: What Is the Relevance to Educational Historians?" *Journal of the History of Education Society* 43, 4 (2014): 431–49, and "North of 60: Some Methodological

Considerations for Educational Historians," *Historical Studies in Education* 27, 1 (2015): 121–29.

Sheila Watt-Cloutier's memoir, *The Right to Be Cold: One Woman's Story of Protecting Her Culture, the Arctic and the Whole Planet* (London: Allen Lane, 2015), is a brilliant and candid personal narrative of value to historians, environmentalists, and the Canadian public in general for understanding the impact of pollutants and global warming on residents of the Canadian Arctic and for understanding Inuit activist responses to climate change over the last two decades. The "I firmly believe" quotation is from page 318.

Among several texts not cited specifically in the essay, Hans-Georg Gadamer's *Truth and Method*, 2nd ed. (New York: Bloomsbury Academic, 2004) and Jeff Malpas's "The Origin of Understanding: Event, Place, Truth," in *Consequences of Hermeneutics: Fifty Years after Gadamer's Truth and Method*, edited by Jeff Malpas, 261–80 (Evanston, IL: Northwestern University Press, 2010) have informed my depiction of the role of time and place in conditioning hermeneutical understanding, or historical consciousness, as a situated practice always framed within the paradox of our own historicity and our own identity. Jonathan Lear's *Radical Hope: Ethics in the Face of Cultural Devastation* (Cambridge: Harvard University Press, 2008) is important for depicting the constructive role of traditional thinking in an Indigenous society facing an unknowable future.

A final note: this essay was written for Peter Seixas's retirement symposium, "Coming of Age: Life/Time/History." I extend my thanks to him for inviting me to present at the symposium, giving me the reason to make time to refine these ideas.

ACKNOWLEDGMENTS

THIS BOOK HAS BEEN a long time in the making. It began with NiCHE, the Network in Canadian History and Environment, a research cluster generously funded by the Social Science and Humanities Research Council. From 2004 to 2014, this group of historians and historical geographers promoted the development of the field of environmental history in Canada. Led by director Alan MacEachern, the NiCHE board included Laura Cameron, Stéphane Castonguay, Matthew Evenden, Liza Piper, Bill Turkel, and the two of us.

As the NiCHE project ran its course, we thought to consolidate or at least represent something of the good that the project had achieved. Conversations between the two of us on bus trips during American Society for Environmental History conferences, and (NiCHE-organized) Canadian History and Environment Summer Schools led us to envisage a volume that reflected on the environmental history of Canada. We hope that this book stands among other things, then, as a reminder of the incidental benefits of getting out of the archives and into the field. With the support of NiCHE, Green College and the Department of Geography at the University of British Columbia, and the Robarts Centre for Canadian Studies at York University, our first step was to organize a series of public lectures divided between the two campuses. There, the ideas in most of the essays collected here received early airings. Encouraged, we moved to bring some sense of the vitality and insight of this work to print.

This book is a showcase. Its range, in time, space, and topic is broad. It is in no sense a complete, comprehensive environmental history of Canada. Our collective intent is to stimulate thought (and encourage reflection) rather than to write the last word on any of the topics broached in these pages; we readily acknowledge that important stories go untold and that those included might have been emphasized differently. No book can do everything.

In approaching potential contributors, we asked colleagues to say something fresh about more or less familiar aspects of the Canadian past. Authors were invited to contribute think pieces on topics suggested by us in view of their individual expertise. They were free to frame their discussion as they wished but were encouraged to offer a view or argument to spur the interest of readers and inspire them to think anew about the environmental dimensions of the matters at hand. Some of the people we approached were unable to join this venture, but our authors include a mix of accomplished mid-career and more-established scholars whose collective insights are given compelling contemporary resonance by the final essay in the volume, prepared for other purposes by Heather E. McGregor but enthusiastically included here. Our basic ambition has been to produce a series of essays in the truest sense of that term: lively, wide-ranging, thought-provoking, and informative reflections on topics of broad significance to Canadians in the twenty-first century.

In addition to thanking our colleagues from the NiCHE executive and all the authors for their patience and forbearance, we also extend our gratitude to all those who have assisted along the way. We thank, at York University, Laura Taman, administrator of the Robarts Centre; at UBC, Green College principal Mark Vessey, Department of Geography administrator Sandy Lapsky, cartographer Eric Leinberger, and adjunct colleague Richard Mackie (for his comments on very early versions of some of the essays); at UBC Press, we owe a special debt to Director Melissa Pitts for her interest in the project and its publication under the On Point Press imprint, to James MacNevin for taking charge of the preliminary logistics, to Lesley Erickson for editorial advice that was both smart and appreciated, and to Ann Macklem and others who saw the manuscript through production.

Beyond this, we have also incurred debts to friends, librarians, archivists, and others across the country who have answered requests of one sort or another. Among them we are delighted to record our thanks to Jessie Amaolo, Raven Amiro, Mary Ruth Amundsen, Emily Antler, Sarah Bankhead, Lev Bratishenko, Christine Braun, Margaret Coates, Patricia Crawford, Geoff Cunfer, Caroline Dagbert, Alessandra Dimaano, Demi Eagland, Sue Fox, Jonathan Goldsbie, Joshua Green, Frank Guillou, Julia Holland, Maggie Hunter, Steven Leclair, Adria Lund, Dan Macfarlane, Christopher Martin, Marcia Mordfield, Patrick Osborne, Derek Pedley, Mark Reid, Sue Plouffe, Stefan Reicheneder, Janet Rogers, Ramona Rose, Susan Schilbach, Janis Schultz, John Shoesmith, Susan Short, Carolyn Soltau, Blanca Stead, Robert Stibravy, Esther ten Bokum, Daniel Tigner, Jamie Trepanier, Melanie Tucker, Kelly-Ann Turkington, Karine Vinette, T.J. Watt, Robin Weber, Bill Waiser, Alan Walker, Weiyan Yan, and, especially, Bonnie Devine.

We acknowledge with sincere thanks the Social Science and Humanities Research Council for their support of NiCHE. We also extend a special vote of thanks to Alan MacEachern for having the foresight and leadership to launch the NiCHE project over a decade ago. A new generation of environmental history scholars is already extending the work represented in these pages, and we see their present and future contributions as one of the key legacies of the original NiCHE project. Recognizing the origins of this book in, and dependence on, the larger community of environment history scholars, all royalties will be directed to a fund in support of UBC Press publications in the field.

CONTRIBUTORS

JENNIFER BONNELL is the author of *Reclaiming the Don: An Environmental History of Toronto's Don River Valley*. She teaches environmental and public history at York University.

CLAIRE E. CAMPBELL's most recent book is *Nature, Place, and Story: Rethinking Historic Sites in Canada*. She teaches environmental history at Bucknell University and focuses on Canada in North America and the North Atlantic.

COLIN M. COATES is the author of *Metamorphoses of Landscape and Community in Early Quebec*. A specialist in the history of early French Canada, he teaches Canadian studies and environmental history at York University.

JULIE CRUIKSHANK is the author of *Do Glaciers Listen? Local Knowledge, Colonial Encounters, and Social Imagination*. She is a professor emerita at the University of British Columbia and her research centres on oral tradition and oral history.

KEN CRUIKSHANK recently co-authored, with his colleague Nancy B. Bouchier, *The People and the Bay: A Social and Environmental History of Hamilton Harbour*. He is a professor of history at McMaster University with research interests in Canadian policy and urban, environmental, and transportation history.

MICHÈLE DAGENAIS's most recent book is *Montreal, City of Water: An Environmental History*. She is a professor of history at the Université de Montréal, where she teaches environmental and urban history.

JOANNA DEAN is the co-editor, with Darcy Ingram and Christabelle Sethna, of *Animal Metropolis: Histories of Human-Animal Relations in Urban Canada*. She teaches environmental history and gender history at Carleton University.

STEPHEN J. HORNSBY is author and co-editor of several prize-winning books, including the *Historical Atlas of Maine*. A specialist in the historical geography of northeastern North America, he is director of the Canadian-American Center and professor of geography and Canadian studies at the University of Maine.

ARN KEELING is the co-editor, with John Sandlos, of *Mining and Communities in Northern Canada*. He is a professor of geography at Memorial University. His research and writing focus on resource development and mine remediation in northern Canada.

TINA LOO's most recent book is *Moved by the State: Forced Relocation and Making a Good Life in Postwar Canada* and she has written on the social and environmental impacts of hydroelectricity and wildlife conservation. She teaches Canadian and environmental history at the University of British Columbia.

HEATHER E. MCGREGOR's publications include *Inuit Education and Schools in the Eastern Arctic*. She is an adjunct professor in the Faculty of Education at the University of Ottawa and her scholarship is located at the intersection of Arctic history, education, Indigenous perspectives, and de-colonizing imperatives.

STEVE PENFOLD's interests include the history of capitalism, energy, culture, and politics. He teaches history at the University of Toronto.

LIZA PIPER is the author of *The Industrial Transformation of Subarctic Canada*. She is an associate professor at the University of Alberta. She teaches and researches environmental history and the history of disease with a focus on northern and western Canada.

JOHN SANDLOS is the author of *Hunters at the Margins: Native People and Wildlife Conservation in the Northwest Territories* and the co-editor, with Arn Keeling, of *Mining and Communities in Northern Canada*. He is an environmental historian at Memorial University who studies northern Canada and conservation history.

GRAEME WYNN is the author of *Canada and Arctic North America: An Environmental History*. A geographer and environmental historian, he writes on Canada and other settler societies. He is a professor emeritus at the University of British Columbia.

INDEX

Note: "(i)" after a page number indicates an illustration.

Ballet Jorgen Company, 178–79
Banff National Park (AB), 166(i), 229, 230
Bardot, Brigitte, 306, 307(i)
Bartlett, W.H., 73, 74(i), 76(i)
Battle for the Woodlands (Devine), 73–78; photos, 50(i), 74(i), 75(i), 76(i)
BC Hydro, 270
BC Spaces for Nature, 309
bears, 229, 230, 342, 343
beavers, 25, 27, 41, 53, 92–93; dams and ponds, 112–15, 113(i); pelts and trade, 101, 109–12; population, 115, 116
Beck, Ulrich, 284
Benjamin, Walter, 97
Bennett, W.A.C., 265
Bennett Dam (BC), 271
Berger, Carl, 63, 329
Big Histories, 11, 13
bird populations, 231–34, 233(i), 235–36, 267–68
Birmingham, Deeno and Dave, 281, 283, 290, 292, 293; photos, 282(i), 291(i)
Blodgett, Lorin, 328
blossom midge, 44
bodily responses: to the natural environment, 293–94; to the man-made environment, 294, 301
Bond-Head, Francis, 126
Borman, Frank, 275
Boucher, Pierre, 56, 58

Bourassa, Robert, 245, 264
Bradbury, John, 207
Brigden, Beatrice, 291
Britannia Beach Mine (BC), 213
British Columbia, 40, 136, 251, 256, 309; population, 148, 161, 185
British Columbia Electric Railway, 244(i), 248(i), 252(i)
British North America (BNA) Act, 223, 257
Bronfman, Samuel, 67
Brook, Tim, 101
Brown, George, 134–35
Brundtland Commission, 72, 95–96, 313
buffalo, 126, 136
Burtynsky, Edward, 178, 211(i)

Cabot, John, 102
Calgary, 184(i)
Canadian Broadcasting Corporation (CBC), 234, 246, 250, 322; Air of Death (documentary), 288, 301; The Nature of Things (TV show), 303–6, 307; A Planet for the Taking (TV show), 305–6; Quirks and Quarks (radio show), 303; Science Magazine (TV show), 303, 304
Canadian Council of Agriculture, 129
Canadian Pacific Railway (CPR), 9, 40, 171, 234; construction of, 181, 227, 228(i)

diseases: cholera, 149–53, 151(i), 152(i); emotional and political consequences of, 159–60; endemic, 144; HIV/AIDS, 156–57; influenza, 144, 147, 155–56, 157(i); introduced to Indigenous populations, 144–49, 160–61; in livestock, 136; origins, 143, 149, 156; pneumonia, 156, 157–58; polio, 153–54, 155(i); poverty and, 142(i); SARS, 158–60; smallpox, 145–46; in trees, 43–44
displacement, 70, 136, 246, 268–70, 321
Dominion of Canada, 61, 223, 256, 324–25
Don't Make a Wave, 289–90, 301
drainage basins, 25, 26(i), 35, 37, 51
drought, 146, 321, 330
drumlins, 35
Drury, Charles, 129
Dutch elm disease, 43–44

Earth, 3, 10, 11, 13, 312–13; history, 24(i), 31(i); seen from space, 275–79, 276(i); systems, 27; temperature, 321, 322
Earthrise (photo, 1968), 275–76, 276(i)
ecofeminists, 282
ecological footprint, 224
ecology, 19, 118, 276, 303; deep, 305; nonequilibrium, 271; road, 230
economic development, 9, 14–15, 78, 173, 245, 340; environmental protection and, 313; mineral production, 204, 207–8; St. Lawrence Seaway

and, 65–66, 70; staple trades, 101–2, 134
economic zone, 103, 107
Edmonton, 194, 302
Edmonton International Airport, 233–34
Edmunds, Jason, 336–37
electricity grid, 247, 249, 255, 256. See also hydroelectric power
elites, 128, 187; urban, 190, 195, 196(i)
elk, 222(i)
Emigrant's Welcome to Canada (Winkworth), 318(i)
energy: ads and logos, 244(i), 248(i), 252(i); conflicts, 253–54, 257; crisis (1970s), 72; distance and flow of, 245–46, 249–50, 251; environmental failures, 248; government involvement, 243–44, 252–53, 257; imports, 255; mining industry usage, 206, 208–10, 217; national dreams of, 255–57; socionatural processes of, 244–45, 249–51, 257; solar, 249, 321; transformative projects, 246–47. See also coal; fossil fuels; hydroelectric power; oil and gas
Energy: The Power of Canada (1989), 243–44
engineers and engineering, 274–75, 281, 282(i); hydro, 9, 65–67, 246, 249, 267(i)
environment: assessments, 96, 214, 237; changing attitudes toward, 9–11, 71–72, 310; disasters, 40–41,

Lind, Annie, 283

literature, Canadian, 6–7, 127–28, 177, 306

Little Ice Age (1550–1850 CE), 135, 320

livestock, 122(i), 127, 130, 136, 143; portraits, 131, 132(i)

Livingston, John, 304–6

local vs global perspectives, 12, 275–77

Locke, John, 59

Logan, William, 34

logging, 307–10; lumber companies, 226; photos, 308(i), 309(i), 311(i)

Lord, John Keast, 62

L'Ouest canadien (1900), 122(i)

Lovelock, James, 312

Lower, Arthur R.M., 9, 11, 175

Lynge, Aqqaluk, 331

Macdonald, John A., 112, 172, 257

MacGregor, Roy, 178

Mackenzie, William Lyon, 132–33

Mackenzie Valley Pipeline Inquiry, 72

Maclean's, 286, 299–300

Macoun, John, 40, 328

Mactaquac Regional Development Program, 266, 270

Maliseet people, 39

Manitoba, 35, 36, 130–31, 153

manufacturing, 70–71

maple syrup, 126

maps, 14; colonial and Indigenous, 73–77, 74(i), 76(i); of dam locations,

273–74; flyaway, 268, 269(i); North America, 105(i), 113(i); Nouvelle France (New France), 51–53, 54–55(i), 56(i); St. Lawrence Seaway and Power Project pictorial, 67, 68–69(i), 70

Maria Chapdelaine (Hémon), 127–28

markets, 13, 105, 118, 133, 255; global, 96, 204, 217; mining, 206–7; oil, 314

Martin, Paul, Sr., 284

masculinity, 281–82, 293

Mason, Bill, 176–77

Masse, Marcel, 243–44, 257

Massey, Vincent, 173–75, 181

materiality, 14, 224, 235, 274

maternalism, 284, 285, 293

Mawson, Thomas, 184(i)

May, Elizabeth, 282–83

McDonnell, Roger, 92–93

McDougall, John, 255

McKibben, Bill, 4

McLuhan, Marshall, 224

McMichael Gallery (ON), 179

McPherson, Hugo, 6

measles, 143–45, 147

Medieval Warm Period (900–1250 CE), 40, 320

Metcalfe, Ben, 292

meteorology, 323–25, 326(i), 327, 330–32

miasmas, 142(i), 149

Michipicoten (ON), 146

microwave technology, 234–36, 236(i)

parks, 36, 176, 180–81, 282, 308. *See also names of individual parks*
Parks Canada, 180, 235
pathogens: complexity of people and, 159–60; eradication, 144; origins and transmission, 16, 43, 143. *See also* diseases
Peace River (BC), 265, 274
Pearl Harbor, 301
Pearson International Airport (ON), 233
Peary, Robert, 335
Peck, Ralph, 274–75
Perrault, Joseph-Xavier, 131
pests, 43–44, 301; grasshoppers, 130
petroleum conservation laws, 253
Phillips, Ruth B., 78
Pine Point Mine (NT), 202(i), 213
Plague City (2005), 159
plains. *See* Prairies
plant species, 53, 56(i), 226; diversity, 230; native and invasive, 43; photosynthesis, 249
pneumonia, 157–58
policy, 95, 96, 255, 256, 310, 313
pollution, 4, 194, 288, 301, 303; controls, 214, 215(i); organizations, 302
Pollution Probe, 302
popular culture, 169, 179
population: "bomb," 10; Indigenous, 61, 78, 144–45, 161; Rust Belt states, 71; settler, 60, 61; urban, 185, 187. *See also* mortality rates

Port Hope (ON), 216
ports, 70, 150
poverty, 142(i), 154, 344; city, 187, 189, 191
power, 17, 87, 331–32; energy and, 244, 247, 251, 257
Prairies, 63, 64(i), 70; agriculture, 127, 130, 134–35, 328; Indigenous peoples and, 110, 112, 126; settlers, 122(i), 329
predators, 227–29, 232
progress, idea of, 65, 161, 264, 305
property rights, 59, 117, 253
protests: logging and old-growth forest, 308–10, 311(i); nuclear testing, 17, 289; student, 302; women's participation, 280(i)
public anxiety, 158–59
public health, 154, 158–59, 160, 189, 197
Public Health Agency of Canada, 160
Purdy, Al, 32
Pyramid Mountain (AB), 235, 236(i)

Quebec, 38, 128, 131, 245; farmers, 129–30; hydroelectricity, 264–65, 271–72; mines, 210–11; Quiet Revolution, 273
Quebec City, 150–51, 152(i), 323
queer theorists, 283

radiation, 284, 286–87, 292, 321
railroads, 205(i), 223, 225–30, 263, 330. *See also* Canadian Pacific Railway (CPR)

wolves, 222(i)

women, 248(i), 266; activism, 17, 280(i), 281, 285–92; bodies, 293–94; connection with natural world, 282–83; Yukon, 85, 90, 97

Woodland peoples, 39, 76–77

Woods, Lake of the (MB), 36, 40, 111

World Described (Moll), 105(i), 113(i)

World Health Organization, 157, 159, 264

Yellowknife, 214, 215(i)

Yoon, Jin-Me, 178

York Factory (MB), 111, 145, 146

Yukon, 15, 34, 213; caribou, 87, 88(i), 95; women, 85, 90, 97

Zelko, Frank, 293

Zeller, Suzanne, 33